CHASING FOUR

CHASING FOUR

A Personal History of Work and Play

Observations, musings, and rants
from the Bronx to the boardroom

By Gene McCarthy

For Gene and Cassie
Touching me, touching you…

To August Lupe McCarthy
Look all around, there's nothing but blue skies…

Life is not what one lived, but what one remembers
and how one remembers, in order to recount it.

—Gabriel García Márquez

TABLE OF CONTENTS

PART THREE: THE REST OF THE PIE

PART FOUR: AS I SEE IT

THE HOME STRAIGHT

WHAT THEY SAY

"I made a movie a long time ago called *Vision Quest*. A character in the film tells an incredible story about Pelé and his athletic prowess. How a single individual can lift humanity up and make us all become more acutely aware of how precious and brief our lives are. 'It's not the six minutes. It's what happens in those six minutes.' While Gene is sharing a story about his youthful pursuit of the four-minute mile, it's not the four minutes; it's how his pursuit of accomplishing that goal would transform his entire life and professional career."

—Matthew Modine, actor, director,
and Emmy and Golden Globe nominee

"While many have held the title of president or CEO, Gene is the rarest of breeds…a true leader. Through empathy, grit, and street savvy, Gene and this book are a testament to what it takes to be an effective leader, an impressive achievement in the challenging athletic footwear industry. Gene is a gifted and prolific storyteller who takes the reader through his life and career journey, his relentless pursuit of excellence, his ability to zig while others zag, and the important lessons he learned along the way. An accomplished athlete and a dynamic executive, Gene's reflections and observations make this a must-read for any aspiring leader."

—Mary Scott, former president of United Entertainment Group

"A CEO has a hard job, but imagine being a CEO who has to motivate some of the most motivated people in the world. They can sniff BS a mile away. G was able to rally me when I was ready to burn the world down. Hopefully, you will be inspired while reading about his journey, because he was a big part of mine."

—Lolo Jones, four-time world champion
and a Summer and Winter Olympian

PROLOGUE

Sometime during the spring of 2017, I received a note from a ghostwriter who had a history of partnering with CEOs to help them add "author" to their résumés. Apparently, he saw a video of a talk I gave at Leaders Week in London and was impressed with my presentation. He also remarked that I had a style that lent itself to being more of a storyteller, rather than a PowerPoint presenter. He then asked if I had ever considered writing a book. While I was flattered and intrigued, I gave it very little consideration since, at the time, I was at the helm of a well-known sports brand, which required absolutely all my mind space.

Nearly two years later, at a plateau in both my life and career, I was contemplating what I would do next. At that point, I had spent nearly forty years with some of the most successful and powerful brands in the athletic industry, with more than half of that time in executive and C-suite positions. While in that moment, I may not have known what I wanted to do next, but I was absolutely certain that I had no interest in joining yet another sneaker brand. I was at a stage in my life where enough was enough, so I now wanted any future reward to come from sharing what I knew, rather than from what I did.

One thing that struck me late in my career was that when I went home every night and pondered the day's events, I found that any conversation or interaction that I had with a young person during that day was way more gratifying to me than if we made a big sale or reported good results to Wall Street. I had always prided myself on being an approachable leader, especially to fresh-faced talent, simply because I was once in their shoes, and I never forgot where I came from. So, as I contemplated my future, I decided that sharing my years of experience with aspiring young people was to be my focus.

Over the years, I had been a guest speaker at some notable universities, and I always left each event feeling incredibly energized. After one of my lectures, I approached the dean of that business school and told him that I found talking to these kids to be way more fun than sitting in a business meeting. The dean said to me, "That's because in a classroom everyone wants to learn from you, whereas in a conference room everyone wants to steal from you." Hmm…I never thought of it that way before.

In 2020, I was asked to speak at Cornell University's Johnson Graduate School of Management. The format was a town hall style, where I was interviewed by the hosting professor before it was opened to the students to ask me anything they wanted. After a few minutes of this lively exchange, the professor, Doris Huang, asked, "Gene, have you ever thought about writing a book?" I told Doris yes, but that's all it was, a thought. Or was it now becoming more than a thought?

Being the good Catholic son that I am, I join my nonagenarian mother every Sunday at mass. Active in her church, Mom knows everyone, or maybe better said, everyone knows Cassie McCarthy. Through her I met a guy, and all I knew about him was that he was a former U.S. Army helicopter pilot who flew hundreds of hours on missions during the Vietnam War.

One day, after mass, the guy approached me and said, "Your mother told me that you are writing a book?" Thanks, Ma! Now, thinking about a book is different from writing one, a distinction that Cassie McCarthy obviously found trivial. I explained to the helicopter pilot that me thinking about writing a book was about the same as me thinking about flying a helicopter. He then told me that he had written three books and was about to start his fourth. It was then that I found out that Chris Komisarjevsky, in addition to being a decorated war veteran, was the retired worldwide CEO of Burson-Marsteller, one of the world's renowned public relations firms. You just never know who might be sitting in the pew in front of you at Sunday mass at Saint Ignatius the Martyr Church.

Chris and I would soon meet every week or so for lunch, and aside from getting to know this very accomplished man, I had a front-row seat as he penned and published his fourth book, *Reputation...First: Building a Crisis Communication Strategy*, which is a wise and thoughtful guide on how to build and maintain strong character, not only for yourself but also for your brand or company.

———

Omne trium perfectum is Latin for "the rule of three." Many people believe that all good things come in threes. Well, first I was approached by a ghostwriter offering to help me write a book, an offer I politely declined. Followed by an enthusiastic Ivy League professor whose relentless encouragement turned my "why?" into a "why not?" And finally, to have the tutelage of an accomplished CEO with "author" on his résumé. Well then, maybe I should write a book! Yet as the Irish are profoundly aware, good things come in fours, just like a four-leaf clover.

On August 5, 1979, *The New York Times* published an article titled "Chasing the Four-Minute Mile Along the Streets of the Bronx." I was its author, and I had just turned twenty-three the day before the article was published. Now, penning one article doesn't necessarily make you a writer, but maybe this was the fourth leaf of my clover, or perhaps the first.

I've chosen to name this book *Chasing Four*, an obvious nod to *The Times* piece from my younger years. Yet it also plays to so much more than my quest to achieve an athletic milestone, a four-leaf clover notwithstanding. It also refers to a part of my business career when it seemed all I did as a senior executive, president, and CEO was to chase the quarter, trying to hit a revenue number every ninety days, only to please shareholders.

Chasing Four also has roots in my personal life, whether related to my role as the overbearing oldest brother to four siblings or the daunting yet rewarding task, later in life, of chasing around four kids of my own. Yet I think that even deeper than that, *Chasing Four* beckons to this obstacle course or roller-coaster ride we are on, which we call life. And it's not lost on me that occasionally, the chase really may have been running away rather than running toward, a lesson that I learned several times over the years, sometimes too late to recognize and course-correct.

As I look back with eyes wide open, it also seems that my entire life was a comingling of work and play. Certainly, there were times in my life when play was a lot of hard work, yet during my working life, there were some moments, albeit too few, when work felt like play. Yet how fortunate am I that my avocation and my vocation ultimately became one and the same. Still, along the way there were plenty of bumps and bruises, highs and not-so-highs, bliss and darkness, as well as moments of pride balanced with bouts of self-doubt, all unique and beautiful to me, like the timeworn scars on a piece of fine leather.

During my chats with the ghostwriter, we had a spirited banter about whom this book would be written for. Well, there are several audiences I thought about while I was writing, yet I always seemed to think about the younger me. What wisdom or foresight could be sent back to me telepathically, sagaciously, via carrier pigeon or, God forbid, electronically…from my future self? But that would totally spoil all the fun. So instead, I hope to share this book with the pioneers who, throughout my life, have beaten their own paths and left a few crumbs and markers along the road so that my journey could have moments of being on good footing. As well, I hope that the young people to whom I dedicate this book will read it and hear only a little about me while pondering a lot about themselves, and all along realizing that it all starts simply with one step.

If an ordinary kid from the Bronx can be blessed with an extraordinary run (pun intended), then so can anybody.

—Gene McCarthy, Long Beach, NY

PART ONE

PLAY IS REALLY HARD WORK

CHAPTER ONE

WALK BEFORE YOU RUN

God, it was hot! You know, that *hot* hot where you feel the heat pressing on your cheekbones. Just like when you open the oven door on Thanksgiving to check on the turkey, when waves of heat attack your face. The *hot* hot where your sweat even sweats. I was in Manhattan, walking in a carefully measured cadence, just brisk enough to create my own personal breeze but slow enough to avoid opening any more pores. I loved this in a perverse, self-torturous kind of way.

Only a few years earlier, when I was in high school, I was walking just like this, three or four days a week, delivering dry-cleaning in the Murray Hill section of the city. I made $1.65 an hour delivering to all sorts of eccentric New Yorkers, as well as to celebrities like Carly Simon and Soupy Sales. The customers were always polite and friendly, but these people never once tipped! Apparently, that ritual was reserved for the holidays, when I was already back at All Hallows High School and no longer a member of the Murray Hill dry-cleaners summer squad.

Now, on this broiling day, I was on my way to *The New York Times* building to meet with a sports editor named Arthur Pincus. I met Art during my time as a student-athlete at Fordham University, where he followed my modest running career. He invited me to stop by if ever I were back in New York. It was only a year earlier, at twenty-one years old and fresh from graduating from Fordham, that I had left the city, the only home I had ever known, to move to Gainesville, Florida, to chase a dream.

Just as my white button-down started to stick to my chest, with the sweat dripping down and pooling in the small of my back, I had finally reached *The Times* building. The cool lobby air was refreshing, but it was no remedy for my "stuck in a rainstorm" look. Even my visitor sticker wouldn't stay on my shirt.

After a quick elevator ride, I soon was seated across the desk from Art. As we ate our sandwiches, Art mentioned that he was intrigued by a quote I gave to a reporter late in my senior year, where I said, "I regret athletically going to Fordham." These six words certainly didn't make me a favorite alumnus, yet at the same time, these words left Art quite curious.

This was during the advent of Title IX, which was the long-overdue legislation that championed equal funding and opportunity for women student-athletes. The Fordham administration's response to this mandate, like many universities at the time, was to defund the men's athletic programs in order to create funding for women's sports. I was known to be a little outspoken on campus during my four years, but this move by the admin-istration was equally insulting to both women and men student-athletes, if not to the entire student body. Hence my quote.

Two months after graduating in 1978, I moved to Gainesville to give my running career "the good old college try" that I never really gave it while I was actually in college.

This move came out of left field for many people in my world. After all, I was a native New Yorker for my entire twenty-one years. And even though I had several scholarship offers to run track at various colleges around the country, wouldn't you know that I would end up choosing a college six miles from my house in the Bronx? But the Gainesville move came from a transformational moment that happened eight years earlier, in 1971, when

I was a fourteen-year-old freshman at All Hallows.

As any sports-loving kid back then would remember, you couldn't wait for *Sports Illustrated* to come in the mailbox every week. In a time when there were only a few television channels and with no information overload like we have today, *Sports Illustrated* gave you the chance to read words that seemed to flow poetically while being accented with vivid photographs that gave you a front-row seat to the big sports moments from just a week earlier. You also had to do something we hardly ever do anymore while reading *Sports Illustrated*: use your imagination.

On the cover of the May 24, 1971, issue was a stunning photograph of two runners in full stride coming off the final turn in a very close mile race. This picture not only captured their sinewy bodies pushed to the extreme but also gave me a sense of their grit and determination that I certainly had not yet experienced in my budding running career. I could almost feel the tension as both runners were reaching for another gear that neither of them probably knew they had. All of this in a single photograph.

The runners were Jim Ryun from Kansas and Marty Liquori from Villanova. The caption below the photo read, "The Dream Mile! Liquori Grins and Wins!" As cool as that headline sounded, it's arguable if Liquori was really grinning. It seemed more like grimacing.

I read the article slowly and carefully, hanging on every syllable. My heart was pounding fast as the writer seemed to describe every step of the four-lap race. Then, to read that Liquori held off Ryun on the homestretch to win by a step while the Philadelphia crowd poured onto the track to swarm Liquori, I just about lost my mind! After reading the article over and over again, I felt the same sensation each and every time. That's it. Decision made. I immediately knew what I wanted to do with the rest of my life. I heard my calling.

Every night, when the church bells rang at six o'clock, all the kids in our neighborhood would run home, inhale supper, and then catch a few more minutes of hanging out in the park until the streetlights came on, the signal to go back home. As the five McCarthy kids and their parents, Cassie and Gene, gathered around a dinner table that could seat maybe four or five uncomfortably, I waited for my opening. While we enjoyed our fish sticks and corn, there was a rare lull in the conversation. I seized the moment and proudly announced, "Everybody, I have something important to tell you. Today I heard my calling like a voice from the heavens! I now know what my future holds. I have decided that I'm going to break the four-minute mile!" The reactions from the other six at the dinner table ranged from bewilderment to eye rolling, along with a little artificial enthusiasm. But I didn't care one bit. You just wait and see. I will show you.

In 1971, the same year of my life-defining *Sports Illustrated* moment, my best mile time was 4:25. Now, keep in mind that only seventeen years earlier, an Englishman named Roger Bannister became the first person in history to break the four-minute mile. It was a feat deemed at the time to be physically unachievable. Some medical experts even thought it was so impossible that a runner's heart might explode. Here I was, a freshman in high school and only twenty-five seconds away from potentially having my heart explode! How cool would that be! What a way to get famous! Imagine the headlines…"McCarthy Breaks Four Minutes. Heart Explodes." Pictures at 11:00 p.m. on *Eyewitness News*.

For the next several years, I would be dedicating every second of my life to chasing four.

As we ate our sandwiches at his desk, Art Pincus was very intent on knowing why I would leave New York for Florida. He mentioned that at twenty-two, I was a little too young to retire, and now that I had my degree, wasn't it time to grow up and put running behind me? Besides, I was a minor track star, not a future Olympian, so why didn't I just stay here in the city, get a good job, and maybe join the New York Road Runners and run races in Central Park on the weekends? Not realizing it then, Art was baiting me, perhaps looking for an angle for a story. When I told him that this was the New York City that the Rolling Stones sang about in their song "Shattered," with rats on the West Side and bed bugs Uptown, he hardly seemed fazed. Then I reminded him that only two years earlier, this was the city where, during the World Series, Howard Cosell declared on live television, "Ladies and gentlemen, the Bronx is burning," as a tenement near Yankee Stadium was ablaze. And despite that there were many parks and green spaces throughout the five boroughs, most were unsafe and in disrepair. That included Van Cortlandt Park, the mecca of cross-country, where the cow pastures that we trained on were always littered with the remnants of the weekend picnics and barbecues. Essentially, New York was a fitness desert.

But I also told Art about how I was inspired as a kid by Marty Liquori, and I mentioned a letter I had written to him upon graduating from Fordham, seven years after seeing the iconic cover of *Sports Illustrated*. I got Marty's address from Brother Naclerio, who taught at All Hallows, yet years earlier he was at another Irish Christian Brother high school in Newark, New Jersey, called Essex Catholic, when Marty was a student.

In that letter I told Marty of my dream to break the four-minute mile, and could I seek his advice? I mentioned that as a high school freshman, I ran 4:25, but when I graduated from All Hallows, my mile time was down to 4:13. Then, in my freshman year at Fordham, I improved to 4:05, but by the time I graduated, my best time was only down to 4:03. I was certain that this would be unimpressive to a guy who broke four minutes in high school, only the third schoolboy ever to do so.

I was pleasantly surprised when Marty, whom I'd never met, wrote me a long letter back. When I wrote to him, I thought that all I would get in return was maybe a list of workouts that I could do on my own. Imagine, then, my shock that in his letter, Marty invited me to move to Gainesville, which he now called home and where he was training as well as running a successful chain of athletic shoe stores, which he cofounded, called Athletic Attic. He mentioned that I could get a part-time job in one of those stores, and it was possible that I could find a place to live with another runner living and training in Gainesville. This was way beyond my wildest dreams.

Upon hearing this, Art Pincus leaned over his cluttered desk and asked me an out-of-the-blue question. "Gene, did you take any journalism classes at Fordham?" Perplexed, I nervously said no. Art then said, "Good. Then you don't have any bad habits. So, here's what we're gonna do. I want you to write down your thoughts about everything you just told me. Use your words; don't try to be an English major or, God forbid, a journalism major, and then let's see what we get."

Once back in Florida, I went through a stack of legal pads and countless pencils and erasers and somehow came up with a story. A friend of mine who worked at the Athletic Attic offices typed it up for me for five dollars. I then mailed my story to Arthur Pincus.

On Sunday, August 5, 1979, just one day after my twenty-third birthday, there was my story on page two of *The Sunday New York Times* sports section. It took up half the page, and it was titled "Chasing the Four-Minute Mile Along the Streets of the Bronx."

I woke up early that Sunday morning, skipped my morning run, and set out on the mission of finding a store in Gainesville that might carry *The Sunday Times*. Despite being home to the University of Florida, Gainesville was a charming, down-home Southern town. It was more about grits, hush puppies, and Spanish moss than pastels, palm trees, and convertibles, like in South Florida.

As I went from store to store searching for *The Sunday Times*, it reminded me of a part-time job that I had in high school. Every Sunday morning, I would get up at 5:00 a.m. and stroll over to Cappy's, a candy store in a shopping center a few blocks from where we lived. Since the many sections of *The Times* were delivered in separate bundles, it was my job to assemble the sections into a complete newspaper for the countless people who would come by after church to buy a lazy day's worth of reading. I recalled one of those Sunday mornings when I took a quick break from my assembly duties and furiously scanned the pages of the sports section. I wanted to see if there was any mention of the Eastern States Cross-Country Championships, which were held at Van Cortlandt Park the day before. By now, my hands were jet-black from putting the paper together; then for a precious moment I was transfixed, almost paralyzed, when I saw a picture of myself right there in *The Times*, hailed as the winner of this prestigious high school race.

After a few unsuccessful stops on my Gainesville scavenger hunt, I finally found a store that sold *The Times*. There were only two copies on the newsstand, but not because *The Times* was popular in Gainesville and had almost sold out. It was because that's all the store carried every Sunday. Naturally, I bought both.

While my article took up the entire bottom half of page two, the upper half featured an excerpt from a yet-to-be-published biography of Thurman Munson, the beloved catcher and captain of the New York Yankees. That Sunday, page two had attracted an extraordinary number of readers because sadly, Munson had died just three days earlier. On days off from playing with the Yankees, Thurman would occasionally pilot his own small plane to fly home to be with his family. On that tragic day, he was practicing takeoffs and landings at his hometown airport in Akron, Ohio, when he lost control and crashed. New York loved Thurman Munson and losing him hit hard.

A week later, it became apparent that my opinion piece in *The Times* also got plenty of attention. My story was centered on the frustration I shared with many aspiring athletes, that in a city like New York, there was little to no opportunity to gain support or to access resources to continue your athletic pursuits once you graduated from college. Well, apparently this struck a nerve with many readers, because a week after my article was published, it was the focus of the "Reader's Mailbox" section of *The Times*. One letter was written by a gentleman who ripped me for what he felt was my undue criticism of the city, and especially the Bronx. The gentleman wrote that when he lived in the Bronx twenty-five years earlier, how beautiful the Bronx was, particularly the Botanical Gardens and the Bronx Zoo. Now settled in a tony part of Connecticut, the gentleman said that I should stop complaining and be grateful for what I had, or rather, for what he had a quarter of a century earlier.

By contrast, the other letter came from a young woman who was doing social work in the South Bronx, which was at the time and still is one of the poorest congressional districts in the country. She empathized with me, mentioning how hard it was for her to motivate the kids she worked with because she had no support or resources, so the kids had little hope.

Two letters from two very different New Yorkers that told a tale of two very different cities.

CHAPTER TWO

HOOP DREAMS

"He looks like a skinned rabbit." Such were the words lovingly uttered by my dad one hot summer day in 1956.

It was a typical New York City summer, or so I'm told, with each day governed by the three Hs…hazy, hot, and humid. My mother was so miserable, late in her first pregnancy, that she took rides on the un-air-conditioned city bus with the hope that the fumes, vibrations, and bouncing over potholes would induce labor. I'm not sure if the bus strategy worked, but on August 4, the first of five McCarthy kids took his first breath at Columbia Presbyterian Hospital in the Washington Heights section of Manhattan.

We grew up in the Bronx, the only borough of New York that is attached to the mainland United States, in an enclave of predominantly Irish immigrant families. We lived first on Webb Avenue until we "upgraded" to a two-bedroom, rent-controlled apartment around the corner on Claflin Avenue. The boys—me, Tom, and John—all slept in one small bedroom, and the girls, Nancy and Katy, shared the other. Our parents' bedroom in apartment 5L was really the living room. The dining room then became our living room, and the table where we ate our meals was in the narrow hallway just a few feet from the front door. And yes, one bathroom.

We all attended Our Lady of Angels grammar school, which, depending on how you looked at it, was conveniently located fifty yards from our apartment building. Each day we were at the mercy of the Sisters of Charity. There were Sisters Genevieve, Monica, and Helen, as well as Marguerite, who, by the way, played the guitar and sang folk versions of church hymns. Sister Marguerite was our very own "Flying Nun," just like on a popular television show at the time starring Sally Field.

There were a few lay teachers at OLA, who were easily recognized by wearing civilian clothing rather than the black habits the nuns wore. We had Mrs. Oakes (a married woman!) as well as Miss McDonnell, who would occasionally tape a red flag on her classroom door to warn everyone that she was in a bad mood that particular day. And of course, there was Miss Duncanson, who not only taught me and then my sister Nancy in second grade, but she also taught our mother in second grade as well.

My first year in grade school was a complete blur, and my grades clearly indicated that. All I did each day was stare out the window…and reflect. When I somehow got promoted to second grade and became a pupil of the legendary Miss Duncanson, I received a stern lecture and loving send-off on opening day from my mom. "No matter what happens, or no matter what anybody tells you, *do not* let them take your pencil out of your hand!" I wasn't quite sure where this was going, but if that was Mom's only advice from her Miss Duncanson experience, I was pretty sure I could handle that. Easy enough, it seemed. Besides, if someone took my pencil, I certainly had a spare or twenty in my knapsack.

What Cassie McCarthy was really trying to tell me was to not let anyone take the pencil out of my left hand and make me write with my right hand. How did I know that being left-handed was a sign of the devil?! Maybe sister Genevieve told us that in first grade, but I was too busy looking out the window, deep in reflection, to pick that one up. Well, aside from the beautiful sight of twenty-five kids learning to write in script with uniformity, in choreographed and sweeping motion, who would have thought that this could also exorcise the devil from within? To this day over sixty years later, I still press so hard when I write that I dent several pages in a notebook, and I have to pause after but a few written words to let my aching hand rest and recover. Oh, the devil's work!

The eighty, um, I mean eight years I spent at OLA went by without much to add to the good old memory bank. I do, though, remember the dark green slacks, tan shirt, and green bow tie, which eventually gave way to the much more fashion-forward navy slacks and white shirt. And right around puberty, the bow tie was replaced by a plaid clip-on long tie.

I also clearly remember Albert Longobardi, who was sitting right in front of me when he threw up on his desk. We had to exit in single file, each one of us passing his desk like it was a funeral viewing, or maybe how cars slowed to see a wreck on the highway. To this day, I can still smell it. And who can forget when Sister Genevieve fell down the stairs leading her first-grade class to recess? The only reason that memory sticks is because Michael Dunn and Nancy McCarthy were first in line and directly behind poor Sister Genevieve. Don't worry, Sister Genevieve was okay. And Nancy McCarthy, to this day, has yet to be struck by lightning.

I remember that summertime in the Bronx was brutal. The three Hs were always dialed up, and the asphalt and concrete were toasty. When I was five-years old, my mom signed me up for a day camp run by the nuns. On my first day, Mom walked me to the corner to put me on the school bus with the other kids for a trip to Rockaway Beach in Queens. Seven hours later, the bus returned, and my mom was eagerly waiting to greet me and hear about my first day of camp. I got off the bus wearing a girl's pink sweatshirt, a sunburn in a matching color, and only one of the two shoes I started the day with. It turns out that I drifted away from my fellow campers and wandered aimlessly for several hours. Apparently, a teenage girl noticed me and somehow returned me to my group. Needless to say, my day camp days were over. We were fortunate though, because our grandfather eventually helped us rent a bungalow for several summers in that same Rockaway

Beach. So for several years, we were able to escape the sweltering Bronx and avoid day camps run by nuns.

————

Sports were important in our house, at least for my dad and the three boys. Every day my dad would read *The Daily News* when he got home from work. He told us to always read the paper from the back sports page up to the front page so we could learn about man's successes and work our way to man's failures.

My dad was a diehard New York Giants fan. He was part of a neighborhood group that had season tickets for the Giants when they played in the original Yankee Stadium. One time my dad took me and my brother, Tommy, to the stadium on a Saturday for what I guess was some kind of promotion sponsored by WNEW radio. I only remember three things about that day. First, it was fifty below zero. Second, for some unknown reason, there was a chimpanzee as part of the event. And third, Tommy dumped his entire cup of hot chocolate inside of one of my snow boots.

When the Giants were on the road, Dad would take over the living room and watch the games on our black-and-white television, an RCA Victor that required a pair of pliers to change the channels, since the original television dial was stripped from furious channel changing. Even today, I still find this perplexing, since back then there were less than ten channels to watch. Dad did a lot of yelling, particularly at any mistakes the Giants made, which meant he yelled a lot, prefacing his comments with a bellowing, *"Jesus Christ!!!"* And not necessarily because he was a good practicing Catholic.

Every day after school, we would run home, change clothes, and go to the park. We called it a park, but it was really a black asphalt playground with a basketball court, swings, monkey bars, and a "park house," a small brick building that had bathrooms and supplies for the "parkies," who were the one or two guys that maintained the park. Yet the park house served another major purpose, as that was where five-year-olds like me went to something called *park school*. It was an alternative to kindergarten, I guess, and it is where I learned the fine art of looking out the window…and reflecting.

Over the years, the park was where we played stickball and "off the point," where we would take a pink rubber ball called a Spaldeen and hit it off the stoop of the boy's bathroom. If you hit it just right, it would sail over the fence and out of the park onto Sedgwick Avenue for a homer. Extra points if you hit a passing bus. Like all kids back then, playing sports was just slightly more important than talking about sports. But there were rules. For example, Yankees or Mets. It was against the law to like both. Same for Giants and Jets, Knicks and Nets, Rangers and Islanders. So if you meet a New Yorker who tells you otherwise, ask to see their driver's license.

Choosing what sports to play was simple. Baseball and basketball. If you had money, then maybe you could play Pop Warner football. I truly can say that when I grew up, I never heard the word soccer, or let alone saw a soccer ball. I played in the Veteran's Little League, named so because of the sponsoring Veteran's Hospital on Fordham Road. You knew spring was coming when you had to go up to Kingsbridge Road and pick up your baseball uniform. When you played in the minors, your team was named after the sponsor, whether it was the local Chinese restaurant or Regan's Bar. When you got to the majors, the teams were named after major league teams, with two notable exceptions: no Yankees or Mets. And no number seven on any team. After all, there was only one Mickey Mantle.

Little League was also a rite of passage for boys to become young men. First there was the uniform, a clear signal that something official was happening. Like a cop or a fireman, the uniform made the boy into a young man. Next, there was the coach. He was somebody other than your father. And he also wasn't the father of a kid on your team. How absurd would that be? I'm pretty sure that my coach, Richie Klein, certainly never had a son or a wife or, God forbid, even a girlfriend! Did Richie even have a job? I don't know, but more important, I didn't care. Richie Klein was our Little

League coach. Period. As a matter of fact, no one ever saw Richie Klein any other place, except on the baseball field.

One Tuesday, we had a six o'clock game on the dusty field next to P.S. 86. The public elementary schools in the city at the time were not named after some historic figure. That was reserved for the high schools. So I guess for eight years you developed "P.S. 86 pride?" At 5:30 p.m., my mom told me to put my uniform on, and I better get going. "Goodbye!" she yelled from the kitchen. "Come straight home after the game!"

The field was right near the 4 train, the Woodlawn line. While I never met Thomas Durkin, my grandfather on my mom's side, he was the motorman who proudly drove that 4 train literally until he died at the all too young age of forty-three. On this particular evening, my dad was coming home from the city on the 4 train. He got off at the Kingsbridge stop and casually sauntered over to watch my game. This was absolutely horrifying to me. It wasn't the pressure of having my dad there. It was the pressure of all the shit I was about to take, at that precise moment and probably forever, from the other kids on the team (they weren't called teammates back then). "Eugene! Your daddy is here! You baby!!!!" How could my dad do this to me? Your parents aren't supposed to go to your Little League games! It was a humiliating and emotionally scarring event in my early life. A catastrophic moment that eventually therapy would try to smooth over. Emphasis on the word "try."

Today, it's considered child abuse if you miss your kid's game, or even if you are fifteen minutes late. And shall lightning strike you if you don't bring a three-gallon jug of electric-blue sugar water and a bag of orange slices while wearing a T-shirt that reads, "GO COUGARS" on the front and "JADEN'S MOM" on the back. And you definitely better be screaming, "Way to go, Jaden!" even if your future number-one draft choice just beaned a batter while pitching, or he swung and missed two feet over a fluttering strike three. Still, trophies all around! Pizza party too! Even if the team lost every single game. Boy, have times changed.

Basketball was to be a vital part of my life. Now, allow me to explain how ludicrous these ten words are. For starters, I am five feet, seven inches and 140 pounds…as an adult. Which is a lot more height and heft than I had when I was eight years old. A small but important detail. Our Lady of Angels had a good CYO basketball program. I wanted in. I needed to be in. Basketball would define me. Fame and glory were the rewards I sought. Not to mention it would set me up to become the starting point guard at All Hallows High School, my number-one choice to continue my education, or better said, the place where I would continue my reflecting while staring out yet another set of windows.

I played for the Our Lady of Angels grammar school varsity. My first year I wore shorts that were so big on me that safety pins were necessary to cinch the waistband so they hopefully wouldn't end up around my ankles. All this just to do the pregame warmups, since I mostly sat on the bench. Yet the status I gained when I went to the park after each game was worth the price. Who doesn't love a man in uniform? Even if it's jerry-rigged like a diaper. Still, lack of talent aside, determination has its rewards, because when I was in eighth grade, I was elected captain of the OLA varsity. Here was my first taste of leadership, even though I didn't know what that meant at the time.

CHAPTER THREE

ON YOUR MARK

After I graduated from OLA, our family moved to a new development in the North Bronx called Co-op City. This was a sprawling community of high-rise apartment buildings with several clusters of townhomes sprinkled in. Hardly quaint, Co-op City was home to about forty-five thousand people, just enough to fill Yankee Stadium. This cement city was built on a marshy tract of land that, only a few years earlier, was home to an amusement park called Freedom Land. Cassie and Gene were eager to provide a better quality of life for themselves, as well as for their beloved kids, so leaving a six-story apartment building and going to a two-story townhome was definitely movin' on up! Foreign to us was having our own washing machine and even a dryer. No more hanging towels and underwear on a clothesline that was strung from my fifth-floor bedroom window and connected to our adjacent living room window. The other foreign object in our new home was something called air-conditioning. More than anything else, this is what made Co-op City my dad's utopia. For us kids, air-conditioning was something we had only enjoyed at the RKO Fordham movie theater, where we would occasionally go to watch a matinee on a steamy afternoon, if only just to keep cool.

Our first night at 18B Cooper Place was in June, with all three Hs raging at full steam. When we went to bed that very first night, the air-conditioning was a welcome comfort. However, when we woke up the next morning, we found ourselves curled up under the covers in the fetal position, with blue lips and chattering teeth. My baby brother, John, came down the stairs ready for school, wearing a turtleneck even though the weather forecast called for temperatures in the mid-nineties with a humidity index to match.

———

All Hallows High School was established in 1909 by Brother Edmund Rice, an Irish Christian Brother who believed there needed to be a religious-centered education for the immigrant poor. The all-boys school was in the South Bronx, just off the fabled Grand Concourse and around the corner from Yankee Stadium. There were a handful of other Irish Christian Brother high schools established at that time. Rice High School was in Harlem, Power Memorial was located on the Upper West Side of Manhattan, and Essex Catholic was across the Hudson River in Newark, New Jersey.

That none of these schools were in the best neighborhoods wasn't the point. The schools went to where the kids were. Or in my case, I went to where the school was, since I was chasing the dream of being the starting point guard for a team whose nickname was the Gaels.

My first week of high school was quite memorable. While I could walk fifty yards from our apartment on Claflin Avenue to my grammar school, getting to All Hallows was slightly more of an ordeal. I woke up at six o'clock each morning, inhaled a Pop Tart, and then caught the number 15 bus that traveled along Gun Hill Road. Then it was on to the D train from 207th Street to 161st Street, the Yankee Stadium stop. I'd then walk a couple of blocks past a bodega, an Orange Julius, a liquor store, and a check-cashing place, as well as the Bronx County Courthouse, before arriving at All Hallows. Door-to-door, an hour and a half.

While we didn't have to wear uniforms, there was a dress code that every student pushed to the limit. We wore slacks with flared bottoms, button-downs with collars so wide that you could become airborne with a good wind gust, and leather shoes with heels big enough to stomp out a good-sized Bronx cockroach. This fashion statement was accented with a necktie that had a knot the size of a four-year-old's fist. To avoid wearing a sport coat, and potentially getting beat up on the subway and having your lunch money stolen, you were allowed to wear an official school sweater, which was a signal to the public-school kids on the train that you dressed this way because you had to, not necessarily because you wanted to.

Your hair style was another thing. Every kid in the seventies wanted long hair, including me. My problem, though, was that my coarse, kinky mop was prone to growing big rather than long. My best friend, Eddie Walsh, sported Rod Stewart hair, while Steve Doran had a Paul McCartney Wings-era mullet thing going a year or two before Sir Paul did. As for me, I'd like to believe that I had Roger Daltrey hair, but the reality was that I looked more like a Chia Pet.

Day one at All Hallows was a blur, just like it had been on day one in first grade at OLA. The difference being that I couldn't stare out the windows like I did at OLA, because the windows at All Hallows were so filthy that the view of the neighboring tenements was more of a silhouette. And by the way, not making continuous eye contact with the strap-wielding Brother Sullivan, also known as Moose, just wouldn't fly. I was terrified.

While heading home on the subway after my first day, I decided to stand and hold a rail rather than grab a seat. When I got to the Kingsbridge Road stop, I felt a sense of relief to be going home, but suddenly my heart started to race, and my face felt flushed. Now, this was a feeling I hadn't quite experienced too much in my tender fourteen years. The only time I'd ever felt anything like this was when I kissed Mary Hayes in eighth grade. But kissing Mary felt way better than this. Without warning, two kids came up to me and grabbed me by the wrist. You see, they had their eyes on the prized jewel I had on my left ring finger, my beloved OLA grammar school graduation ring, a seven-dollar gift from my parents. Just as I was about to surrender the one and only piece of jewelry I had ever owned, a man wearing a fedora came up and brandished a small pistol, which scared the living hell out of my two assailants. They took off like there was no tomorrow, which there might not have been if the man in the fedora had his way. The man said to me, "Piece of advice, son. If you're gonna ride the train, then leave the jewelry at home." He then just casually walked away.

Not me. I just stumbled home in a zombie state. I would say absolutely nothing about this to my parents. If they knew what happened, they would have immediately taken me out of All Hallows and crushed my goal of being the starting point guard. Yet ever since that very moment, I have trained myself to take inventory of my surroundings and try to find out who is friend or foe before the subway doors close. Later in life, this ritual would prove helpful, as I would make a habit of taking a good hard look everywhere I went, especially before the conference room and boardroom doors closed.

The other big event during week one of my foray into the South Bronx was freshman field day at All Hallows. On this day we had classes in the morning, and then we switched into our gym uniforms and walked down to Macomb's Dam Park, which was in the shadows of the original Yankee Stadium. Macomb's was a decrepit place that was decorated with all kinds of trash that was usually associated with the creatures that pop up from the manhole covers after the bell tolls midnight. It had a cinder track, which, due to little if any upkeep, seemed more like the sand at Orchard Beach than cinders, whatever that was supposed to feel like.

I wanted absolutely nothing to do with field day. First, it was embarrassing enough walking through this very tough neighborhood wearing our gym uniforms, which looked like navy-blue underwear. Second, this field day didn't include baseball or basketball, so how could this have anything to do with sports? I immediately needed an exit strategy, like maybe catching the flu or even asking to be excused because I had a chronic heart condition. No matter what, I wanted out.

As I was preparing my escape, a very large and looming figure began to speak. He was a calm and steady man, and his voice seemed, in a way, almost soothing. "Welcome to freshman field day," said the man in the long black gown and white collar, a stopwatch hanging around his neck. His name was Brother Pat Morkan. While he had a towering presence, his Irish eyes were always smiling. Obviously, while he was a man of the cloth, I would eventually learn that Brother Morkan could also seem like your favorite uncle, or maybe even like a next-door neighbor, depending, of course, on the quality of your neighborhood. But because I didn't know any of this at the time, his next few words escaped me because I was too busy looking for a window to stare out of, or maybe to jump out of. But I did perk up when I heard that you must compete in two events, and then you could go home. Music to my ears! I immediately decided that I would compete in the very first two events, even if they were the pole vault and the hammer throw, and then I would be off to the subway and ready to face, if need be, my two assailants from a few days earlier. Because now, that seven-dollar ring with the emerald stone was safely on the hand of Mary Hayes.

The first event at the freshman field day was the 440-yard dash. After asking a kid standing next to me what that meant, I learned that it was one lap around the track. Okay, seems achievable. A whistle blows, and off we go. Well, off went everybody else. As the eager freshmen tore around the first turn, I just relinquished myself to jog my way in. I just had to compete in two events; no one said a word about winning two events, and then I'd be off to the train. But about halfway through, I noticed an immense amount of fatigue that suddenly reduced these "fastest out, fastest in" track stars to maybe needing emergency care when or if they crossed the finish line.

Now, with about 330 yards covered and 110 yards to go, I felt a burst of energy and a feeling of euphoria. Was I really going to win this thing?! I crossed an invisible finish line and hit an imaginary tape near where that giant man in clerical garb was staring at his stopwatch. I looked to him for a reaction, some sign or just some kind of recognition. Nothing. Not a raise of an eyebrow, no subtle curling of the lip. Nada. Zilch. Morkan just shouted, "*Okay*! Next race is the 880!"

Since 14-year-olds usually resort to reacting way more than to reasoning, I gave little thought to my lack of conditioning and got right on that starting line, waiting for the whistle to blow. Once again, the speedy boys darted out, giving no consideration whatsoever to the fact that looking good at the start of a race was slightly less important than looking good at the finish. I continued to trot, admittedly looking more like a show horse than a racehorse, and certainly not looking like a stallion. But my eye was on the prize, the D train.

As I rounded the bend on the final lap, I discovered that I was the proud owner of not one but two rubbery legs. I immediately thought of the Gumby toy I played with as a kid, but I probably looked more like his buddy, Pokey. Still, I somehow crossed the finish line in second place and then immediately bent over and began to inhale way more oxygen than I was exhaling. Once I gained my balance and felt I could utter something close to a sentence, I approached the large man in black and said, "Brother…I did…two…events…May…I…be…dismissed?" "Congratulations!!" replied Brother Morkan. "Welcome to the All Hallows cross-country team!"

Once again, I went into reaction mode rather than opting for reasoning, a skill that would come to me way later in life. I began to tell the world's largest penguin that running cross-country would be entirely impossible, as I was to be a vital part of the All Hallows basketball team! I was adamant. "Brother, you don't understand! It is my calling and my purpose on this earth to be the point guard!" Brother Morkan replied with no show of empathy and said that I would be running cross-country that fall, and was I at all aware of the fact that he was also my math teacher? Now, within seconds, a rare moment of reasoning overcame me and eradicated any notion to just simply react. I put two and two together, which at the time was the extent of my mathematical prowess, and decided that I would run cross-country. I would be a show horse, get a good math grade, and maybe have an hour a

day during Brother Morkan's riveting math class to look out the window...
and reflect.

For the next three weeks, the All Hallows freshman cross-country team
had practice every day after school, either at Macomb's or at another place
in the Bronx called Van Cortlandt Park. We would run in circles or in a
straight line for an hour every day, while three times a week we would run
the back hills at Vanny, as we called it, and that was the definition of practice.
Not very exciting, to say the least. It was then that it dawned on me that
being a track coach may just be the easiest job in the world. All you had to
do was tell a kid, "Son, go on out there, stay to your left, and get back here
as fast as you can!"

On a cool fall Saturday morning, we had our first cross-country meet at
Van Cortlandt. At precisely ten o'clock, about one hundred freshmen from
the Catholic schools from the five boroughs of New York City all lined up,
stretched out in a long horizontal line. There was no whistle this time, but
instead, there was a starter's pistol. Holy hell! A gun in the Bronx that was
used for something good!?

The gun sounded, and one hundred kids in their standard issue gym
uniforms exploded across the cow pasture, as it was called, converging after
a quarter mile onto a rocky horse path that would accommodate maybe two
runners at a time, shoulder to shoulder. Then, after about nine minutes and
change, something magical happened that would transform me.

I came in first!

Instantly, I became intoxicated with the idea of winning. Not necessarily
for the glory of it, but more in the sense of achievement and accomplishment.
At that stage of my young life, I never saw myself as having any sort of talent.
I believed that was something for others to discern and decide for me. But
it was the pure and simple notion that hard work brings reward, and that's
how I got the buzz. Just a few months later, in the spring of 1971, when I
was mesmerized by that cover of *Sports Illustrated*, I found the inspiration
and motivation to keep putting in the hard work.

In high school, I stayed consistent with my grammar school strategy and did my fair share of gazing out the musty classroom windows, but now, rather than reflecting, I was daydreaming about my own version of "The Dream Mile."

When the bell rang at two-thirty, it signaled the end of the day for all the students. For me, that bell said the day was just beginning. Every day during cross-country season, we would travel across the Bronx to workout at Vanny. Every so often we would train at Macomb's, the scene of the famous freshman field day where I signed a pact with Brother Morkan: the promise of an excellent math grade in exchange for hard workouts and great racing on the weekends. Even though Macomb's was only a few blocks away from All Hallows, I hated it. I just felt more in my element training at Vanny, where I memorized every detail of the back hills—the rocks, gullies, crevices, leaves, twigs, and branches—so that by race day, I felt like the course belonged to me.

For some young runners, cross-country is a drudgery, something you must endure in the fall while you wait for track season. For suburban kids, cross-country usually means having a dual meet on a local municipal golf course against a rival high school. For New York City kids at the time, cross-country was something we took very seriously. It was a sport, not just a way to get in condition for track. And Vanny was a real cross-country course, rugged, rough, and hilly, not manicured fairways with gentle slopes. At Vanny, you competed as much against the racecourse and its elements as you did against the other runners. And since Vanny was considered a mecca for cross-country, every Saturday in the fall there was a championship invitational, where it was common for over one hundred schools from the East Coast to descend on the park to compete in dozens of races.

In my senior year, I won all seven major invitational meets at Van Cortlandt, including the New York City Catholic School Championship and the Eastern States Championship. My best time that fall was the third-fastest ever on the course, behind Dave Sandridge from Maryland and a guy named

Marty Liquori. Suddenly, running took on another dimension for me. This modest success put me in a position to possibly earn a scholarship and go to college, becoming the first person in our Irish immigrant family to do so.

When fall gave way to winter, our training and racing shifted to the 168th Street Armory in Washington Heights, which was just across the street from Columbia Presbyterian, the hospital where the "skinned rabbit" was born. Today, the Armory is a state-of-the-art indoor track and field venue that hosts over one hundred track meets a year, including the fabled Millrose Games. In the seventies, the Armory was a storage base for military vehicles and equipment for the state's militia, and later for the National Guard. By the eighties, the Armory was a homeless shelter.

We would train at the Armory Monday through Thursday and then race on Saturday. The track was an ancient wooden floor that was eight laps to the mile. The surface was slippery and splintery, and the air was a toxic combination of diesel fuel and oil from the tanks and trucks. If you didn't know how to negotiate the turns, you could easily take a spill and be rewarded with painful splinters that the hospital across the street could remove and then give to you in a vial as a reminder of how to take the turns.

By the spring of my senior year, I was one of the fastest milers in the Tri-State area. Because of this, I was being courted by many colleges and universities. This was uncharted waters for me and my parents, as they didn't attend college, nor did my straight-off-the-boat grandparents. Going to college, never mind on a scholarship, was something completely foreign to the McCarthys.

My high school coach, John Mulligan, was my agent of sorts, and he decided which schools he would allow to speak to me and my parents. For all high school seniors, the process of choosing a college can be a daunting and stressful experience. You fill out dozens of applications, submit hopefully good grades, write flowery essays, get letters of recommendation, and then hope and pray you get accepted to a few schools. On the other hand, if you are a promising student-athlete, you go through a courting process that runs the gamut from getting a love letter from a coach all the way to having coaches and alumni kissing your ass, and your parents' asses too. Mulligan managed this three-ring circus, and he eliminated the clowns and sword swallowers, only letting my parents meet with the lion tamers.

There were two coaches that initially impressed me, yet one of these coaches impressed my parents more. One was Fred Dwyer, the head coach at Manhattan College, which for some mysterious reason is in the Bronx rather than Manhattan. Fred, in his day, was a great miler at Villanova, where he was coached by the legendary Jim "Jumbo" Elliott. And just a year earlier, in 1973, Manhattan College won the NCAA Indoor Championship team title. Yet the real appeal to me was that Fred had been Marty Liquori's coach at Essex Catholic when Marty first broke four minutes as a high schooler.

The other coach was Tom Byrne at Fordham. Gene and Cassie felt very comfortable with him, especially after he took the three of us out for a nice and expensive dinner. Tommy was sociable and entertaining, and he put my parents at ease. It also didn't hurt that Tommy and my dad enjoyed a well-made Jack Daniels Manhattan or two. But I was also intrigued that Tommy was coaching a guy named Marcel Philippe. Born in Queens to French immigrant parents, Marcel was one of the top 800-meter runners in the country while at Mater Christi High School. Even though he had just graduated a year earlier from Fordham, Marcel was still training with the team under Tommy's tutelage. This presented me with the chance to train with a great runner who was almost certain to become a French Olympian just a few years later.

———

I stood by myself anxiously waiting for the service elevator. I was in the loading zone in the bowels of Madison Square Garden, the world's most famous arena. It was a brutally cold February night, and I had taken the bus and the subway to the Garden, as I was to compete in the inaugural

High School Mile at the Millrose Games. Since 1914, the feature event at Millrose was the Wanamaker Mile, and for years, this was the hottest ticket in town, always a Garden sell-out. This year, 1974, was no different. The Wanamaker Mile always closed the show, and this year the very first High School Mile would be featured right before the main event.

The elevator arrived, and I stepped in, a bundle of nerves. There were already several athletes and coaches on the giant elevator, with one interesting-looking guy standing out from the rest. With a head of red curls and wearing oversized glasses while reading a book, there he was. Marcel Philippe.

I never said a word to him, but I took it as a sign, and it was at that moment when I decided to go to Fordham.

I kept this decision to myself through the spring of my senior year. This turned out to be a huge mistake. As I continued to run well, more and more colleges were calling and trying to visit with me, which was a big distraction. One day, Fred Dwyer, who, to say the least, was a straight shooter, approached me and asked if I was going to choose Manhattan College. Now, Fred posed this more like a statement or directive than a question, so I definitely didn't say yes, but I definitely didn't say no either. Which Fred, being the mind reader that he wasn't, I guess took as a yes.

Later that spring, after I made a formal commitment to Fordham, I was doing a workout by myself on the cinder track at Vanny. It just so happened that a few Manhattan College guys were working out at the same time. As I jogged a lap in between my 440-yard intervals, who decided to jog next to me? Fred Dwyer, wearing a shirt and tie and holding a stopwatch. Let's just say that based on his red face, bulging eyes, and loud, colorful language, Fred was not congratulating me on my decision to go to Fordham.

CHAPTER FOUR

A NOT SO ROSY HILL

Fordham University's Rose Hill campus is in the North Bronx. Flanked by the New York Botanical Gardens and the Bronx Zoo, Fordham feels like an oasis in the middle of the tough, working-class Belmont neighborhood. Eighty acres of neatly manicured lawns graced with beautiful nineteenth-century architecture, the Fordham campus is highlighted by the iconic Keating Hall, with its clock tower and palatial steps. Keating Hall sits majestically over Edwards Parade, the grassy quadrangle in the heart of the campus.

Outside of the iron gates was the real Bronx. Roosevelt High School was just across the street on Fordham Road. Just behind the high school was Arthur Avenue, with its legendary Italian restaurants. To New Yorkers in the know, this was the *real* Little Italy. There were also the neighborhood bars, where the regulars tolerated the Fordham kids, especially on Thursday nights, back when the legal drinking age was eighteen. And then of course, there was White Castle, whose legendary little square hamburgers were very popular, especially after midnight and after one beer too many. It's a little-known scientific fact that White Castle hamburgers were designed to taste good only after a night of drinking.

Like any other kid going to college, I was anxious, apprehensive, and full of fear. But thanks to receiving an athletic scholarship, I became the first member of my Irish immigrant family to be able to attend college, and that filled me with pride. Yet the scariest part was moving away from home and living in a freshman dorm on campus. There was a bright side, because at home I shared a bedroom with my two brothers, whereas at Fordham I only had one roommate, Jackie Lynch, who was also on a track scholarship. What proved to be most daunting was that I felt an immeasurable pressure to earn my scholarship each and every day and live up to the expectations of my coach, Tommy Byrne, while also certainly not letting my parents down. I was not emotionally prepared for any of this.

When I was in high school, the Monday through Friday ritual was to rise and shine, ride the bus and subway, attend classes, ride the bus and subway again, go to track practice, more bus and subway, home by early evening, dinner alone, homework, and then bed. Saturday was race day. Sunday was rest day. As I look back on those times, I realize that when I went to Fordham, I was very immature and socially underdeveloped. After all, I went to an all-boys Catholic high school and participated in a sport where you trained every day and competed virtually all year round. I had no time to build friendships outside of my teammates, and while I had a girlfriend, I never really saw her. My teammates were my only gang, and while those friendships were some of the best I've had in my life and still remain to this day, it was a small, tight circle with very little variety. The harsh reality was that I experienced little else outside of school, running, and riding mass transportation. So to make it through Fordham, I had a lot of growing up to do.

Lucky for me, being on the track team provided a little insulation from many of the freshman pressures. First, I had an instant set of new friends, my teammates. Second, being on the track team kept me busy and was a good distraction. Third, the upperclassmen on the team could hopefully help me navigate and acclimate to college life.

My running went well in my freshman year. In the fall, we qualified for the NCAA Cross Country Championships, the first time a Fordham team had ever done so. We were all thrilled and ready to compete on the national level, until we got the sobering news that the school's athletic department decided not to fund the trip. No NCAAs for us. The athletic director, Pete Carlesimo, didn't see the value in non-revenue-generating sports. Pete himself was a former football player and happened to be the father of the future legendary college and NBA head coach P.J. Carlesimo. Pete often saw track, tennis, and other sports as barely a grade higher than intramurals. I wish I had known this before I chose Fordham.

Dejected, our team gathered in C-House, which was a dormitory on campus where some of our teammates lived. Rather than having two students to a room like the freshman dorm, this was a house of suites where eight students could live together in an apartment-like setting. I guess this was my first experience in the C-suite. As we sat in the living room of C-4, wallowing in our anguish and lamenting our fate, somebody came up with the idea that on the actual day and exact time of the NCAAs, why don't we have our own race and then compare our times to the finishers in Bloomington, Indiana?! Somehow, though, this idea morphed into our team running as a form of protest against the athletic department for its decision not to send us to Bloomington. We then decided that we were going to run a twenty-four-hour relay around Edwards Parade, which was adjacent to the Rose Hill Gym and was home to the offices of Pete Carlesimo and his staff.

We started our relay in late morning to coincide with the start time of the NCAAs in Bloomington. One by one, each member of our team would run a few laps around Edwards Parade then pass the baton to the next guy. Originally this stunt went largely unnoticed, but then word spread across campus, and we were eventually joined by some students as well as athletes from the other sports. They did everything from cheering us on to bringing us food and beverages, and some even chose to run with us. As the sun set and classes were all but over for the day, our protest was starting to gain momentum.

In the fall of 1974, the Vietnam War was winding down, but the sentiment and tension about the war were still present on every campus in America, including Fordham. So the idea of staging a protest was still considered radical, no matter the cause. It was also a time when the track guys were the cool guys on campus. I know, hard to believe. The legendary Steve Prefontaine, from the University of Oregon, was our patron saint. Track guys on campuses all across America were the ones with long hair, mustaches, beards, Levi's, and ear piercings. The football and basketball players, on the other hand, had crew cuts, sported letterman jackets, and wore khakis. While I will never speculate as to who was for or against the war, there was definitely a vivid distinction in how we looked compared with other student-athletes at Fordham. Just even walking to class, you could tell who was on the track team and who wasn't. Boy, looking at college athletes today, it is clear that this axis has swung a full 180.

With nightfall upon us, a few cars came out near Edwards Parade to shine their headlights on our relay. Even people from the neighborhood were coming by to see what was going on. But it was a visit to Rose Hill that evening by a guy named Gerald Eskenazi that made a difference. A well-known sportswriter for *The New York Times*, Gerry had received a phone call about this protest toward Fordham's athletic department, so his curiosity brought him to campus along with a photographer.

When the sun came up the next morning, our twenty-four-hour protest relay was winding down, but our troubles with the athletic department were just beginning. *The Times* ran a story along with a photograph. Gerry's piece only quoted one Fordham runner, its new freshman star. "We are running for ourselves," I said. "No one seems to care that we qualified for the national championship." Of course, this drew the ire of Mr. Carlesimo, so I was advised to shut up, put my head down, and just go to class and run.

Just a few months later, our two-mile relay team qualified for the NCAA Indoor Championships. John Jurgens, the Trammel twins, Alex and Eric, and I were hopefully going to Detroit to compete against the best Division

1 teams in the country. This time the athletic department was swift with its approval. So that March of 1975, the four of us, along with our coach, Tommy Byrne, flew from LaGuardia to Detroit. This was only the second time I had ever been on an airplane.

My first plane trip came a few months earlier, during my senior year of high school, when I was invited to compete in an international prep meet in Chicago. That trip remains a fond memory for me because after having flown several million miles to all corners of the earth, that flight to Chicago inspired the wanderlust that is still with me to this very day. Yet there is another memory from this trip that had nothing to do with the flight.

If all went well, and the flight back to LaGuardia arrived on time, I would have a small window to get home, change my clothes, and then race from the Bronx to my high school graduation, which was to be held that evening at St. Patrick's Cathedral on Fifth Avenue in the city. During that mad dash in the car with my parents, I was hoping I could mention to them one tiny little detail from my trip to Chicago. Now, this was going to be hard to do because, let's just say my dad, well, he liked to yell at other drivers, just like he yelled at the television on Sundays when the Giants made one of their many mistakes.

You see, when I was in Chicago, the meet director asked to see me before I flew home. He began, "Since you are the only New Yorker here at the Chicago Invitational, I have a great opportunity for you and your family! Wouldn't it be just a wonderful experience if you were to host for just a few days at your home in New York, the two runners from Germany who also competed here in Chicago? They have never been to New York, so we've arranged for them to fly home next week from JFK. What a fabulous cultural moment it would be for everyone!"

Now I remember this not sounding at all like a question, so I definitely didn't say yes, but I guess the meet director thought it was definitely not a no, which to him was definitely a yes. When I mentioned all of this in the car to Gene and Cassie, there was a considerable amount of nonverbal communication going on. There was a long, and I mean a long, moment of silence, yet no yelling or taking the Lord's name in vain. After all, we were on our way to St. Patrick's, and it wasn't a Giants game. So, my parents definitely didn't say no, which, if I took a page out of the meet director's book, meant it was definitely a yes? Or at least it was not a no. Actually, they didn't say anything. Not a word. Just a lot of unnecessary accelerating and braking by my dad and plumes of smoke coming out of his ears.

Two days later, the McCarthys welcomed Helmut Stenzel and Michael Lederer to our home, which had three bedrooms, each already occupied by at least two or three McCarthys. Small detail. Helmut and Michael got one bedroom, while me and my brothers slept in the living room. Turns out after all, it was a great experience, despite adjusting to a few little cultural nuances, like when our German guests would walk buck naked in the hallway from the shower to the bedroom every day.

———

My freshman year at Fordham ended much better than it began. Aside from establishing myself as a rabble rouser, our two-mile relay team just got nipped at the tape, losing to Princeton in the NCAAs at Cobo Hall in Detroit. A friend and native New Yorker, Craig Masback, ran the anchor leg for Princeton and was just two steps ahead of our own John Jurgens. This not only earned Jurgens, the Trammell twins, and me All-American status, but along with Princeton, we had one of the fastest two-mile relay teams in the world that year.

Later that same year, I finished sixth in the mile at the IC4A Championships held at William and Mary University in Williamsburg, Virginia. Villanova's Eamonn Coghlan won in under four minutes, making this my first time competing in a sub-four-minute mile race. My time was 4:05, which was a dramatic improvement over my 4:13 high school time just a year earlier. After a very long car ride from Virginia back to New York with assistant coach Jim Mitchell and John Jurgens, who ran 4:01 in the very same race, they dropped me off at my house in Co-op City, since the dorms at Fordham were closed for the summer. I quietly entered the house around 2:00 a.m. and crashed into the lower bunk bed in a bedroom that had been hostilely taken over while I was away at college by my brothers Tom and John.

I must have woken up my dad, because he came into the bedroom, and as he stood there, a silhouette in the dark except for the glow of his cigarette, I told him about my race in Virginia. He had no words, but I detected a faint smile in the dark. I then said to him, as he walked to the door to return to bed, "Dad…only five seconds away." I loved saying those words to him.

The summer break between my freshman and sophomore years gave me a chance to catch my breath and reflect on the year that was, and to prepare for the year that was to come. Now that I knew what to expect from college, I felt a lot less anxious about returning to Fordham. In my first year, I had managed to get decent grades, I had made new friends, and I even had a beautiful girlfriend. Now here I was, returning with some idea of what I wanted to study; I was a little more socially mature, and I had a 4:05 mile time.

Five seconds away.

————

The first Saturday following Labor Day, Tommy Byrne had us do a time trial through the back hills of Van Cortlandt. The weather that day fit neatly into the category of gross and disgusting. The temperature was in the high seventies, low eighties. There was a thick cloud cover blotting out the sun, and there was a dense air that, well, made even your sweat *sweat*.

We had an impromptu start to the time trial, dashing across the cow pasture and heading directly toward the narrow horse path and the back hills. The collegiate cross-country course at Vanny was very different from the course we raced in high school. For starters, the college course was five miles, twice the distance as in high school. In a college race, you made a loop around the cow pasture before entering the back hills, whereas in high school, you sprinted across the pasture in a quick minute or so. Once you got to the horse path in a college race, the course was longer and had more hills and a tougher terrain than what the prepsters travailed. And the college course had a moment of truth, which the runners called Cemetery Hill. Originally named Vault Hill in 1749, this was the site of the burial ground of the Dutch settlers, the Van Cortlandts. This hill was beyond steep, and for every runner, it was make or break.

This time trial was important to all of us, as it would give each teammate a chance to see not only what condition you were in but also how you measured up against everyone else. Since the path was narrow, you were forced to form a single line with your eyes trained on the uneven terrain while you tried to stay within striking distance of anyone in front of you. Once you exited the hills and back onto the cow pasture, you could close in on the leaders if you had any gas left in your tank.

One nice surprise when we gathered that September day was that we were joined by Bobby Byrnes, who had graduated the previous May. Bobby was our cross-country captain a year earlier, and he certainly came out that day for the camaraderie, if not to just bust balls. During my freshman year, I was a target for Bobby's razzing, but he also was there to help me with anything that had to do with math, as that was his sweet spot and my sour spot.

Not surprisingly, on that day, some of us were in better condition than others, so we were spread out through the hills. One by one, we eventually crossed the finish line, with our drenched cotton T-shirts stuck to our skin from sweat and the hazy, moist air, while soiled with trail dirt and debris.

We were all breathing heavily, yet we were relieved that we were done for the day. As we milled around, waiting for everyone to finish, a runner from another school suddenly ran up to us, out of breath, and frantically asked, "You guys are from Fordham, right?! Well, one of your guys collapsed in the hills, and he looks like he's not breathing!!" Instinctively, we sprinted across the pasture, heading back into the hills, retracing our steps, and became instantly panicked when we found Bobby Byrnes lying flat on his back.

By this point, a few lagging runners were there to help Bobby by trying to perform CPR, while some of us were rubbing his legs to hopefully get his blood flowing. Eventually paramedics did show up on foot, since the path was too narrow for an ambulance. We all stood there traumatized by this horrific moment as we watched the paramedics put an oxygen mask on our former captain.

Once the paramedics took Bobby on a stretcher, we all scrambled to get into a few cars, and then we raced to Montefiore Hospital, hoping to see him and make sure he would be all right. We gathered outside the emergency room, and as much as we tried, they wouldn't let us in, since we were covered in mud and drenched in sweat. We stood waiting for what seemed like an eternity when suddenly the door opened, and a nurse came outside. At this point it had just started to rain. When she saw our hopeful faces waiting for any word of good news, she just started to cry and walked back inside.

Without a word, we knew we lost our brother Bobby.

This was something no one was prepared for, especially me. How could you be so young and athletic, with your whole life ahead of you? This was just not supposed to happen. A few days later, the funeral mass for Bobby was held at the University Chapel, which was located on Fordham's campus and just steps away from C-House, where I now lived. As I walked toward the church and saw the large crowd in front of me, I suddenly became overwhelmed with grief and began to cry uncontrollably. Tommy Byrne saw me and walked me back to my dorm. I never went to the funeral.

A week later, there was a beautifully written tribute to Bobby in the Fordham student newspaper called *The Ram*. I was honored to have been quoted in the article:

"Bobby was a valiant person whose devotion and hard work attitude was admired by all of us who knew him. When he won the Metropolitan two-mile championship last February, I was probably more excited than he was, because I could appreciate all the hard work that he put in to get that title. That was one of the many moments that made me feel proud to know Bobby Byrnes. I hope someday I can be like him."

As I reflect, and while I didn't know it at the time, Bobby Byrnes gave me my very first real lesson in this thing called leadership. While I was named captain at All Hallows, I assumed it was mostly because I was the fastest kid on the team. It never dawned on me in my teenage years that being a captain was more than just a symbolic honor. It was Bobby from whom I learned more from what he did than what he said. As an example, when we would finish practice at Vanny, all of us would just pile into cars and take the short drive back to campus. Often, Bobby would skip the ride and just run back. He never said a word; he would just be off on his way. Over time, some of us would join him on the jog back, and not because he invited us or told us to, because he never did. It was just because some leaders don't lead. People just follow.

With Bobby gone, I relied on Marcel Philippe for leadership and guidance. While he had enrolled at Fordham Law School, which was at the Lincoln Center campus in the city, Marcel, his schedule permitting, would train with us whenever he could. We became fast friends, particularly during the semester breaks, when we would work out together and then spend the down time just hanging out. While Bobby Byrnes gave me a starter class in leadership, it was Marcel who helped me build my confidence. Up until this point, I ran all my races out of fear, trying to conquer my self-doubt. Or maybe I was just trying to win every race in order to keep my scholarship? Maybe more so, I was just trying to impress my dad. Marcel didn't help me chase those pressures away; he taught me how to manage them and how to run for me and not for anyone else. Marcel helped me to put everything in perspective.

Despite the influence of Marcel, the rest of my time at Fordham gradually went from being a labor of love to becoming a chore. My spirit had been broken when we lost Bobby Byrnes. Then Tommy Byrne and his wife,

Mary, lost a baby at birth, which took the wind out of Tommy's sails. For a while, our wonderful assistant coach, Jim Mitchell, ran our workouts, but the optimism that I once had was slowly waning. Still, there were classes to attend and fun to be had. After all, this was college. But for me, the magic wasn't happening.

In my senior year, I managed to get my mile time down to 4:03, when I finished second to Peter Gaughn from Manhattan College in the Metropolitan Championships. I'm pretty sure Fred Dwyer loved that. Still, instead of being excited, I felt more of a sense of failure, since I ran 4:05 three years earlier as a freshman. My final race as a college senior was at the IC4A Championships, held at Franklin Field on the campus of the University of Pennsylvania, and home to the famous Penn Relays. Graduation from Fordham was just the week prior, on a beautiful May afternoon on Edwards Parade, the site of our protest relay nearly four years earlier. Alan Alda, the television star and Fordham alum, was our commencement speaker. During the ceremony, I was honored to receive the prestigious Terrence O'Donnell Award, presented to "The Fordham athlete who best exemplifies the qualities of sportsmanship, loyalty, dedication, and self-discipline." So the IC4As would be my last hurrah as a Fordham Ram unless I ran fast enough to qualify for the NCAAs.

On Friday, I ran the opening round of the 1,500-meters, where I qualified easily for Saturday's final. I spent a restless Friday night with the weight of my world unintentionally yet undeniably on my shoulders. To this day, I am completely capable of taking all my worries, both big and small, and neatly stacking them into a massive pile. Then I tend to stare at and fixate on that pile. School's over. No more college lifestyle. Move back home. Friends are shotgun sprayed into the real world. No job waiting. And Saturday could be my last race…ever?

Saturday comes, and I head to the paddock with the other 1,500-meter finalists. It's a hot but dry day. Cassie and Gene made the trip to watch me run. And as usual, I really wanted to make my dad proud. We put on our spikes and tore off our sweats, and we were led to the top of the backstretch and to the starting line. We settled in and lined up, heads down, waiting for the gun to sound.

Now, the 1,500 is an interesting race. Slightly shorter than a mile, the 1,500 is considered the premier race of track and field around the world. The 100-meter race is all about speed. The 400 is speed and stamina. 800 meters is speed and endurance. But 1,500-meters is all stamina and endurance, but it's your instinct that can win or lose a race. There is no time for thinking in the 1,500, just reacting.

The tempo of the race was decided almost immediately when the front-runner revealed himself. I settled in toward the middle of the pack, and the pace seemed comfortable to me. After 800 meters, some runners became restless, and they picked up the pace. As we came off the turn, heading for the bell lap, I suddenly stepped off the track and stumbled onto the infield. My knees buckled, and I gasped for air. I was then ushered off the track and taken into a locker room, where I was put under a cold shower. As I settled down, I saw my mom standing by the door, noticeably frantic. Assistant coach Jim Mitchell then came into the locker room with an incredulous look on his face. Not at all fazed by my mother being there, he goes off.

"You quit!! I cannot believe it! You just...quit!!"

He was right. I gave up. I quit.

CHAPTER FIVE

BELL LAP

H e cried. Like a baby.
　　　My dad stood at the top of the stairs, about to leave for work. As was ritual, my mom would send him off with a kiss and a worried gaze into a cruel working world that over the years showed him very little mercy. We all knew that having to provide for a family of seven was daunting for my dad. Yet we conveniently ignored the fact that he often feared failure, while he carried the burden of not letting his family down.

Yet on this summer day in 1978, and just two months after graduation, I was standing with my mom to send him off to work, yet also to say goodbye. A few hours later, I would be leaving for Gainesville, Florida, with a one-way ticket. Like it was for most men of that era, to cry was rare, never mind in front of others, as it was considered far from masculine and a pure sign of weakness. So this was a moment. For both of us.

As he descended the stairs, his crying seemed uncontrollable. Still, he went out the front door to catch his bus to Manhattan. Only a few hours later, I would descend those very same stairs and step out of that same front door. But unlike my dad…I wouldn't be coming home for dinner.

Our relationship, as with many fathers and sons, was complicated, not necessarily because of our differences but mostly because of our similarities. So here we were, saying goodbye, or was it so long, which was what our family resorted to saying to each other when facing long separations. Yet it was important for me to take the bold step to try to finally be different than my dad. Like him, I was also scared to death to walk out that door. He may have been worried about his workday, but I was worried about my future. Deep down, what motivated me to leave that day wasn't just to chase the dream of breaking the four-minute mile, but rather to gain his approval and to make him proud of me.

In the two months since I had disgraced myself by dropping out of my final collegiate race, I spent a lot of time beating myself up. I created a pile of what I considered to be my failures, both big and small, and poured gasoline on them. But I never lit the match. To this day, I can usually handle criticism simply because no one could be as hard on me as I can be on myself. So the idea of moving to the Sunshine State and chasing my dream of breaking the four-minute mile became less of a romantic story with a fairy-tale ending and more of a need for redemption.

After changing planes in Atlanta, my Eastern Airlines flight finally landed in Gainesville. As I would find out later, if you died in Gainesville, you would have to stop in Atlanta on your way to heaven. Once the plane door opened, I was immediately suspended in a state of culture shock. We descended the aircraft steps (where was the jetway?!), and I picked up my duffel bag not on a carousel inside the terminal but on a table outside on the tarmac, with a crooked umbrella hovering over it.

I was met outside by a guy named Bruce Kritzler, whom Marty Liquori had sent to collect me. A completely laid-back and gentle guy, Bruce was the manager of the original Athletic Attic store, which was ground zero for a chain of successful running shops that seemingly blossomed overnight throughout the country. The original store was in the attic of Bill Pinner Shoes, a women's-only shoe store run by its charming and charismatic namesake. Athletic Attic was founded by Marty with his partners, Jimmy Carnes and

Gerry Shackow. Jimmy was the former head track coach at the University of Florida and future head coach of the 1980 U.S. Olympic track and field team. Jimmy had the gift of Southern charm along with the perfect lilting southern accent. Gerry, a lawyer by trade, was a Midwest transplant who provided pragmatism and structure to the trio. Both Carnes and Shackow had a style and manner that cut nicely across Marty's "shoot from the hip and be hip while you shoot" New Jersey posture. These three guys couldn't have been more different from one another, and not only in their backgrounds but also in their personalities. But it worked.

As we drove, Bruce told me about this exceptional running community I was about to join. There were many future and present Olympians that trained together and often socialized with one another, notwithstanding a few rivalries here and there. Frank Shorter, Jack Bacheler, and Barry Brown were just a few of the names that domiciled here, not to mention the dozens of transient wishful stars who would come to Gainesville for a few weeks, and sometimes for a few years. There was the benefit of the university's fast tartan track, miles of trails and seldom-traveled roads for long runs, not to mention a mild Central Florida climate.

While I was so enamored with Bruce and his chamber of commerce speech, I was still a little fuzzy on where I was actually going to live. We then pulled up to a small, nondescript house in an equally nondescript neighborhood. As my culture shock was now at full tilt, I happened to notice a side yard with extremely tall grass and weeds. In it I saw a tall and slim shirtless guy, profusely sweating while whacking the grass with a golf club. Bruce casually told me that this was my new home, and this was my new roommate, Steve Foster. Quickly I realized Steve wasn't working on his golf swing, and if he were, I would've suggested he take a lesson or several. Now, while growing up in the Bronx, I never actually knew anyone who had a lawn, but I knew enough to know that a good lawn usually isn't three feet high and that a lawnmower is a way better way to maintain a lawn than furiously swinging a golf club.

As he extended his damp, dirty hand, he said, "Hi! I'm Steve. Welcome to Gainesville!" Oh boy, I thought.

"I'm Gene. Nice to know you." (I think...?) "So, what's going on?" I asked awkwardly.

"The lady that owns this house called me and told me to mow the lawn, or I would be evicted. So I'm doing the best I can. Now that you officially live here, are you ready to pitch in and help?!" he asked. "Sure!" I mumbled, while thinking if I should grab a driver or a wedge or maybe just offer to caddie?

As I stood there in suspended animation, I immediately searched for an escape route, briefly reminiscing about my All Hallows field day. Sadly, my only escape route evaporated. Bruce Kritzler and his very large, old, un-air-conditioned clunker was long gone. Welcome to Gainesville. Dad would be so proud.

Steve Foster was from Ohio and just a few years older than me. He moved to Gainesville to be a part of this elite running community, and he was a member of the legendary Florida Track Club. Just a year prior, Steve had run a 3:55 mile. So up until now, I had only been in a race where the winner broke four minutes, but here I was, about to live with a sub-four-minute miler who did yard work with a 7-iron.

Once I was settled in, or said another way, less traumatized, I finally met Marty Liquori in person. I was a bit nervous, but I was captivated by the idea that here I was, standing in front of and talking to a guy that I had seen on a magazine cover nearly eight years earlier, which was a moment of epiphany for a young teen. Over those previous years, I religiously followed Marty's career and read about all his races. Whenever his races were televised, I would drop everything to be glued to the TV. No matter whether he won or lost, I was a student of his every move.

Aside from being only the third high schooler in history to break the four-minute mile, Marty was, at the time, the youngest runner to have competed in an Olympic 1,500-meter final, which he did in Mexico City in 1968. Marty was also ranked number one in the world for the mile in both 1969 and 1971. As he got older, he switched his focus from the mile to the longer 5,000-meters, which was the mile three times over and then some. Just a year before I finally met Marty on that steamy July day, he had been ranked number one in the world in the 5,000. But at that moment when I met my hero, none of his world-class performances seemed to matter that much to me. It was right there and then that I realized my intrigue was with his willpower, determination, and grit. In other words, how he did everything was suddenly more important to me than his glorious outcomes.

———

I reported in late afternoon, as instructed, to the track at the University of Florida for my very first workout. Well, actually, I was given a ride by my roommate, Steve Foster, since I didn't have a car, a small detail that I never considered before relocating to a rural area. It also should be noted that I didn't have a driver's license, another small detail. My dad, to his credit, had taken me to a driving test in the Bronx a few years earlier, even though I never had a driving lesson. That's a large detail. Obviously, as you've probably surmised, I didn't pass. But what you don't know is that my test was over in eight seconds or less, since I put the car in *reverse* rather than the preferred *drive* and crashed into the vehicle behind me. Maybe worse than failing was knowing that the kid waiting in the car behind me was going to fail his test too, due to broken headlights.

The drive home with Dad was extremely quiet until about twenty minutes in, when he spontaneously burst into hysterical laughter. It caused me to laugh too, and it definitely broke the tension. He wasn't laughing, however, a week later, when it cost a thousand bucks to fix his beloved Dodge Aspen.

———

As any runner would know, before a track workout you would typically warm up. It might begin with a bit of stretching; then you would jog a few laps on the outside lanes of the track before beginning your workout, like twelve times one lap at fifty-six seconds with a half lap jog in between. That wasn't exactly how Marty and the guys approached warming up. Instead, everyone would gather in the parking lot, shoot the breeze for a bit, and then eventually Marty would literally start to shuffle, barely a jog, while the small group would shuffle right behind. I don't think I have ever run that slow in my life. Being a forefoot striker with a relatively high knee lift, this made me feel like I was going backward. Curiously, we didn't go on the track for our warm-up, but rather onto a narrow, sandy trail that would take us around Lake Alice, which was in the center of the Florida campus. This very still and calm lake, dotted with lily pads, was accented on its banks with willow, oak, and maple trees, all decorated with Spanish moss. This was something I had never seen before (add another entry into the culture shock journal), even though the New York Botanical Gardens were across the street from Fordham's campus.

As a kid from the Bronx, in addition to my ignorance of all things botanical, my experience with wildlife was equally underdeveloped, even though the famed Bronx Zoo was also across the street from Fordham. Up until this point in my life, my idea of wildlife was limited to rabid pigeons and squirrels, cockroaches, and of course, dumpster-diving rats. Occasionally I recalled seeing a horse, but there was usually a police officer on its back.

From what little research I did about Florida before I moved there, I remembered reading that any body of water larger than a puddle would probably be inhabited by an alligator. During my first warm-up shuffle around Lake Alice, that theory was completely dispelled. There were no gators in the lake. That's because they were all sunbathing along the trail that we were jogging on!

As I found my rhythm with my training partners and new friends, I anxiously awaited the big reveal. The secret sauce. What made these guys so good? Undoubtedly, they were all gifted and talented, but that was merely the price of entry. Even though the workouts were nothing special, you certainly had to have the goods just to keep up. I soon began obsessively observing how these guys behaved. I paid little attention to their stride or arm carriage and focused more on trying to find a pattern to their psyches. I was convinced this was what made these guys some of the best runners in the world. Because of this, each workout for me was equal measures physically challenging and mentally stimulating.

On the long afternoon runs, the conversation was always social. Barry Brown could talk for an entire fifteen-mile run, on a variety of topics and with little punctuation. The original human run-on-sentence. When Barry spoke, though, it was hard to tell if Marty was listening or if his thoughts were somewhere else. Later, Marty would fondly say of Barry, "He's like a car radio. You turn him on for the entire ride. Sometimes you listen and sometimes it's in the background…but it's always there." For me, the big question was, what was Marty thinking about when Radio Free Barry was playing in the background?

There was a side to Marty that ran parallel to his legendary running career, and this also intrigued me. Early on in his life, Marty had a goal of becoming a millionaire by the time he was twenty-five. That's a good amount of money in today's world, never mind in the early seventies. Yet the money wasn't his only goal. Just like in any of his races, the preparation and path to a victory were where he got his satisfaction. Money was merely the happy result of bringing a great idea to life. While I didn't know it at the time, Marty was the first entrepreneur I had ever met. And this was before I had ever heard that word or knew what it meant.

Over time I started to realize that the things that made Marty a world-class runner were no different from the disciplines he used in his very successful business pursuits. Sure, he had all the textbook characteristics: hard work, determination, perseverance, discipline, and motivation. But he had one more gear that separated him from the pack. He deeply believed in something that he was committed to, even if the odds were stacked against him. As a matter of fact, when the odds weren't in his favor, that's when Marty was at his best. He also worked both ends against the middle. He turned being an underdog into an advantage, while he could also silence the naysayers when he was the favorite.

When he was injured and couldn't compete in the 1972 Olympics, Marty parlayed that downtime into becoming a *Wide World of Sports* commentator, working alongside television legends like Howard Cosell and Jim McKay. So Marty was still at the Olympics while not necessarily in the Olympics. And while having athletes do TV analysis was nothing new, Marty worked with the very best in the field. Never the B-team. And by the way, Marty wasn't just a member of the A-team; he was exceptionally good at it.

Aside from his success as a founder of Athletic Attic, which at one point grew to over one hundred stores, Marty was always thinking about, considering, and pursuing ways to optimize an idea and turn it into an opportunity. This was my first glimpse into something called vision. It's a word thrown around way too much today, even though it's a talent, if not a gift, reserved for an exceptionally small part of the population. His endeavors would only become pleasing to him when the path he took to success was equal to its financial reward. Like anyone, Marty liked easy, but he was never afraid of hard. He was always thoughtful about his pursuits, and he never had regrets for the ones that failed. While very few people on the planet (most particularly me) would never be remotely as successful an athlete as Marty Liquori, I still was determined early on to learn and live by his credos so that just maybe, I could find some success on the track as well, eventually, as off it.

———

While dreaming seems timeless when you're asleep, it abruptly ends when you wake up. When you are daydreaming, there is a time frame, usually measured with a sundial or an hourglass. The best songs about dreams coming true usually clock in at around three minutes. I had only one dream, and I wanted it to be measured by a stopwatch and to precisely end at 3:59.

Aside from a dream, I had a timeline as well. I planted my flag in Florida in the summer of 1978 and had given myself two years for two reasons. Like many aspiring athletes, the culmination of being the best you could be meant peaking in the summer of an Olympic year. While it was impossible for me to represent my country at the highest level, I still wanted to train with and draft off those who would likely become Olympians. As Freddie Patek, the five-foot, five-inch former MLB shortstop once said, "I would rather be the shortest player in the majors than the tallest player in the minors." The other reason I gave myself a two-year window was that at some point, adulthood had to kick in.

When I was in college, I never had the discipline to put in the hard work, particularly when it came to morning runs or every-other-afternoon long runs. I measured my own fitness and preparedness by how I did my track workouts. If I could run eight quarters in say, fifty-four seconds, then I would convince myself that I was ready for my next race.

With Marty, we spent the entire summer and fall doing a five-mile run every morning and then another ten miles in the afternoon, Monday through Friday. Saturday was reduced to an easy ten miler in the afternoon, followed by a long twenty miles on Sunday morning. It was one thing to manage my culture shock living in a new place, but it was a jolt to my body and my mind to run over one hundred miles per week. In college I had convinced myself that fifty miles a week was more than enough.

While everything was new to me, I had to bite the bullet and just follow the bouncing ball. If this was how the best in the world do it, then I had to have complete faith in the system. This is where I first learned the idea of trusting the process. Still, the process was just that, a process. It wasn't ironclad. You had to adjust along the way, and you had to see things coming and shift to avoid them. Running one hundred miles a week also meant finding time to rest and recover. It seemed like being perfectly fit teeter-tottered on the brink of chronic fatigue or even getting sick. I learned that the workouts would break you down, but the recovery was where you would build strength and stamina.

Diet was another thing. In the late seventies, I ate to satisfy my hunger. I put no real value on what I was putting into my body. Barry Brown would always say, "If the furnace is hot, it will burn anything." Today's athletes have carefully measured diets. All science, but certainly not a whole lot of fun. I also came from an era where the trainer would give us salt tablets if we were sweating too much. Today, that would be unheard of! But that's all we knew. Then I met Dr. Cade.

Dr. Robert Cade was a professor of medicine and nephrology at the University of Florida. In the mid-sixties, one of the University's football coaches approached Dr. Cade, wondering why his players couldn't pee after long practices. Dr. Cade established and led a research team that studied dehydration, using the Gator football team as its subject. Central Florida had its own brand of heat and humidity that was way more intense and denser than back home in New York. Also, the football team practiced and played its games at Florida Field, which was nicknamed the Swamp, where the heat and humidity were extra brutal since the field was well below street level. To replenish the lost fluids, Dr. Cade invented something called Gatorade, a concoction of glucose and electrolytes, which today is a staple at every sporting event from little league and peewee football all the way up to the NFL and MLB.

Crazy as it sounds now, in all my years of training, I never once considered hydration as part of my conditioning. When we were in high school, we would all stop at a bodega after practice and get a sixteen-ounce Coke or Pepsi to quench our thirst. Not to mention a bag of Doritos, I guess to replace the sodium we didn't know that we had lost.

I once heard Dr. Cade speak at a Florida Track Club meeting, and I was instantly captivated. I then immediately introduced myself to him. He was colorful and acerbic, while he also reminded me of Truman Capote if he were to be reincarnated as a scientist. Over the years, I would go visit with Dr. Cade, always fascinated that he was equal measures intellectual and entertainer. I learned a lot from those visits with him, well beyond the stories about his game-changing remedy for dehydration.

———

When I was in high school and college, we seemed to have a race or a meet every weekend. Cross-country in the fall, then indoor track in the winter, followed by outdoor track season in the spring. In New York City every meet was as major event, attracting schools and stars from all over the Tri-State area and sometimes beyond. As I've said, the kids in the suburbs had it easier, as they would maybe have a dual meet against a crosstown school while occasionally venturing into the big city for a major race or meet with top-tier talent.

In Gainesville, three-quarters of our time was spent on conditioning and preparation, not racing. We did not run cross-country at all. The risk of injury was not worth it. We may have run a race or two during the indoor season and a few more in the spring, but this group was preparing for the summer, where there was a circuit of races, particularly in Europe, where there was stiff international competition, not to mention lucrative under-the-table prize money for the biggest stars. I was absolutely not in this category, so my emphasis changed to being a training partner for Marty when he came home in between his summer world travels.

My first year in Gainesville was largely spent adapting to this very different running regimen. My times were improving, and I was gaining confidence, particularly when I competed against runners who were clearly better than me. When I was in high school, I was usually one of the fastest runners in any race I was in. During my post collegiate years, I was often one of the slowest or least experienced runners in the field. I grew to really appreciate this way more than being the guy to beat. Years later, this feeling would become my sweet spot and comfort zone, particularly in my business career. I crave to this day being around people who are different, better and smarter than me.

It was at this time that I also started to grow up. I graduated from living in a house with a high-maintenance lawn to a bigger house with high-maintenance roommates. Eventually, I found my own apartment. One huge mistake I made back then was to let my friend and training partner, Charlie Duggan, convince me to share my second bedroom with two friends of his from Connecticut, who wanted to get a taste of this elite running experience. When these two guys arrived, I immediately had regrets, especially when they gave me a housewarming present: a Styrofoam cooler packed with frozen hamburger patties that they stole on their last day from the Burger King where they both worked.

Another maturing moment was getting my driver's license. Taking the test in Florida was a little less intimidating than in New York. For starters, the test was in a huge parking lot where you maneuvered around orange cones, whereas in New York you started under an overpass and immediately drove onto the city streets and then the expressway. Another major difference was that instead of the standard parallel parking, which was make-or-break in New York, the state of Florida simply required you to park between two white lines, like you were at the mall. No problem! I passed on my first try, and more importantly, I didn't hit any other cars during the test. Now, at the time, I still didn't have a car, but first things first. Then my dad somehow found $1,000 that he didn't have and sent it to me. Grateful, if not astonished, this brought me to tears. That was a lot of money back then for anybody, never mind for Gene and Cassie. I bought a '68 Volkswagen Beetle from a guy I knew. He said it was his grandmother's, and she only drove it to the grocery store. I believed him. It was painted a dull white, maybe a Maaco or Earl Scheib special? It had "four on the floor," whatever that was, and no air-conditioning. There were a few dings here and there, probably from those stray shopping carts on those infrequent grocery store trips, which I regarded as testimony to this car's character and maturity. I added an eight-track player and suddenly, this baby became mine!

———

If there ever was a time to focus and block out everything else, it was now. The summer of '79 through the summer of '80 would be my most important year ever. In my mind, this was going to be life-defining. Once I reached my twenty-fourth birthday in August 1980, I hoped to have realized my decade-long dream of breaking four.

It would also be a point in time to make major life decisions. Do I continue this frivolous athletic pursuit? Where would I call my home? How would I make a living? And maybe bigger than all of that, I had to really get to know myself and reveal a new identity rather than hiding behind my extended childhood, also known as being a track athlete.

Marty had planned that we would train without racing through the fall and then run a few high-level races in the winter. In February 1980, there was a big meet called the Brooks Invitational, named after a running shoe company led at the time by a guy named Jerry Turner. Founded in 1914, Brooks initially made ballet slippers. And while over the years, Brooks has had a few reincarnations, there were several notable moments in its history before it became the top-shelf running brand it is today.

Early in its history, Brooks expanded into other categories, starting with roller skates, as well as football and baseball cleats. As legend has it, in 1962 Jerry Turner somehow finagled his way into the New York Yankees clubhouse. He eagerly showed his cleats to any player that might listen to his sales pitch. Roger Maris was not interested at all, but Mickey Mantle loved them. And here is the amazing part. Mickey, as the story goes, wrote Jerry a check for $44 and bought two pairs! In the modern world of sports marketing, this would be considered a very tall tale, and that's saying a lot because the athletic footwear industry loves to just make stuff up.

The other game-changing moment for Brooks was when Jerry met Marty Liquori and, with Marty's input, introduced in 1974 a running shoe called "The Villanova," named after Marty's alma mater. Jerry, and of course Marty, would have preferred the shoe to be called "The Liquori," but the amateur athletic governing bodies at the time would have nothing of it. It proved to be wildly successful, not just because of how comfortable it was but also because it capitalized on this new consumer trend called "the running boom," which, by the way, is a curious label, since many of its fanatical participants were just really jogging or shuffling along. Still, it was all about health, fitness, and sheer capitalism.

The Brooks Invitational in 1980 was more spectacle than track meet. The venue was the enormous Houston Astrodome, which was the world's first multipurpose domed sports stadium and served as the home of the NFL's Houston Oilers and ultimately MLB's Astros. Dubbed "the Eighth Wonder of the World," one of the Oilers executives remarked at the time that if the Astrodome was the eighth, then the rent was the ninth.

The meet promoter was a guy named Ron Stanko, a former classmate of Marty's at Villanova, who possessed a style of "go big and when you get there, then go even bigger." Stanko sold the idea to CBS-TV to air a few events live on its weekend *Sports Spectacular* show. One of the events would be the mile, featuring some of the fastest milers in the world. While that clearly didn't include me, Marty asked me to be the rabbit, essentially to set a pace for this incredible and talented field. Of course, I jumped at the idea, not just because I would be on the starting line with some of my idols (not to mention a few of my friends) but also because it was going to be live on TV. I knew I would make Gene and Cassie proud back home in the Bronx and give them bragging rights to all the neighbors…even if I was just the rabbit.

There was one other moment in my running career that gave the McCarthys a chance to boast to all their friends. You see, back then, it was hard to brag about your kid's athletic prowess unless he played football, baseball, or basketball. For example, Pat Harris, who lived on the sixth floor of our apartment building on Claflin Avenue, played on our CYO grade school basketball team. Eventually he went on to star at West Point, where he played for the legendary Hall of Fame coach Mike Krzyzewski. Not bad for a kid from the Bronx. Now, telling your neighbor that your kid ran a 4:13 mile just didn't have the same ring to it as twenty points, ten rebounds, and eight assists. But if there was one way to get anyone's attention anywhere in New York City, it was these three words: Madison Square Garden.

When I was a high school senior, I was one of eight runners invited to compete in the inaugural High School Mile at the famed Millrose Games. As was traditional, the Garden was sold out and stuffed with suits, beers, cigarettes, and cigars. I remembered that each of us in that race was petrified because it wasn't often that seventeen-year-olds had eighteen thousand sets of eyeballs trained on them.

A mile race outdoors is four times around a 440-yard track. In the Garden, a mile was eleven laps around an elevated board track that was banked on each turn. Since the Garden was home to the Rangers and Knicks, events like Millrose were crammed in between hockey and basketball games. Because of this, the board track wasn't necessarily assembled with precision, so it was important to take a quick jog on the track before your race so hopefully you could find the dead spots.

When the starter's gun sounded, I reluctantly took the lead. I kept that lead through the bell lap. On the backstretch I could feel the energy of the Garden crowd, since with one hundred yards to go it could be anyone's race. And as the only entrant in the field from one of the five boroughs, I felt that I needed to make the Garden crowd beam with pride, especially Gene and Cassie, who were there with some of their friends up in the cheap seats.

As I came off the final turn, I noticed out of the corner of my right eye that the crowd was beginning to stand and roar. In that split second and with forty yards to go, that slight tilt of my head cost me as my nemesis from Long Island, Mark Belger, passed me on the left and beat me by a step. The Garden erupted, Belger was victorious, and I was stunned. Did this really just happen?

One of the tuxedo-clad meet officials, Kurt Steiner, grabbed both me and Mark by our wrists and told us to take a lap around the track. We got a standing ovation. All these years later, I still get chills just thinking about it. For Mark, it was, of course, a victory lap. For me, it was a lap for Gene and Cassie and all their friends up in the nosebleeds.

As we lined up in the Astrodome, all I could think about was immediately getting to the front, even if it meant giving an elbow to the guy lined up next to me, who just so happened to be John Walker, the New Zealander who was the first person to break 3:50 in the mile. As I sprinted to the front before settling into my pace, something unusual was happening. None of the other runners were keeping up with me. It certainly wasn't that the pace was too fast, as I hit the first quarter in fifty-eight seconds, which was pedestrian for this group of runners. By now, I had a ten-to-fifteen-yard lead, which perplexed everyone, including Dick Stockton and Jim Ryun (yes, the other guy with Marty on the cover of *Sports Illustrated*), who were calling the race live for a national television audience.

Maybe some of the guys like Steve Scott or Eamonn Coghlan were tired since they had raced the night before in Los Angeles. Or just maybe it was something else. As it turned out, Eamonn had suddenly decided after the LA race that he was pulling out of the next day's race in the Astrodome, which horrified CBS, as he was the big draw for this live TV event. Nicknamed "the Chairman of the Boards" because of his unprecedented success on indoor tracks, Eamonn was also handsome and charismatic, which was topped off with his smooth brogue from his native Ireland. Apparently, CBS made some *concessions* to Eamonn to get him to Houston. This apparently rankled the other runners, who decided to dog the slow-starting Coghlan rather than stay up with me, the rabbit.

I took the field through the half mile in 1:58, which is what I was asked to do, as the gap between me and the world's best was starting to close. I then moved over to the outside lanes and let the field pass me. Don Paige and Steve Scott made it a show for the viewers, with Scott edging Paige at the tape in 3:54. Eamonn Coghlan was one of the last to finish. A week later, *Sports Illustrated* ran a piece and I was mentioned. Unfortunately, the writer said that I did "an ineffective job" as the pacesetter. If only he knew the backstory.

One month later, a big blow came to every aspiring U.S. Olympian. President Jimmy Carter had announced that the U.S., along with some other nations around the world, would boycott the Moscow Olympics due to Russia's then-occupation of Afghanistan. This was devastating, especially for Marty, as this may have been his last chance to add Olympic gold to his storied career. He certainly was very accomplished up to this point, but Olympic success had eluded him. It was also at this point when I came to realize that I was fueling my modest goal of a sub-four-minute mile not just on great workouts but from feeding off the energy and determination of the guys I trained with. Now I worried that their energy would fizzle. Yet since I had already quit once a few years earlier, folding up the tent now was not an option for me.

In April 1980, I ran in the Ben Franklin Mile at the Penn Relays, the same venue where I had quit my last collegiate race. Gene and Cassie came to watch me run, which was thrilling, since I hadn't seen them that often since moving to Gainesville. At the bell lap, I was near the front of the pack. I felt great, and I realized that all my hard work, as well as my mental preparedness, put me exactly where I wanted to be. On the backstretch, as some of the runners made their moves, I stutter-stepped and briefly broke my stride, but I still finished a respectable fifth, with the winner being Craig Masback.

As I crossed the finish line, somehow, through the dense crowd, I saw my dad, definitely a *Where's Waldo?* moment. As our eyes met in the distance, he was holding a stopwatch, and he was shaking his head, no. I ran 4:01. Just a stutter step away from realizing my dream.

Since it was an Olympic year, there weren't many opportunities left to race the mile, as most meets switched to 1,500-meters since that was the distance raced in the Games. Marty thought I was ready to finally make my childhood dream come true, so he had an idea. Why don't we have our own impromptu mile race on the track at the University of Florida? We would have it on a weekday evening to avoid the blazing Florida sun. And since running was so popular in Gainesville, it was almost guaranteed to have fans come out simply by just spreading the word.

The race would include several of my training partners, but Marty felt that the field needed someone who was in sub-four shape, so he invited an old college teammate of his who now lived close by in Atlanta. His name was Dick Buerkle. A colorful and outgoing guy, Dick sported a completely shaved head way before it became popular, and he took a lot of razzing for it. Unbeknownst to his classless hecklers, Dick had alopecia since he was twelve years old. Those taunts fueled his determination and made him one of the toughest competitors in our sport. In 1978, Dick broke the world record for the indoor mile, but that wasn't his most astonishing achievement. When he attended Villanova, he was a walk-on rather than a heavily recruited scholarship athlete. To walk on at any Division 1 college or university was a monumental if not impossible task, especially at Villanova. So I was thrilled when Dick agreed to come down to Gainesville to help me.

However, a small problem developed just two days before my shot at making my dream come true. Walking barefoot in my apartment and not paying any attention, I tripped over an ironing board. Now, what an ironing board was doing in my apartment forever remains a mystery, but my middle toe on my left foot swelled to the size of my big toe. I immediately called Marty. He called Dick. No need for him to drive five hours from Atlanta. All bets were off. There would be no shot at my dream.

In late June of 1980 and at the very end of two years chasing four, I flew to Eugene, Oregon, for the U.S. Olympic Trials. For every athlete, these Trials were certainly bittersweet; however, for some, this was their Olympic Games.

I raced in one of the two semifinals for the 1,500-meters. The idea that this may be my last race flooded my mind. My semifinal heat was stacked, and it included Steve Scott, Mike Durkin, and Steve Lacy, who a few days later would become the 1,500-meter contingent to go to Moscow…if there were an Olympic Games for American athletes.

When the race was over, I finished a dismal eighth. I pulled off my track spikes without even unlacing them, and I slowly walked barefoot on the outside lane of the track. This was certainly nothing like my *victory* lap at the Millrose Games. My whole life seemed to flash before my eyes. Was this it? Was this the end? I visualized myself as a fourteen-year-old at Van Cortlandt Park, standing in my gym shorts, nervously waiting for the gun to sound. I had a flurry of thoughts about my Fordham years. Especially when I quit. Now here I was at the Olympic Trials, physically and mentally if not spiritually spent. The tank was empty.

On the backstretch, I saw Marty standing near the track. Our eyes met. Mine were relinquished. His were proverbial. "Enough is enough," he said.

PART TWO

WORK SHOULD BE MORE LIKE PLAY

CHAPTER SIX

FROM WORKING OUT TO WORKING

During the summer of 1980, I spent more time deflecting rather than reflecting. I was in denial that I was at a crossroads in my life, so I spent most of my time having fun, which there was plenty of in a college town. I also was content with my job, where I had advanced from selling shoes in the Athletic Attic store to running the warehouse at the company's corporate headquarters. At one point, I even had an office. Before this job, I didn't really have much of a résumé, even though my employment career began back when I was ten years old.

My first job was at Bernie's in the Bronx. Now, everyone called it Bernie's, but it was really the neighborhood drugstore (nobody in the Bronx ever called it a pharmacy, never mind an apothecary). Bernie was the pharmacist and store owner, who also lived in the neighborhood. My job was to deliver filled prescriptions to the homes of the elderly and the shut-ins, as Bernie called them, three days a week after school. If we weren't busy, Bernie would send me across the street to the park to play rather than have me just sit around the store. If a prescription were to be delivered, Bernie would cross the street and yell my name through the park fence. I was paid five dollars a week.

Bernie's was no different than today's pharmacy, as he sold everything from toys and perfume to gum and candy. And there was even a phone booth, all of this jammed into an eight-hundred-square-foot store. This phone booth played a significant role in every neighborhood boy's rite of passage. You see, up until fifth grade, you were considered a little boy, especially by the sixth, seventh, and eighth graders. But if you wanted to play stickball and basketball or just sit on the park house steps with the big boys, then you had to pass an initiation test.

You were instructed to bring a dime to the park one day, and then a couple of the big boys would walk with you to Bernie's phone booth, where you would insert the dime while one of them dialed a phone number. When someone answered the phone, you were instructed to ask, "Is this Dr. Lipschitz?" When the person on the other end answered in the affirmative, you would then say, "Well, if your lip shits, then my ass whistles!"

Click. Call over.

I will readily admit that I didn't really get the joke until later in life, but who cares? I was now officially a big boy, and all it cost to join this prestigious club was ten cents.

In addition to delivering dry-cleaning and assembling *The Times*, my early working career included a stint at Baskin-Robbins, where I learned that crafting the perfect ice-cream scoop wasn't some special twist of the wrist. Instead, it was perfecting the art of having more air than ice cream embedded inside the scoop. Success wasn't measured in how much ice cream you gave the customer, but rather in how much the customer thought they got. Here was my first experience that led to my obsession with how to make a profit.

––––––

One of the most complex decisions any athlete must make is when to end a career, to retire, to move on. Do you end a career when you win a championship, a title, or a medal? You know, go out on top? Do you retire when your body tells you *no mas*? That's a tough call because many athletes don't listen to their bodies. Or do you move on because it's time to start something else? This is a difficult decision for many athletes since it requires the reconciliation of the mind and the body.

I wasn't quite ready to let go of my identity as a competitive runner. After all, this was all I knew, or how I was known, for most of my twenty-four years. I certainly was not past my prime as a middle-distance runner, but I didn't see how I could keep at it. I did have my warehouse manager job, a modest apartment, and my car. And yes, there were still great people to train with in Gainesville. Still, my inner voice kept nudging me to commit to another couple of years. That was a good thing. The bigger issue for me was that this was a very selfish lifestyle, and there was little room for other things in my life. I also had to pause and ponder if I was happy living in Florida, or did I miss New York? Most importantly, I had to consider if there was another side of me that I needed to explore or perhaps even invent. So maybe it was time to invest another ten cents and move on from being a young runner to becoming a mature professional.

I visited Snelling & Snelling, an employment agency in Gainesville. In those days, agencies like these were only concerned with filling jobs, rather than today's approach of searching for talent and launching careers. Back then it was called "manpower." Today we have a "workforce." After the husband-and-wife team who ran Snelling asked little more than how old I was and if I had a college degree, they set me up for an interview a week later.

The interview was with a company called Pitney Bowes, and the role would be sales representative. The job would require me to visit small businesses in the local area and sell them copy machines and postage meters. It sounded good, especially the part about potentially making $18,000 a year. As they explained it to me, all that I had to do was tell office managers that Pitney Bowes copiers were faster and better than their current Xerox or IBM machines. And wouldn't they prefer our postage meters instead of licking stamps all day? Simple enough.

My interview was scheduled for one morning at a Denny's restaurant, where I was to meet the Pitney Bowes sales manager. I had no idea who he was or what he might look like, but the couple at Snelling told me not to worry, that I would figure it out.

When I walked into Denny's, it took mere seconds to realize that the guy in the starched white button-down shirt with the crisp blue silk tie and the perfectly coiffed hair must be the guy from Pitney Bowes. Or viewed another way, he was the only guy in the restaurant that wasn't wearing a tank top, cut-off shorts, and a trucker hat.

I walked over to the booth where he was sitting, and after being greeted with a firm handshake and a sparkling smile, we began to casually chat. Now, where I come from, most kids grew up playing hide-and-seek or cops-and-robbers. This guy, on the other hand, looked like he grew up playing office. I would bet that for Christmas, there was a briefcase and a fountain pen under his tree. After an hour or so of what seemed to be random conversation, we walked out of Denny's and stood in the broiling parking lot, where I sweated profusely while the Pitney Bowes sales manager somehow stayed perfectly starched and coiffed.

He then said to me, "When can you start?"

Gulp.

"Uh, in two weeks," came my nervous reply. And just like that, I suddenly had a big-boy job.

After the first month, it began to dawn on me that this was not going to be my jam. I would arrive every morning to this musty office and join another sales associate and two copier repair guys. Really good guys, but not my crowd. Then we would each venture out to make cold calls while the repair guys fixed all the broken machines that the previous sales guy sold in.

Here I was in my little white VW Bug with an eight-track player, a demo copy machine in the back seat, and a postage meter on the passenger seat. Also in the back seat was a fresh shirt and tie because I would usually sweat through my first shirt by noon. While my car had great music, it had no air-conditioning. Not a small detail. Particularly when you had a job in

Central Florida that required you to wear a shirt and tie.

Yet none of this was why I hated the job. The real reason was that I just did not have a personal passion for the product. Believe it or not, there were many guys who geeked out on copiers and postage meters, but more so, these guys just loved the idea of creating a need that didn't already exist. They were jazzed by the art of the sale. This was a major life lesson that I'm grateful came to me early on.

While I was dreading each day as a copier salesman, I tricked myself into believing that this was the price you had to pay to get a weekly paycheck. Certainly, work was not supposed to be fun. After all, that's why it's called work, right? The paycheck wasn't a reward for a job well done. It was hush money. Just go home and keep the whining to yourself.

One day I received a call from a guy named Norm Froscher, who was the sports editor at the local newspaper called *The Gainesville Sun*. Norm had apparently read the piece that I had written for *The Times* and asked if we could meet. I went to visit *The Sun* office, which was exactly how you would expect a newsroom to be in the early eighties. Metal desks, flickering fluorescent lights, stacks of folders and papers everywhere, the smell of burnt coffee and cigar smoke, and of course a watercooler. Norm was a small guy with an exceptionally large mustache, which seemed menacing, particularly when he spoke. He told me that while Gator football was the town's true passion, he was also aware that there was a large running community in Gainesville, and boy, would he love to sell them some newspapers. Would I be interested, Norm asked, in writing a weekly column for the paper? I would get paid $20 a week just for writing a thousand words! The column would be called "Making Tracks," and its focus would be on anything that I thought local runners would enjoy reading. Norm might have changed my grammar and punctuation here or there; otherwise, I had creative freedom to write whatever I wanted.

For me, the best part about writing for *The Sun* was that I could maintain some type of relevance in the running community, rather than just being known as an okay runner who retired too soon. *The Sun* column was surprisingly well received, even though trying to come up with a fresh topic every week was much harder than I imagined it would be. Still, it was a welcome respite for a full-time postage-meter salesman.

Later, I met a guy named Bill Abrams at a Florida Track Club meeting. Bill had an idea. Why don't we have a weekly television show on the local Cox Cable affiliate and also call it *Making Tracks*? Bill would be the producer while D.J. Head (yes, his real name) manned the camera, and I could be its effervescent host. Wow! Here I was, a future Pulitzer Prize-winning newspaper columnist, and now I get to be a television star too?! Suddenly, I had a new identity besides being a washed-up miler turned copy-machine guy.

One great moment in what quickly turned into a mediocre television career happened at an indoor track meet at the University of Florida. Sitting in the stands at the Stephen C. O'Connell Center was none other than the former New York Yankee great Roger Maris. He seemed relaxed and was enjoying the meet when I shyly and timidly approached him to say hello while trying not to be another annoying Yankee fan. Surprisingly, he couldn't have been nicer. At the time, Roger and his brother Rudy owned the Budweiser distributorship in Gainesville, not a bad place to sell beer. It turns out that this arrangement was made late in Roger's career, when he played for the St. Louis Cardinals, who were owned by the Busch family of the famous Anheuser-Busch dynasty.

I then asked Roger if I could interview him for my TV show. If it didn't take up a lot of time, Roger said that he would be delighted. I made up less-than-compelling questions on the fly, like "Why are you at the track meet?" and "How long have you lived in Gainesville?" Now that I'm on a roll with one dumb question after another, I asked Roger if he missed baseball. Reasonable question, right? He looked at me, laughed, and then bellowed, "Christ! No!!" Maybe Roger was channeling a little of my dad when he was watching the Giants on TV. Not surprisingly, that part of the interview was edited out from the next week's show.

A few months later, I did go over to Roger's office to meet with him and his brother Rudy. Trying to put my college degree to work, I proposed that they hire me to do marketing for their beer distributorship. Rudy wanted to know what the heck marketing was. Roger, on the other hand, was very polite and told me that with forty thousand thirsty college kids and a legal drinking age of eighteen, he really didn't see the need for any marketing. Still, I was proud of my proposal, and I thought that selling beer with a Yankee legend would have been the job of a lifetime.

———

I was now eighteen months into my Pitney Bowes career, and I still had my side hustle with my newspaper column and TV show. Then I received a phone call from someone at Nike. He got my name from the sponsored-athlete department, as I had been one of the track guys receiving free gear from Nike for quite some time.

My relationship with this disruptive upstart brand began in 1975, just a few years after the company was founded. A runner I knew from Villanova, Phil "Tiny" Kane, introduced me to a guy named Geoff Hollister, whose job was to find the next generation of track and field talent and introduce them to Nike by giving away free shoes. Nike called it "word of foot" advertising. Geoff originally was hired by his former University of Oregon track coach, Bill Bowerman, and his partner, a former Oregon runner named Phil Knight, as they were the West Coast distributors for a line of Japanese running shoes called Onitsuka Tiger. At the time, Bowerman and Knight's company was called Blue Ribbon Sports, presumably named after the prize you may get after you win a race, or perhaps more likely after a very popular beer, Pabst Blue Ribbon. I fondly remember, as a freshman in high school, taking the subway downtown to Paragon Sports, where I bought my very first pair of running shoes. They were Tigers. When Blue Ribbon Sports changed its name and became Nike, Geoff Hollister was employee number three.

The guy calling me from Nike wanted to know if I knew anyone who lived in Florida that had a running or sports background and maybe a business or marketing degree. Nike, as it turns out, was in the process of building a team of "tech reps" to be in key markets across the country. The program was called EKIN, which is Nike spelled backwards, to signify Nike's earnest desire to never lose touch with its grassroots efforts while the company was growing by leaps and bounds.

Incredulously, I said to him, "Hey, what about me? I check all those boxes!" He really didn't say too much after that except thank you and that he would pass my name along, which, at that moment, felt like an empty promise.

Weeks went by without a word. I knew that I didn't want to be at Pitney Bowes any longer, and I was very motivated and excited to belong to a company whose product I was passionate about. Another life lesson here. I also had to keep reminding myself that leaving someplace and going someplace are two completely different things. All the while, I remained hopeful, if not prayerful, because I was sure that this phone call had to be an omen. Certainly, this was meant to be. I was so convinced (read: wishful) that this would come to fruition that I even prepared my tearful resignation speech from Pitney Bowes. Tears of joy, of course.

Two excruciating weeks had passed when I finally got a call from an assistant at Nike who asked if I would like to fly to Oregon to be interviewed for the EKIN position for the state of Florida. Well, of course! What took you so long?! I'm on my way! I flew from Gainesville (first making a connection in Atlanta, of course), all the while looking out the window and marveling at this vast expanse of land below without a home or building in sight. Did people actually live in the Midwest, I wondered…or was it just a place where you changed planes?

I arrived in Portland and was picked up at the airport by a guy named Brad Johnson, who was second-in-command of the EKIN program. A warm and friendly guy, Brad immediately put me at ease as we drove through a very scenic, lush, and very damp Portland on our way to Beaverton, where Nike was headquartered. I had only been to Oregon once before. It was two years earlier, when I ran in what turned out to be my final competitive race at the Olympic Trials in Eugene, which is a two-hour drive south of Portland. When I was in Eugene, I didn't make it a point to check it out or sightsee, as I was there for a singular purpose, to run my best. So in essence, this was my first official trip to the state of Oregon.

My vague recollection of Eugene is that it was a college town with a vibe similar to Gainesville. The other thing I remember is that they were filming a movie on the site of the Trials called *Personal Best*. Directed by Robert Towne and starring Mariel Hemingway, the movie focused on two athletes who were both vying for a spot on the Olympic team, so the U.S. Trials and particularly Hayward Field proved to be an authentic setting for the film.

As Brad and I headed toward Beaverton, I was having a moment not too dissimilar to when I first arrived in Gainesville. This was simply not like any other place I had ever been to before in my life. Today, most people recognize Portland as a cool hipster town with excellent restaurants, downtown living, bicycles versus cars, and an outdoor lifestyle, with a stunning view on a rare clear day of a snowcapped Mount Hood. However, Portland, never mind Beaverton, was nothing like this in 1982. When one fellow East Coast native had moved to Oregon a few years earlier, I asked him, what was his biggest adjustment? He said the time difference was a bit of a struggle. Because when it was three o'clock in New York, it was 1967 in Oregon.

After a quick stop at the Beaverton Red Lion Inn to drop off my bag and freshen up, Brad drove me to the office for my interview. Nike's headquarters at the time were just two very basic buildings called Murray 1 and Murray 2, named for the street where the buildings were located. At that point, my experience with interviewing was, let's just say, not very extensive. When I was in college, I had an interview for an entry management position at a department store called Bamberger's, which thankfully didn't go well. And my Pitney Bowes interview was merely about my qualifications as a schmoozer to get past a receptionist. So needless to say, I was really nervous because I didn't know what to expect, and I really wanted this job.

Brad escorted me to the office of Pam Magee, who was in charge of the EKIN program. She wasn't there when we arrived, so Brad told me to make myself comfortable until she returned. Pam joined Nike in the early days and worked alongside Geoff Hollister in athlete promotions. Pam was a very outgoing and gregarious girl from New Jersey who was a perfect fit to work with Nike's women athletes. As Joan Benoit Samuelson, the gold medalist of the very first ever women's Olympic Marathon, can attest, Pam was like your friend, sister, confidant, and confessor…as well as your shoe company rep.

An hour or so had passed, and still no sign of Pam Magee. People walking by began to wonder who this stranger was, sitting in Pam's office all afternoon while there was no Pam. Eventually, I went to the restroom, and Brad happened to walk in. "Hey! How did it go?" he cheerfully asked. "Well, I haven't seen her yet." Brad, slightly puzzled, just sighed, and he eventually drove me back to the Red Lion. He told me to relax until the three of us would meet for dinner just a few hours later. Conveniently, the restaurant was connected to the hotel, so I eagerly showed up a few minutes early.

Soon after, Brad arrived, and we got a table. As we waited for Pam to join us, Brad and I got to know each other. He told me about his background and gave me his perspective on Nike as well as some insight into the EKIN program. The conversation was thoroughly enjoyable, as were the several beers we consumed. Eventually, the phantom Pam arrived, a little flustered, but as I would soon learn, that was her style. We continued our "get to know you" chat and shared stories about our upbringings while the conversation and the drinks flowed.

Before I knew it, dinner was over, and we said our goodbyes. I walked back to my hotel, a little fuzzy, and not just from the drinks. Was that an interview? I wondered. There were no questions about my current job, no query about my education, and not one trick interview question like "If you were a tree, what kind of tree would you be?" There was no mention of next steps or a potential second interview. Just a hearty goodnight and best wishes for a safe journey home.

The next morning, I flew back to Gainesville, slightly perplexed but still hopeful that all was good. After all, this was my destiny. As I settled in for the long flight, I thought a lot about the night before. Maybe this is just what interviewing is supposed to be like in the eighties. Are you charming enough to get past the receptionist and get to the office manager to sell a postage meter? Good, you're hired! Are you fun to talk with over dinner and drinks? Good, you're hired! Or maybe this just was all too good to be true.

A week later, Brad Johnson called me. "Gene, we'd like you to join Nike and be our EKIN in Florida." I didn't realize it at the time, but this one short phone call would put me on a journey that would last for the next forty years.

CHAPTER SEVEN

GO WEST, YOUNG MAN

Ending my short and insufferable career at Pitney Bowes to join Nike brought along a few subtle lifestyle changes. My '68 VW Bug was now replaced with a brand-new, shiny Toyota Tercel, and yes, with air-conditioning. The copier and postage meter demos were no longer crammed into the back seat of my Bug. Instead, several duffel bags of Nike's latest shoes, along with some giveaways like keychains and pens, fit neatly into the Tercel's roomy hatchback. My shirts and ties were now in the back of my closet rather than in the back of my car, where I hoped they would stay forever except for the occasional wedding or funeral. So now, my new daily uniform was a Nike polo shirt along with some crisp Bermuda shorts and, of course, a pair of the latest and greatest Nike shoes. While these changes were more like upgrades, there were several other not-so-subtle differences between my former and present world.

First, my sales territory at Pitney Bowes was based in the greater-Gainesville area. I rarely had to drive any farther than twenty miles to make a cold call or visit an account. With my new role at Nike, I was required to cover the entire state of Florida, from Pensacola to Key West, which happened to be a mere 832 miles apart. The second big difference was that my apartment, and maybe more so my car, would now serve as my office. While I wouldn't miss the cigarette smoke or the smell of copier toner at the Pitney Bowes office, I must admit that I liked the idea of having a place to start and end my workday. Years later, I would come to value the separation of my work and my home, as it would prove crucial for preserving my well-being. Another huge difference was my clientele. No more eye-rolling receptionists or condescending office managers who couldn't wait until I left. My new audience of running-store managers and salesclerks were always thrilled to see me and often wanted me to stay as long as I could. However, the biggest difference was that I was now in my element, and I was with my people. I felt blessed that my vocation and avocation were now suddenly one and the same.

The essence of being an EKIN was to espouse the virtues of Nike to shoe-store salespeople and running enthusiasts alike. I did learn early on, however, that tech talk, even about cool running shoes, could be just as exciting as watching paint dry, so I slowly began to turn my clinics into performances of sorts. Tapping into my family tradition of Irish storytelling, I found that it was easier to keep the attention of a part-time, minimum-wage salesperson if I told colorful stories about these new shoes rather than just reading them the ingredients on the label. More often than not, the kid on the sales floor would not only remember the story about the shoe, but perhaps they wouldn't forget the storyteller.

Being an EKIN soon became more of a lifestyle rather than a job. When I visited stores, it was often after closing time, since giving a clinic during the day could be disruptive to the business. I also often worked on weekends, when I attended road races and set up a little booth to display our shoes. This was always my favorite part of the job because after a race, I got real honest feedback from hot and sweaty runners who felt entitled to share their unfiltered comments with me simply because they had parted with their hard-earned money to buy their precious Nikes.

Since we were all in our mid-to-late twenties, it didn't suck to be an EKIN, especially when we were off the clock. While at the time, many of our former college classmates usually had good jobs and their own versions of success, they may not have enjoyed the social status that we did. At happy hour it just seemed more fun and interesting to say to your pals that you worked for Nike, rather than a big corporation like, say, Pitney Bowes. Telling people that you worked for Nike did have its hitches, though. People, all too often, would ask you if you could get them a job, as if pulling strings was in your power. And then, of course, there was always the inevitable question… "Can you get me a free pair of shoes?" The best way to answer this I learned from my great friend Freddie Doyle, who was the EKIN in New England. Whenever he was asked this question, Freddie would dryly reply, "If I worked in a bank, would you ask me for free money?"

The tricky part was managing the fine line between being who you are while not falling into the trap of becoming what you do. Staying vigilant to this distinction came back to me as a compliment many years later.

As in any business, it's a tradition to host key customers over dinner. I was never a big fan of this, but it was part of the job. The real intent of these dinners was to leave the title on your business card at coat check and then break bread and enjoy a nice bottle of wine while getting to know your guests a little bit better. For some retailers, these dinners were a nice break from a meal at home. For others, it was a chance to go over the top on their host's credit card, when someone might order the most expensive thing on the menu, like lobster, even if they were allergic to shellfish. And then, of course, there were times when a dinner might follow a tense business meeting. For me, the food at those dinners often had no taste.

Late in my career and after one rare, pleasant dinner, I joined the CEO of a powerful retailer in the bar for an aperitif. He was in a reflective mood when he said to me, "You know, Gene, when you were at Nike, I always liked you because you never were a Nike guy. You were always just a guy from Nike." While I was flattered by this, I'm not sure this was something I was aware of or did cognitively. Yet I'm pretty sure that this was a distinction that I learned when I gave those countless clinics at all those little running stores throughout Florida at the beginning of my career.

———

The popularity of Nike had a big effect on me and the other EKINS and how we were perceived on the front lines. In the major markets, we were considered the face of Nike. The same might be said of the Nike sales reps, but the difference between being an EKIN and a sales rep was that each shoe in a salesman's sample bag had a price tag attached, whereas for the EKINS, each shoe in our bag had a story inside. A sales rep's audience was the buyers who usually were sitting in a stuffy office above the store. Now, at the time, and before the reliance on data and analytics, it seemed to me that the basic qualifications needed to be a buyer were to have amnesia, to be hard of hearing, and to never use a pen, only a pencil with a good eraser. An EKIN's audience were the salesclerks on the shop floor. However, I would quickly come to see that the most precious audience was the runners who purchased our shoes. They were the ultimate judge and jury, and without them, the food chain would just seize up, and the whole thing would cease to exist. Years later, it was shocking for me to see that some of the brands that I eventually worked for truly believed that the definition of success was just making the sale to the retailer. For me, that wasn't the finish line; it was just the first lap. Throughout my career, no matter which brand I worked for and no matter what title I had, I always relished hearing from the people who bought our shoes, and not just for their insight, but also as a constant reminder to me of why I was doing this in the first place.

———

I stayed in my role as Florida's EKIN for about four and a half years. By today's standard, that would be considered an eternity. The program was originally designed for grassroots marketing, but it quickly evolved into becoming a farm system for future talent that would eventually work either in sales or in one of the various divisions at Nike's headquarters. Many future EKINs may have been in their jobs only for an average of two years or less, as the company needed lots of talent to keep up with its phenomenal growth.

Here, for the first time in a while, I was faced with making a big decision. Do I invest in my career and relocate to Oregon, which, as a place to live, was the polar opposite of Florida? Do I trade my nomadic work routine for the confines of a cubicle? Or do I become a journeyman EKIN and potentially fall into the rut and the trappings of just phoning it in, before phoning it in was a thing? As I pondered these questions, I would often look back on the other jobs that I'd had, going all the way back to working for Bernie at the drugstore. I even considered my time as an athlete, which to me was work. As I reflected on my past occupations, I certainly considered the task I was charged to do, but more so for whom I was doing it. This is when I realized that I had a few coaches and managers over the years, but I also had the rare privilege of experiencing true leaders, like Bobby Byrnes at Fordham. This was an important epiphany for me at the time. I may have been a little unsure back then of where my true talent may lie, but I was completely certain that I didn't want to be managed. Instead, I wanted to be led. To me, a manager ran the business while a leader moved the people.

It was 1986, when I was offered a position as a retail-marketing manager for Nike in Oregon. Obviously, this meant not just a job change but a life change. I was about to trade the road for an office, shoe stores for conference rooms, road races for meetings, and runners for coworkers. During my four years in Florida, there were many visits to Portland for sales meetings and other events, and I must admit, these visits were always enjoyable and lots of fun. Yeah, sure, the climate in the Pacific Northwest might require me to make the switch from sunscreen to a SAD lamp, but that should be no big deal. I surmised that by that point, I had been to Portland at least twenty times, and I didn't melt or wither away. And besides, after eight years in Florida, wasn't I really tired of the sunshine and balmy winters anyway? After all, the weather in the office in Oregon was always a temperate seventy-two degrees, with cloudless ceilings and abundant fluorescent lighting. So even though deep down inside I was hesitant, if not a little scared, I convinced myself that I had to take this big leap. Nothing was ever going to be perfect, and it wouldn't be forever, right? Besides, I hadn't earned the right to be able to pick and choose the next steps for my career. I had been fortunate that my first job at Nike came to me. The second job required that I come to it. There was a life lesson I learned a bit later on that I wish I knew when I was much younger to help me process this daunting idea of relocation.

While living in New Jersey, our daughter Ashlee, who was twelve years old at the time, made her Confirmation, which is the third of the three sacraments of initiation into the Catholic Church. The other two are Baptism and Holy Communion. The presiding bishop was from Antigua, a beautiful, small island in the Caribbean that I had once visited and with which I was familiar. During his homily, the bishop spoke fondly of his island and its beautiful beaches and resorts, but in order to make a point about the plight of its people who called Antigua home, he chose to tell a story (a man after my own heart).

The bishop began...

"There was this man who unfortunately died, and he found himself in a very long line, waiting to get into the pearly gates of Heaven. Suddenly, someone tapped the man on the shoulder. As he turned, he saw an angel. The angel said, 'Waiting in line will take a very long time, so if you'd like, I have a place where you can wait, and when your name is called, I will come and get you.' The man found this to be a reasonable offer, so he followed the angel to an elevator. Once on the elevator, the man was alarmed to see only two buttons: one for Heaven and one marked Hell. The angel selected Hell, and the elevator made a quick descent. The man immediately panicked, but then he thought, how could you not trust an angel from Heaven? The elevator doors opened, and to the man's surprise, there was a very floral and aromatic scent. Beautiful women and handsome men, all wearing pristine white robes, were lounging in plush sofas near a fountain flowing with sparkling wine. The man eagerly settles himself into a comfy chair when the angel says that she will come back for him soon. A few hours go by before the man receives a tap on his shoulder, and the angel tells him it is time to go. Reluctantly, the man gets on the elevator, and as the door begins to close, he takes one last look at the paradise he was leaving behind. As he steps out into Heaven, he turns to the angel and says to her, 'You know, on second thought, I think I want to go back down to Hell. It was not at all what I expected. I really enjoyed it and felt very comfortable down there.' The angel says, 'Okay, suit yourself.'

"The man eagerly gets back on the elevator, and after a speedy ride, the door opens back in Hell. He feels a burst of blistering heat, and there is a noxious, putrid odor. There are horrible, evil creatures roaring loudly, while people are on the ground writhing in pain and suffering immensely. The man now turns and quickly dashes back toward the elevator, but it has now become an impenetrable iron door that is padlocked shut."

The bishop then went on to explain to the confirmands, "My dear children, the moral of the story is…that visiting a place and living in a place are two incredibly different things."

Amen.

———

Looking back now, moving to Oregon was a big and bold move for me, and not just because it was a new job. Over the course of my career, I would eventually live in all four corners of the country…from Florida to the Pacific Northwest, New England, and then all the way to Southern California. Not to mention a few other places in between, including Maryland and New Jersey. I even spent a few years in the Midwest, and not just because I needed to change planes. I would come to value living in different places and experiencing new cultures and climates. It would help me to broaden my perspective on life, for sure, but I also believe that everywhere I'd lived added a dimension to how I was going to do my job. In this world we live in today, where remote working and virtual meetings are considered modern and progressive, I worry that young people will miss out on how living in different geographies and working in different environments can not only expand their prowess but also help shape one's greater being. When you move, you get the chance to reinvent yourself or become more of yourself. In either case, it gives you a new chance to make your mark.

––––––

Winding down my time in Gainesville before relocating to Portland took a little more energy than just packing a few bags. It was time to end my moonlighting gigs, writing a weekly newspaper column and hosting a weekly television show. Most regrettable, though, is I had to step down as president of the fabled Florida Track Club.

Jimmy Carnes, then the head track coach at the University of Florida, along with former college runner turned environmental engineer Jack Gamble, founded the Florida Track Club (FTC) in 1965. The original idea was to form a club for postgraduate elite runners, who could train together while benefiting from Gainesville's mild year-round climate. To adhere to the strict code of amateurism that was in place at the time, Gamble had arranged for part-time jobs at the university's Plant and Grounds Department so the athletes could supplement their income. He also had arranged with some local hotels for these runners to stay in unoccupied rooms. To help organize the club as an entity, Carnes and Gamble recruited a local runner with a law degree; his name was John L. Parker Jr., and he drew up the club's original charter. Soon after, Parker would write a wonderful book called *Once A Runner*, which was loosely based on the FTC and the colorful characters who made up its inaugural team. John's book became, and still is, a cult running classic, and it gave way for him to pen several more books. Two of the club's most prominent members were Frank Shorter and Jack Bacheler, the latter who himself created the FTC's iconic Florida orange logo. Over the years, the FTC would expand from its elite athlete roots to also include avid everyday runners from Gainesville's sprawling running community. During this expansion, Dr. Robert Cade became a big financial supporter of the club, albeit a low-profile one.

I attended one last FTC meeting before moving to Portland and was surprised and deeply touched when I received the "Dr. Robert Cade Award" for my service to the club as well as to the local running community. Along with a plaque to commemorate this special moment, I received an FTC racing singlet with "Past President" emblazoned on the left chest, a prized possession of mine to this very day.

As I was leaving the meeting, Dr. Cade stopped me and asked, "May I give you some advice before you embark on this next leg of your long run?" Appreciating the kind gesture if not also the metaphor, I, of course, said yes! Who wouldn't want advice from the man who invented Gatorade?!

"Let me tell you a story," began the good doctor (another man after my own heart). "When I was in the late stages of creating Gatorade, I brought some samples to a Gator football practice. I asked some of the players to drink it before the practice began. One big guy, a lineman, I presume, took a sip, immediately spit it out, and said, 'Ugh! This tastes like piss!' I then looked at one of my assistants and said, 'Good. We're on the right track!'"

Dr. Cade then went on to explain that the original formula for Gatorade would often taste chalky if you drank it casually. It only became palatable when you were dehydrated or depleted. That's why pediatricians eventually recommended giving Gatorade to feverish babies. So after a hard practice, the texture of Gatorade was notably different than before practice. I guess that's the same science used to explain why White Castle hamburgers tasted way better at midnight, after a few beers too many, than if you ate them for lunch.

After hearing this entertaining story, I asked Dr. Cade what advice he was giving me.

He laughed and told me that his story was the advice. He winked and said, "From time to time, there will be moments in your future when this story will all make sense to you."

I certainly didn't know it at the time, but this simple story from this very interesting man would serve me at key junctures throughout my career and my life.

CHAPTER EIGHT

OUTDOOR CAT

There was little time to get settled in Beaverton, even though Nike proved to be quite generous with its relocation policy despite my entry-level manager position. Comfortable temporary housing, a rental car, and other amenities made it a little easier to focus on my new role and learn the lay of the land.

During my first few weeks, Nike had hit an unexpected rough patch. With business results missing forecasts, there was the unusual and painful reduction of staff, or in my dad's parlance, layoffs. Back in a time when Human Resources was simply known as Personnel, the process went like this: if your name was called, you were instructed to drive to the pizza place down the street. If you weren't called, you were told to stay at your desk until someone summoned you. One by one, each unfortunate employee heard the canned speech and then received paperwork and a cardboard box to collect personal effects from their workstation. Then you grimly left the office for the very last time, only to arrive home at an unusual time of day, which certainly is off-putting. Since I was at the pizza place, I wasn't there to witness this, but I was ridden with shame and guilt because I had just arrived at Nike for a shiny new job while others were losing theirs. It also reminded me of times when my dad came home after suffering the same fate while we were a young family.

As my fellow survivors and I headed back to the office, we drove past the Nike employee store, where we were shocked to see some of our fallen comrades trying to get one last chance to shop at a discount and to stock up on holiday gifts.

Having a routine while always being on the move was innate to me. Sitting at a desk wasn't. At times this reminded me of study hall, and other times I felt like a child on time-out. Back then, there were no convenient distractions like a computer or a mobile phone. It was the day and age of typewritten memos delivered through interoffice mail, which was just some young kid pushing a cart though the halls. It was also a time when looking busy seemed to be just as important as being busy. The occasional meeting was usually a welcome distraction, but some of these meetings were painful and agonizingly long. I began to wonder if every Sunday evening, it would take some of these people two hours to watch *60 Minutes*. But sometimes this gave me a chance to resume my hobby of staring out the window... and reflecting.

My task, on the other hand, was very exciting. Nike was just a few months away from introducing its very first visible-air shoe, the Air Max, with its revolutionary design created by the relatively unknown Tinker Hatfield. The Air Max was the centerpiece of a collection of shoes known as "Air Pack." The intention was for the Nike sales force to sell retailers the entire collection, with nonnegotiable minimums. This proved difficult since most retailers had no problem with a minimum as long as it was for one shoe only, the Air Max. The Air Pack also included another shoe called the Air Trainer, which Nike believed should be in a new sport category that didn't, or as some would say, never existed, called cross-training. I distinctly remember a snarky comment from one sales rep who said, "There are probably more people in America who cross-dress than cross-train." Still, it was an attempt to create a new form of fitness and generate new open-to-buy dollars.

My role in this thrilling launch was retail marketing. It fell on me to go out on the road, visit the biggest shoe sellers in America, and wax poetic about the Air Pack collection while introducing them to the accompanying in-store displays that we would soon be shipping to their stores. This part of my job was right up my alley. It was my EKIN job on steroids. The roll-out of this comprehensive initiative was grueling, but once again, it was a game changer for Nike. Selling multiple sport categories with vivid in-store displays not only drove revenue but also gobbled up market share. What was most important were the optics to the consumer, as the shoe wall in every store was now seemingly dominated by Nike. This was when I first learned that creating mindshare comes hand-in-hand with earning market share. The Air Pack launch also gave Nike a ton of momentum. I usually loathe sports analogies, but just like momentum can change the course of a game, it can also accelerate a brand to seem bigger and stronger than its actual size and revenue.

As the Nike brand grew, so did its need for more talent. Once the launch of the Air Pack was complete, I was then assigned to my next tour of duty, as the customer service manager for our national accounts such as Foot Locker and JCPenney. This was my first experience managing people. Now, the only way to get this kind of experience was to get this kind of experience. The job mostly entailed wearing different hats and at times being a parent, sibling, psychologist, and minimum-security prison guard. Occasionally, all hats were worn at the same time. Each day required a special cocktail of leadership and management, with a splash of negotiator, mediator, and consoler mixed in. And that was just for the employees. The national accounts were a whole other story. They all desperately needed Nike, but they often resented our success and their dependence on us.

What I learned during my three-year assignment in Beaverton was that I wasn't wired for office life, at least at this stage in my career. I missed the road, with its diversity and energy. In the office, you often killed the clock. On the road, the idea was to beat the clock. In the office, you did work. On the road, you did business. And it seemed that all the meetings I attended in Beaverton generated more questions than answers. I would leave some meetings feeling like I knew less than when I walked in. The answers, I was certain, were in the streets.

When I was ten years old and delivering a prescription drug with a name impossible to pronounce, it only meant something when I saw the face of the sickly old woman at her front door. In high school, the dry-cleaning I delivered was merely fabric in a plastic bag until I met the man who wore the suit. Now, with what could be a promising career with a soon to be iconic brand, I had to make sure that no matter what job I had at any given moment, I promised myself to never lose sight of the value of the road and the people along the way. That's where the answers were, and usually not in plain sight. I was suddenly convinced that it was impossible to see the light from the confines of any company's headquarters. You can create the dots there, but it's on the road where you connect them.

At this early point in my career, I realized that I wasn't ready to be domesticated. I just wasn't good at being a desk jockey. My senses needed to be constantly aroused, and my curiosities needed to be continually explored and satisfied.

Shakespeare once wrote that a cat does indeed have nine lives.

"For three he plays, for three he strays, and for the last three he stays."

My first three lives were spent playing, chasing four. Now, for my next three lives, I had to stray. I had to roam and be adventurous, but I also had to be smart enough to go home from time to time for a good meal. Late in my career, and in the last of my three lives, I did my best to be the cat who stayed. However, when I was confined and housebound as the co-president of Timberland, my glorious assistant, Marie, would look at me and simply say, "It's time." And off I would go, into the market for a few days to refresh my senses and get my rhythm back.

Like an outdoor cat.

CHAPTER NINE

BACK ON TRACK AND IN THE FIELD

The names…Heavy G, Coach, Joey Bag O'Donuts, Geno, Curtis, Pedots, Fordo, Albee Sure.

No, these aren't the names of the guys who used to loiter on the corner in my Bronx neighborhood. Nor are they hit men, consiglieres, or underbosses of a Mafia family, although some of them very well could have been. These were just some of the larger-than-life personalities who were sales reps for the Nike Mid-Atlantic region. These were my partners in crime (pun intended) on my next adventure. NKMA (Nike was obsessed with acronyms) covered a sales territory from central New Jersey to northern Virginia and, for some reason, the island of Bermuda (maybe because it was in the middle of the Atlantic). The main office was in Mt. Laurel, New Jersey, a suburb of Philly, with a satellite office in Columbia, Maryland. I was excited to join this team for a couple of reasons. First, it brought me back to the East Coast and close to New York and my family. Second, I was back in the streets, and I was selling something slightly more exciting and desirable than a postage meter. However, I was dismayed when I was assigned to cover the southernmost part of the territory, Washington, D.C., and northern Virginia. I was also responsible for Bermuda. Maybe a gift of sorts, I guess to ease the pain a little bit.

While I was grateful for the opportunity, I briefly felt like I was being banished to the hinterland, and I worried that I would become an afterthought. You know, out of sight...out of mind. When I approached my boss, John Petersen, to ask him why he put me there, his answer surprised me. "Gene, I put you down there because it's the farthest away from the Mt. Laurel office, and that way I don't have to worry about it." So instead of being out of sight and out of mind, it was more like distance makes the heart grow fonder. This was a nice compliment and a lesson that I would refer to and deploy many times as an executive myself.

John Petersen began his tenure in the seventies, working in a Nike store in New Hampshire. Like many employees during those times, John eventually held a variety of positions and was always happy to go wherever Nike needed him. He was tall, athletic, and fiercely competitive, yet his management style was somewhat understated. While John was a man of few words, it was what he didn't say that said the most. Once you figured this out about him, it became crystal clear how he expected you to do your job.

I learned a few tricks of the trade from John, and none of them were about how to sell. He believed that every salesperson should have his or her own unique style. He was no fan of cookie-cutter presentations. Do it your way. Just hit the number, and hit it responsibly. How you got there was up to you. John was very hands-off, and if he thought that you were drifting off course, he would gently guide you back on track while letting you feel that you had directed your own course correction. Said another way, John Petersen handed you a rope and gave you two choices: lasso a stallion or hang yourself. It was all up to you.

My biggest takeaway from working for JP was how he valued character, especially honesty and integrity. That mattered way more to him than skill. He believed that you could teach skill. Honesty, John believed, was a family trait, learned at the dinner table and not in a classroom. This lesson would always stick with me, and years later I would remind my kids that their résumés may get them an interview, but it's their character that will get them the job.

John Petersen was hands down the best boss I've ever had.

———

In some circles, the word "salesman" doesn't always hold prestige. As a kid I developed a wariness toward this profession even though it's the second oldest in the world, going all the way back to the Garden of Eden (the first profession, of course, being gardening).

The Fuller Brush sales guy would knock on our apartment door and schmooze my mom while my dad was conveniently at work and try to sell her cheap cleaning supplies. When I was at Pitney Bowes, I would get a taste of this firsthand when the receptionist would see me coming and alert the entire office, "Warning! Incoming salesman!"

Even within Nike, there were mixed feelings about the sales team from some of the other employees, who considered salespeople to be generally underworked and overpaid and thought that we were more lucky than good. There was no real selling involved. After all, it was Nike…the product sold itself. So the assumption was that the job was merely order-taking, and the only thing that the salespeople had to do was show up. This couldn't have been farther from the truth. In fact, in the mid-nineties, Nike was growing so fast that we were literally turning down business. The job was more marketplace management than snake-oil selling. Feed the beast, but don't stuff the turkey.

The office in Maryland was a far cry from the drab Pitney Bowes office. While it was a place for me to begin and end my day when I was on the road, visiting customers, the office also had several showrooms, which allowed retailers to come in and see the full breadth of the line on display. Otherwise, a salesperson would traditionally schlep sample bags through the back door of a store and display the shoes on the cold, musty floor of a space-constricted stockroom. Sometimes you had to pay a kid to watch your car in some of the tougher neighborhoods. The showroom created more of a presentation setting, which let the salesperson control the environment.

While I've learned so much from so many great people over the years, the most consummate salesperson I've ever known was a guy named Jeff Tapkas. While I eschew nicknames almost as much as I do sports analogies, everyone called Tapkas "Coach." Maybe more than a nickname, it was a way to pay homage to the best seller among us. And he obligingly called everyone Coach. I mean everyone. And having coach-like qualities was hardly the point.

"Good morning, Coach, how ya doing?"

"I'm great, Coach. Good to see ya!"

We even called the UPS guy Coach, not to mention our office manager, Coach Dottie.

Coach Tapkas came to the office every single day, whether he had appointments scheduled or not. No matter, he was impeccably dressed, always wearing a starched, fitted dress shirt with his initials embroidered on the sleeve. Necktie, of course, and a sport coat, even if it was ninety-five blazing degrees outside. On the rare occasion of a blizzard or some other weather calamity causing the city to be shut down in a state of emergency, Coach would still make the trek to the showroom from his personal world headquarters in Crownsville, Maryland, in his spotless Lexus. On those days, he just might break his own dress code and show up in a crisp polo shirt and cashmere sweater. I even remember one time, in a softball game at a sales meeting, when Coach played catcher in perfectly pressed tan linen shorts. Ever the competitor, Coach slid into home in those shorts while taking out the opposing catcher, a woman named Pat Zeedick. Coach was safe, and his linen shorts, unlike Pat were not mussed. In the unlikely chance that Coach Tapkas would rent a car, he probably would hand wash it before he returned it.

Always one to own the room during a sales presentation, Coach would seethe when an account would mosey on into a showroom before the pitch began and start looking at the hundred-plus samples on the wall. To prevent this, he bought navy-blue, king-size bed sheets and covered all the samples so no one could see them. As he presented the line, he would remove the sheets one at a time so the buyer couldn't skip ahead. This famously became known as the "unveiling." He began every presentation with a review of the account's prior purchases and then informed them how much they were going to book for the next season. He wouldn't pass out the catalog or begin his pitch until there was crystal clear agreement on the dollar amount to be booked. When he did eventually give the buyer the catalog, he denied any page-turning until he said so. Also, to the buyer's surprise, or maybe dismay, Coach had already marked the catalog, having noted the styles and colors that he mandated the account to buy. However, he would never write the anticipated quantities in the catalog, just in case the buyer wanted more than what he expected. Coach fervently believed that the selling didn't begin until the buyer said no.

At Pitney Bowes, the notion was to wear the customer down. In the Tapkas church of selling, the religion was to overwhelm the customer. Ray Kroc, the founder of McDonald's, once famously said, "The art of salesmanship was letting the customer have it your way." (Ironically, a twist on this quote became a longtime slogan for Burger King). Coach himself believed that selling wasn't just style, but rather, it was a discipline and paying attention to details. Many salespeople showed the line and hoped for the best. Tapkas planned for the best and then demanded the best possible outcome.

He was also fond of saying that if you "watched the nickels and dimes, then the dollars would take care of themselves." These were words that Coach certainly lived by. For example, at the end of every sales meeting, which was usually held at a hotel or resort, the last task for the NKMA team was to pack up the hundreds of footwear samples so they could be shipped back to our showroom. Coach would also collect all the pens, notepads, and even bowls of candy that the hotel provided and pack them up to ship back to the showroom. The nickels and dimes, so to speak. He also often said that his goal in life was to run out of money and breath at the exact same time.

For many of us in the Nike sales ranks, Jeff Tapkas's legacy will be as the purveyor of a one-shoe program that eventually would become iconic in the sneaker world for decades to come. The Air Force 1.

First introduced in 1982, the Air Force 1 initially saw modest sales. A year later, it was marketed in a Nike poster featuring a handful of NBA players, who posed in dress suits while wearing the shoe. This was before Air Jordan, at a time when Converse and Adidas dominated the basketball category. And yes, it was a time when kids bought posters and hung them in their bedrooms. The shoe was briefly discontinued, but in 1986, Tapkas had an account in Baltimore called Rudo Sports who wanted the Air Force 1 to be reintroduced as an exclusive for their stores only. The small chain was run by the founder's son, Harold Rudo, whom kids in Baltimore called Mr. Shoe. Tapkas's persistence ultimately wore down the Nike product team, and Mr. Shoe got his exclusive. The rest became history.

By the time I joined NKMA in 1989, the Air Force 1 was still highly exclusive, but now it had been offered to a handful of accounts in my territory. The first of these accounts was in Washington, D.C., called Snyder Shoes. Like Rudo Sports was in Baltimore, Snyder Shoes was D.C.'s ground zero for cool sneaker culture. Its owner, Mark Van Grack, was finally granted permission to carry the Air Force 1 mostly because of one particular detail… the kids in Baltimore didn't give a rat's ass about D.C., and the kids in the district felt the same about Baltimore. Even though the cities are only forty miles apart, they might as well have been Venus and Mars. The allure of the Air Force 1 wasn't necessarily in its styling but rather in its scarcity. No one played that hand better than Jeff Tapkas. His message was that he owned the shoe, and the retailers merely rented it.

While I loved my time in Nike Mid-Atlantic, I learned that there was a not-so-subtle difference between being a salesman and having a sales background. I'm grateful for my sales learnings and experiences while I was there, but I am not worthy of the title salesman. I will leave that to Coach Jeff Tapkas.

CHAPTER TEN

RIDING THE BUS

The alarm blared like an air raid siren.

Clock said 4:30 a.m.

The view out the window read pitch-black and with daylight coming no time soon.

After a brief moment of confusion, I realized that I was not in Gainesville, where I would wake up at 5:00 a.m. every weekday to get in a five-mile run before jumping on my bike and heading to my warehouse job at Athletic Attic headquarters. To avoid talking myself out of that early-morning run, I would go to sleep in my running clothes, leaving nothing left to do when I woke up except to lace up my shoes and open the front door.

That very first step decided the day.

But Toto wasn't in Gainesville anymore. He was in South Jersey, and he was due in the big city by 8:30 a.m. sharp. And I don't mean Philadelphia, which was fifteen miles away. I mean the other big city, the one that allegedly never sleeps, just waiting for the guy who had barely slept. I would get in my car and drive twenty minutes to the Greyhound bus depot in Cherry Hill, where I would get in line to catch the 6:00 a.m. bus to New York City, which was a mere ninety miles away. The ride could be an hour and a half on a good day, and good days were far and few between. And every day was far between South Jersey and the Big Apple.

The bus had its rules, but you had to learn them on the fly, as there was no official handbook. Some of the seats were unofficially reserved for the lifers, those sad souls who made this journey every single workday for decades. Also, talking was not allowed. And reading a newspaper was strictly prohibited for two reasons: the rustling of the pages as you turned them, as well as the overhead light that you would need to read, would disturb those who somehow could get some shut-eye in this rolling sardine can. I was always amazed how anyone could sleep on this bus, because the seats were way narrower than what you squeeze into in coach class on an airplane. And there were no armrests to divide you and your fellow schlepper. Besides, the endless potholes on the Jersey Turnpike made the bus feel like it had square wheels.

When the bus pulled into Port Authority on 42nd Street, I had to make a mad dash to catch another sardine can, the 1 train, downtown to 18th Street. Then it was a walk to the Nike NYC office, which was located on the corner of 18th and 6th. The length of the walk was never measured in time or distance, but rather was decided by the elements you braved, and I don't mean the weather, but that too. Once I arrived at the office, it felt like it was lunchtime, and I would often eat the sandwich I made the night before by 9:00 a.m.

This grueling routine was the penance I had to pay for a whole year, as I was promoted from being the East Coast footwear sales manager to become a senior sales manager for the team that called on New York-based Foot Locker, which was Nike's largest customer worldwide. You may be wondering why I would make this torturous hike, and why wouldn't I just move closer to the city? Certainly, a relocation would have allowed me to get more beauty sleep, while it would also help to avoid the onset of thrombosis from being crammed into the bus. However, HR had assured me that this assignment would be only for one year, and this was the pathway to a more prestigious director-level role. So I endured.

Sales may have been in my job title, but selling was hardly the task while handling the massive Foot Locker account. In the nineties, Nike had become so dominant in the marketplace that we spent more time managing the business for sustainable growth while ensuring that Foot Locker was differentiated from other retailers. This wasn't necessarily just to give Foot Locker an advantage but more to allow the independent retailers to thrive as well. Sometimes this went a little too far. Looking back, how much did the cool kids really care if Foot Locker had a blue sneaker while another store down the street had the same style in green? It was more to fuel a buyer's ego and give the store managers bragging rights, rather than to just make sales. Don't get me wrong; I do believe in segmenting the market, because if everything were orange, then there would be no orange. Or, said a bit more succinctly by Larry Cooper, an independent sneaker store owner in Secaucus, New Jersey, and part-time philosopher: "Gene, when you have a barbecue, and everybody brings potato salad, then it ain't a barbecue."

Larry was the type of store owner I enjoyed the most. Ever the hustler, Larry would cross the Hudson River, into the city, and then camp out in front of the big hotels. He would then bribe the tour-bus drivers with fifty bucks so they would make a detour into nearby Secaucus and stop at Larry's store so the tourists could shop until they dropped. Larry even sold Samsonite luggage in his store to make it easy for the overzealous South American tourists to carry their loot back home. If the tourists went crazy, Larry would sometimes give the bus drivers a piece of the action over and above the fifty bucks.

It was Larry who once perfectly summed up the sneaker business when he told me, "Gene, there are only two types of shoes in the industry. Shoes that sell, and shoes that don't sell."

Sneaker words of wisdom for the ages.

———

Abraham Lincoln once said, "If I had only an hour to chop down a tree, I would spend the first forty-five minutes sharpening my axe." This was how we managed the Foot Locker business. Seventy-five percent of the time was spent planning and strategizing, while the rest of the time, we were meeting with Foot Locker's buyers and executives. We looked at the business surgically, as we were placing an assortment rather than selling a bunch of shoes. This very simple premise of "strategy first" was a core competency at Nike. Yet what I found very surprising in my post-Nike career was that building strategies wasn't always the standard for some of Nike's competitors. Now, I know this assertion will be met with huge levels of disagreement from some other brands, but within that small community of former Nike managers and directors who would make the blasphemous move to work for a Nike competitor, they know exactly what I mean.

Way too often during my post-Nike life (yes, there is life after Nike), some brands' strategies were merely tactics dressed up in their Sunday best. A strategy, though, is like a boomerang. You toss it out there, and it circles right back to you as a reward. A boomerang that doesn't come back to you is merely a stick. Tactics are just plain old sticks, like uncooked spaghetti thrown at a wall. Tactics should be the offspring of strategy. And a strategy without tactics usually becomes a binder that collects dust on a shelf in a manager's office.

One of the brands I led late in my career was obsessed with the "Big B," hitting the mystical milestone of a billion dollars in revenue. I had asked the chairman, "That's great, but what's the strategy?" He told me, "That *is* the strategy."

Revenue is nothing more than the result of a strategy.

Back in the eighties, Nike even became obsessed with this mad dash to hit a billion dollars, but only after being caught off guard when Reebok surged past Nike on its way to its own first billion. Because of Reebok's achievement, it became so important to Nike that when we eventually did hit a billion, everyone in the company received a plaque commemorating this magical moment. Soon after, though, Nike would realize that chasing revenue was tactical, and while it may have brought short-term success, it potentially could make the longer-term volatile.

Years later, I was at Under Armour when it reached its first billion dollars. With a young employee base that was used to double-digit year-on-year growth, this was a milestone that Kevin Plank wanted everyone to be a part of. All the employees assembled in the gym on the UA campus and watched a real-time video from the nearby distribution center. Kevin and his longtime partner, Kip Fulks, proudly loaded a box onto a FedEx truck, the shipment that would push Under Armour over the billion-dollar threshold! I will admit that I found this moment very exciting, whereas when I was at Nike for its first billion, I recall feeling like it was more of a relief than a victory. Similar to Nike, every UA employee received a commemorative medallion, which was inscribed with the words, "What Got Us To The First Billion Will Get Us To The Second." Shortly thereafter, Under Armour had appointed a new (and not for long) chief marketing officer. When he became aware of the medallions, he issued a mandatory recall from every employee, and he was vigilant to make sure every single medallion was accounted for. He believed, and rightly so, that what any brand needed to do to hit the next billion had little or nothing to do with how the brand got to its first.

Not long after Nike passed a billion dollars, the leadership team made a major pivot from chasing the big bucks to becoming a brand that created big ideas. The formula was relatively simple: discover, identify, or invent an opportunity or concept and then vigorously vet it. The team would then create a plan and rigorously test it before launching. Yet maybe the most important virtue for Nike was having the fortitude to stick with it. The magic potion here wasn't necessarily just the big idea but rather the discipline to execute and be relentless in pursuit. To this day, I believe this is what distinguishes Nike from Under Armour, and most certainly from Reebok.

———

Honestly, my long year on the Foot Locker business wasn't very enlightening, at least as it related to the art of selling. Certainly, working on a business of that size had its challenges, but essentially it was just a few more zeros and commas that separated Foot Locker from the independent retailers I serviced back in NKMA.

What turned out to be the most enlightening part of that year was spending time with the people who designed and created the shoes we sold. Making, or should I say building, a shoe is tedious and laborious since, after all, a shoe is a three-dimensional object that requires equal measures creativity and engineering. I think today, this point may be lost on many young, aspiring shoe designers who create flat images on a MacBook Pro and then just add color. To highlight the point, it's important to note that the legendary Air Jordan designer, Tinker Hatfield, graduated from the University of Oregon in 1977 with a Bachelor of Architecture degree. Sure, it's great to have a good-looking shoe, but the damn thing must work so you can run faster and jump higher.

————

The year commuting to New York had taken its toll on me. Up before dawn, home around 8:30 p.m., and then a quick dinner and bedtime. This was a routine that reminded me of my four years at All Hallows High School. It wasn't much of a life; it was more of a zombie-like existence. Yet like in high school, this was all meant to be a means to an end, with a brass ring to grab as the reward.

Because of Nike's phenomenal growth in the nineties, many people's careers were accelerating as well. This meant that my next role would be at the director level, but it also meant a move back to Oregon. This didn't thrill me, as we had four kids who were in their formative years, which made relocation much more complex, as their lives were evolving with friends, schools, and activities. Yet I also knew that I couldn't ride that Greyhound bus anymore.

So moving back to the West Coast was a painful but inevitable decision.

Just like anyone who is exploring a job change, I had to make sure that I clearly saw the difference between leaving my job and going to another job and that all my energy was focused on running toward rather than running from.

CHAPTER ELEVEN

AGGRAVATION CAUSES THE PEARL

I n the fall of 1997, Nike created the Jordan Brand. While Air Jordans were first introduced in the winter of 1985, it remained a subcategory of sorts, embedded within the Nike Basketball division. The idea was that the Jordan Brand would become its own business unit while it had the benefit of Nike's infrastructure. The brand would outwardly appear to be independent while not quite seceding from the union. It was more like when a teenager gets a driver's license; you had to tell your parents where you were going, you had a strict curfew, but you paid for your own gas. The strategy behind having it as its own standalone business was so the Jordan Brand could focus on dominating the basketball sneaker market at $100 and above while Nike focused on all price points below $100. This land grab would potentially gobble up all the open-to-buy dollars in the category and block out the competition while essentially creating a monopoly for Nike Inc. Yet the overarching plan for Jordan with its premium pricing (read: expensive) was to grow the very lucrative basketball pie rather than slice it.

A little over a year after its inception, the brand's director of sales left to join the Nike Golf division, a plum assignment if you played golf. It's a unique category in the sports industry because your golf game matters a little more than your sales skill set. The lower your handicap, the more desirable a candidate you'd become. However, to have a good golf game and a low handicap requires you to play a lot of golf. To my knowledge, the game of golf is quite time-consuming as opposed to, say, a thirty-minute run at lunchtime, and it is mastered and enjoyed usually during daylight hours. So is work. You get the idea.

I was approached by HR to see if I would be interested in the Jordan sales director role. In a relatively short time, I had built a strong sales résumé, first as a field sales rep, then as a regional manager for the East Coast, and then as a senior manager for Nike's largest account. So this opportunity seemed like the natural next step for both me and Nike. After conferring with Patti and the kids, I formally and enthusiastically expressed my interest in the role.

At that time, the Jordan Brand had its first president, and his name was Larry Miller. A self-described street-tough kid from Philly, Larry had a strong background in finance, first at Campbell's Soup, whose headquarters were in Camden, New Jersey. Larry then eventually landed in Portland, at Jantzen Sportswear, before joining Nike in Beaverton in its apparel division.

The woman from HR met with Larry in his office about the vacated Jordan sales director role and said, "Larry, I've got great news! We have a great candidate for your job opening." Larry perked up with interest. "Great! Who is it?" She replied, "It's Gene, from Nike Mid-Atlantic." Larry's eyes widened, and he said, "That's great! I love Gene!"

Now, details being what they are, it's important to mention here that there were two Genes in Nike Mid-Atlantic. One was named Gene Smith, a handsome and muscular man standing at six feet, two inches. This Gene happened to have been the captain of Georgetown University's basketball team in the Patrick Ewing era, when the Hoyas won the NCAA Championship. The other Gene was a five-foot, seven-inch, 140-pound track guy.

HR told me of Larry Miller's robust response, so I immediately flew to Oregon to have my meet-and-greet with him. Now, cut to the scene when I walked into Larry's office. Imagine, if you can, the look on his face. Aghast?

Stunned? Bewildered? Perplexed? Maybe all the above. The look I saw on his face said, "Damn. I got a runner, not a baller!" At that point, I'm pretty sure it would have been futile to tell Larry that I had been the captain and starting point guard at Our Lady of Angels grammar school.

Still, he hired me.

Once settled in my office in the Jerry Rice building (no, not the Michael Jordan building) on Nike's sprawling campus, it didn't take me long to figure out why my predecessor exited stage left for the golf division. Sure, he may have loved golf more than basketball, but the bigger reason why he left was because as the head of sales for Jordan, he had little or no leverage. While the Jordan product team had full responsibility and accountability for the product lines they created, it was the Nike sales force that we relied on to sell Jordan product into the market. You see, as the head of sales for Jordan, I was a party of one. My responsibility was to create sales plans and assortments that were crafted to expand and grow the Jordan Brand business. But since I had no ordained authority to tell the Nike reps what to do, my directives were usually seen as just cute suggestions. If the Nike reps chose to cherry-pick the Jordan line, which at the time they often did, they would use the classic Air Jordans as a lever to get the buyer to load up on Nike rather than to buy the new products that the Jordan team had created. My problem was that I was a conductor, but without an orchestra.

Over time I did solve this. I assembled a small group of street-savvy sales reps to peddle an ill-fated line of Jordan apparel called Two-Three. The original concept was to create an off-the-court clothing collection for Jordan lovers. Comprised of dressy knits, fine cotton, and denim, the line failed like a missed buzzer beater. But…I still had a sales force. So in the thick of the night, using a little East Coast hustle and West Coast slyness, I transformed this group of street singers and subway buskers to become the orchestra that would sell Jordan footwear. In the blink of an eye, Nike sales reps would suddenly become competitors of sorts with this newly christened Jordan Brand footwear sales force. With no surprise, my popularity with the

Nike sales team plummeted like an air ball in a dark arena.

There was another dilemma that all of us in the brand were facing. When I joined Jordan in 1999, it was the same year that Michael retired from the NBA, and for the second time. Many will remember that Michael had abruptly retired a few years earlier, just before the 1993–94 season to play minor league baseball, only to then return to the Chicago Bulls in March of 1995. He would then lead the Bulls to three more championships before his second retirement in '99. Before there was the term GOAT (Greatest of All Time), Michael's name was used as the benchmark for greatness. Sports fans everywhere would say, "Who is the Michael Jordan of baseball? Who is the Michael Jordan of football? Who is the Michael Jordan of hurling?" And so on.

Yet with his retirement came a lull in the popularity of his famous sneakers, some of it due to Michael being out of sight and therefore out of mind. But also, because of Nike's bravado, there was a notion that when Michael retired, the world would come to a complete stop, and everyone on the planet would buy a pair of Air Jordans. Hence, the market was oversold, and this once-prestigious brand was now being widely discounted.

The Jordan Brand had a core team who, for the next six months, had a choice: right the ship or write your résumé. This time in my career, though very difficult, had a huge impact on me. While my time in Nike Mid-Atlantic was the most fun, my experiences in Jordan were my most rewarding, with learnings that I would refer to for the next twenty years.

Ted Clarke was our CFO, an avid weight trainer who dyed his dark hair yellow. Chuck Smith was our manufacturing and operations guy, whose Southern accent always made you smile, even when he was telling you to go to hell. Keith Houlemard, who later would become president of the Jordan Brand, was a cool, smooth dude who had the unenviable task of running Jordan apparel, which wasn't nearly as popular as Jordan footwear. Mark Riley was our inspiring footwear chief, who always made chicken salad out of, well, you know what. Our head of marketing was Greg Johnson, a dignified and holy guy who, unlike the rest of us, provided a very calming presence. And finally, we had Mary Slayton, our strategist and brains of the organization, who was wildly logical and kept the rest of us from becoming our own worst enemies. Often, the seven of us would gather in a conference room for hours and feed off each other, pondering the what-ifs and the why-nots but never asking, why us? And when we needed a sermon from the Mount, there was Howard White, who unequivocally was the heart and soul of the Jordan Brand. The brand could live without any of us, including Larry Miller, but without "H" there would be no Jordan Brand, neither in the beginning or especially today.

For me, though, our conference room was often filled with theories and possibilities while the answers were still in the streets. I went on the road to check the pulse of our brand, with my first stop being New York to see some powers that be at Foot Locker. I had a meeting with Tim Finn, then the president of the Foot Locker division. He was thirty minutes late, so I sat awkwardly in his office, unsure when or if he would show up. Only a few months prior, when I oversaw the Nike business for Foot Locker, I probably wouldn't have had this inconvenience. Finally, Tim casually breezed in, plopped in his chair, and without the prerequisite "Hello, how are ya?" bluntly said, "So, what's up with Mr. Ball Park Frank?" which was a smarmy reference to the off-the-court Michael. At that moment, it seemed that our brand had no pulse.

During the twilight of Michael Jordan's career, he had a ton of endorse-ments, ranging from quarter-pounders, hot dogs, and phone cards (remember those?) to cereal and underwear. And lest you forget, Michael had starred in a movie with one "cwazy wabbit." This posed a huge problem for our gang of seven, because without Michael on a basketball court, he was potentially becoming a cartoon character himself. Keith Houlemard put it best when he said, "We can't let him become Mr. Coffee," a reference to the legendary baseball great Joe DiMaggio, who was known during his career as the "Yankee Clipper." Eventually however, he became known to millions as a coffeemaker pitchman. This is when it was decided that the future of the brand needed to be about the essence of Michael Jordan rather than about Michael himself.

At first, we did little things that went a long way, such as not using the standard-issue Nike business card. Instead, we created a Jordan Brand version that was black and silver, which was a distinct contrast to the Nike cards, which were a pale tan and featured the iconic Nike Swoosh in its warm red colorway. Instead, our cards prominently displayed the now famous if not ubiquitous Jumpman logo, with no reference to Nike at all. This subtle change was particularly helpful to me when I visited retailers, as it helped over time to create the notion that Jordan was truly a standalone brand. Another change was designing our own shoebox. Up until that point, Air Jordans came in Nike shoeboxes. Using the same black-and-silver colorway with a silhouette of a serious-looking Michael Jordan peering at you, it gave you the feeling that Michael was somewhat mysterious. This played into the idea of the essence of Jordan rather than Jordan as product pitchman. These small tweaks were just like one twist of a Rubik's Cube; it still may look like a block with colorful squares, yet it's radically different than before the twist.

Another big moment came when our leadership team spent two days with SY Partners in San Francisco. Founded by the brilliant Keith Yamashita in 1994, SY Partners worked with CEOs and their leadership teams to help recalibrate and refocus brands so they could have resilience moving forward. While our brand had momentum, there were little cracks and stresses that needed to be mended before they became fault lines. As Paul McCartney once said, "You're supposed to fix the roof on a sunny day." The time spent with SY and Keith was challenging, as there were a lot of big personalities in the room. Yet luckily, sometimes conflict can cause clarity, while other times aggravation can cause the pearl.

This vigorous group exercise began with everyone offering up words or attributes that we associated with or described Michael Jordan. There were no parameters for this exercise, just a few intense hours of free-forming and playing word association. The hard work began when we had to whittle this list down to ten or so words from the hundreds contributed by the team. When done, we had a filter for the Jordan Brand.

On the final day, it was time to give the filter a test. Keith Yamashita asked us to name world leaders that would pass through the filter and thus could become a member of Team Jordan. Or how about athletes from other sports? You would be surprised at who didn't pass through the filter. For example, Tiger Woods certainly was the best golfer in the world at that time, but the filter required more than just being the best. It demanded that you were Jordan-esque. This stringent cover charge permitted the brand to create an *illuminati* while also allowing us to expand the Jordan Brand outside of basketball, get into other sport categories, and potentially grab once off-limits open-to-buy dollars. You want a piece of the baseball cleats market? Great, then let's sign Derek Jeter, the Jordan-esque player for the Yankees. Major League Baseball, here we come! How about signing the colorful Randy Moss of the Minnesota Vikings? Hello, NFL! This successfully ignited a brand reach for Jordan beyond basketball, which today includes almost all major sports, including college football, which I find intriguing since the Jumpman logo is a silhouette of a guy about to dunk a basketball.

Another critical component of the Jordan strategy was to have a brisk go-to-market cadence. So if the massive Nike brand was to be a relentless flow of product, then Jordan should be more like flash flooding. In other words, if Nike basketball shoes were meant to liquidate at retail, then Jordans should evaporate.

It's been said that an object in possession seldom retains the same charm it had in its pursuit. That wasn't true of Air Jordans. Once in possession, they exponentially increased in value, but more importantly, they increased the owner's personal value. Jordans gave you prominence and bona fide street credibility. When you wore your Jordans, you now were instantly cool even if you weren't. But one thing that was true: the pursuit of a pair of Air Jordans was just as important as the capture.

It's the oldest trick in the book: short the supply to create the demand.

Deprivation does, after all, cause craving. For example, Disney did this in the nineties when it announced that some of their classic movies were only going to be available on DVD until a certain date before they would be locked in a vault forever. If you wanted your kids to watch *Aladdin* whenever they wanted to and in perpetuity, you'd better hurry to the video store, Mom!

––––––

When I speak to college classes, I sometimes like to give this pop quiz:

A man creates a novel and interesting product, and he chooses to sell it only to independent specialty stores while ignoring the large retail chains. He gives each store a limited amount of his product, and he forbids the stores to sell it for anything below a certain price (by the way, that's illegal, but I digress). This creates a little tension for the retailers, but when they sell out of their initial order within days, they call the man and double their first order. The man ships them a second order, but rather than doubling the first order as requested, it's only 10 percent larger. The second order also sells out, but now it's beginning to leave the customers anxious and a little angry. When the third shipment arrives, which is now double the original order, there are people lined up outside the stores to be the first to buy this coveted product. When the customer demand is once again not satisfied, the lucky people offer to sell their precious purchases to the unlucky people at double the price they originally paid for it, essentially creating a black market. When I ask the students what product I am talking about, they are almost always shocked when I tell them:

Beanie Babies.

––––––

To riff a little on the musings of the wise philosopher Larry Cooper from Secaucus, New Jersey…sure, there are two types of shoes, the ones that sell and the ones that don't sell. But adding to that, you don't necessarily always make money on the shoes that sell, but you do absolutely lose money on the shoes that don't sell. And unlike wine, most sneakers don't get better with age.

At that time, the goal for the Jordan team wasn't to make the brand the biggest in the Nike universe but rather the prettiest. The best way to dress up a brand is by making it profitable. Having little or no inventory on hand after a product launch is a recipe for profitability, hence the idea of evaporation versus liquidation. Satiate the thirst of the market rather than overserve it. Now don't get me wrong; revenue is obviously vital since, after all, it is the proud parent of profit. But being big doesn't mean you can't be pretty at the same time. Yet if the goal is to only obsess over revenue and hope that all else follows, it's a fool's errand. The key for the Jordan Brand's success was its strident discipline toward profitability, coupled with a shrewd laser focus on creating demand by limiting consumer access.

Years later, when I joined other brands, it bewildered me when revenue seemed to be the lone measure of success, the Holy Grail. At one brand that I was heading, I was in a meeting with our sales leadership team. The team gushed about one key retail partner, and they proudly boasted to me that this account did $25 million in annual revenue with our brand. While I found that notable, I was quick to query as to how much money we made on that $25 million in sales. I received puzzled looks from the leadership team before one sales leader rhetorically asked, "What do you mean? It's a $25 million account!" I then asked them, What did it cost us to buy that revenue? What were the initial margins on the product we sold them? Did they return any unsold product? What discounts and dating did the retailer receive? What other incentives did we offer? Did we provide marketing dollars and in-store displays? How much did it cost us to have dedicated sales execs on the account? Did we entertain them with steak dinners and expensive wine? Several weeks later, I received a comprehensive audit of this $25 million account. Bottom line, we barely made a profit, which meant that the $25 million in revenue was like empty calories; while filling, they didn't really count. If you go to the bank with a bag of revenue, the teller will politely smile and say, "That's very nice, but can you go back to the office and then bring me the bag that's marked profit?"

————

Many might argue this, but I believe the Jordan Brand is an anomaly in the world of signature sneaker brands. Many of Nike's competitors wrongly believed that all you had to do was simply put a name on a shoe, and it would sell millions. This book doesn't have enough pages to list all the signature sneakers that have come and gone. For the Jordan Brand, the pace to market and the rigid distribution were certainly the vital business acumen, but it was the storytelling, along with capturing the essence of the man, that was the jet fuel. An Air Jordan was a story with a shoe attached, where many other signature shoes were merely a price tag with a shoe attached.

To me, one other signature shoe that may be worthy of comparison to Air Jordan is the Puma "Clyde." First introduced in 1973, this suede low-top was inspired and worn by the New York Knicks' flamboyant point guard Walt Frazier. Up until this point, there was really no such thing as a signature sneaker save for Converse's Chuck Taylor All-Stars, but that goes way back to 1922. The "Clyde" moniker came from Frazier's penchant for style and fashion off the court, where he stood out in the New York night-life after every home game, wearing dashing suits, accessorized with bold neckties with matching pocket squares, and most importantly, topped off with a strategically tilted fedora. The "Clyde" tag came from the New York media as a reference to the movie *Bonny and Clyde*, which was a big hit a few years earlier when Warren Beatty played the part of the impeccably dressed outlaw Clyde Barrow. As Jordan would do for Chicago decades later, Walt Frazier was the floor general who led the Knicks to the franchise's only two championships. And like Jordan, Frazier's compelling off-the-court persona, both during and after his career, has allowed his personal brand to thrive decades after its inception.

To me, the concept of a signature sneaker has become a blur and a bit of overkill. Today, it seems like we are just stroking egos and coddling our superstars, or sports-marketing assets, as they are called in business-school lingo, by giving them their own shoe or exclusive colorway. Is this really important? Sure, there is a sneaker-freak community that obsesses over this stuff. But for the big brands, these signature sneakers may move the needle, but few, like Air Jordan, are game changers. Most other brands use signature sneakers to buy relevance rather than drive revenue. The same goes for all these collaborations with music artists and fashion brands. It's more like the soup of the day at your favorite restaurant. Take yesterday's perishing ingredients, put them in a blender, and serve up the old while calling it something new.

CHAPTER TWELVE

FROM THE BASKETBALL COURT
TO FEDERAL COURT

With the Jordan Brand firing on all cylinders, it was starting to get a little crazy. Telling Michael Jordan that his latest namesake shoe had once again sold out within hours was becoming standard, if not redundant. Yet the energy around an actual product launch was hard to describe to him. Michael was conditioned to focus on how many pairs were sold, with little emphasis on how they were purchased. So rather than just sharing the sell-through results with him, I proposed that we take him on the road so he could see a launch rather than just hear about it. To his credit, Michael had mandated that the launch of any new Jordan shoe should only happen on Saturdays so kids wouldn't be tempted to skip school to wait in a queue to buy his latest release. So off I went on a reconnaissance mission to find a location where one of the most recognizable people on the planet could safely and quietly show up at a shopping mall. On a Saturday.

A month was spent scouting out different locations that had easy access to a sneaker store with an even easier exit, and with the right amount of security to pull this off. I looked at a half dozen cities and ended up settling on the very first one I saw, the Beverly Center in Los Angeles. Eight stories tall, the Beverly Center wasn't just home to many great stores but had the full Foot Locker fleet: Lady, Kids, and Men's Foot Locker, plus its sporting goods nameplate called Champs. The Beverly Center was also a magnet for all types of celebrities who loved to shop but even more loved to be seen shopping.

The day before our planned stealth visit, we met with mall security. Having superstars come to the Beverly Center was nothing new to the chief of security and his team. When he asked which celebrity was coming to visit, I was coy and wouldn't tell him, as I feared the word might get out, and our mission would be spoiled. Instead, I asked the chief, Who was the biggest celebrity ever to come and shop at the Beverly Center, and how did it go? More importantly, I wanted to know how his team handled it. He told me that the celebrity was Janet Jackson, and they had no warning. According to him, all went smoothly, calling it "an organized frenzy." I assured him that our mystery guest was arguably bigger than Janet Jackson, but the good news was this time he would not be blindsided. We arranged a time and crafted a plan for the next day's visit with fingers crossed, hoping that security would be more like the Secret Service and not like Paul Blart in the movie *Paul Blart: Mall Cop.*

Saturday at 1:00 p.m., I waited anxiously with two mall security guards at a service entrance to the mall, right near the dumpsters for the food court. This may sound less than perfect, but who would ever expect Michael Jordan to drive up to a food-court dumpster? A few minutes late, but right on time by LA standards, Michael pulled right in, driving a shiny new Land Rover with two friends in tow. The six of us then boarded a service elevator, which ever so slowly took us up a few floors, where we entered the mall through nondescript metal doors. We then headed for the nearby Champs store. Now, this was 2002, and cell phones were still coming of age, while cameras in phones were rare and primitive. As we approached the store, the first reactions of the mall shoppers were of shock and awe. The second reaction was that all phones were out and flipped open to spread the word. Michael

Jordan was at Champs?! As the crowd swelled, Michael casually entered the store and put his arm around one young girl from the sales staff. After asking her name, he said, somewhat awkwardly, "Well, darling, tell me, what's selling?" She gazed right up at him, batted her pretty brown eyes, and coolly answered, "Anything with your name on it!" Words that earned that girl the famous ear-to-ear smile from the greatest player ever to play the game. Meanwhile, the LA cell phone towers were lighting up, and we were now quickly eclipsing the Janet Jackson frenzy. After a few minutes, and with Michael absorbing it all, mall security was becoming anxious, so we headed back to the elevators. As our small entourage was briskly walking, there was a mom with two small kids, oblivious to who was just a few strides behind her. One of her kids, maybe six years old, stopped dead in his tracks and stared up at Michael, who bent down to say hello. The little boy just looked at him and said, "Merry Christmas!" It was early October.

As the elevator slowly descended, Michael said to no one in particular, "Man, I can't remember the last time I was in a shopping mall, even just to go to a movie." Words that I'm sure he still mutters to this day.

By the way, the total elapsed time from when the Land Rover arrived at the mall dumpsters to its departure: thirteen minutes.

———

A less glamorous Saturday morning mall visit happened in Oakland. There was no Michael on this visit, but there was plenty of frenzy.

It was around this time that a launch of the latest Air Jordan started to become more stressful than exciting. For mall managers, these launches had become a nuisance rather than a marketing event. Having at least a thousand kids lined up to buy way less than a thousand pairs of shoes was nothing but disruptive to the normal flow of mall business. Customers shopping the other mall stores were complaining about all these kids and how it was interfering with their own shopping experience. Even when the malls set up stanchions to create some sort of order, many older mall shoppers were still angry or intimidated. We decided to partner with the Foot Locker team, as well as mall management, and concluded that we should have Air Jordan launches earlier in the morning, preferably before the mall opened for normal business hours. Since the shoes usually sold out in less than an hour, we decided that the launch could begin at 8:00 a.m., which would leave plenty of time for the mall to recover and be ready for its regular shoppers at 10:00 a.m.

A small group of us made a plan to show up at this mall in Oakland at 6:00 a.m., just so we could get our bearings and hopefully be able to say hello to the store managers and staff. When we arrived, we were shocked to see well over a thousand kids outside the mall entrance, all pushing, shoving, and elbowing their way to be in the front when the doors opened. There was nothing orderly about this whatsoever, and there was no sign of mall security anywhere to be found. It seemed more like a mosh pit at a concert, as the kids seemed anxious and agitated rather than thrilled. At around six-thirty and with no apparent warning, the mall doors opened, and suddenly it was like the running of the bulls in Pamplona. It was pure bedlam. Right in front of me, a young girl, about twelve years old, had been shoved to the ground, and her chin split open on the hard tile floor. No one seemed to care, so I helped this poor kid and took her to the mall office, hoping to get her some type of medical help. She was sobbing incessantly while a woman in the mall office attended to her chin. Once she calmed down, she told me she had been separated from her older brother. Almost as important as losing her brother, she became frantic that she now couldn't get a pair of Jordans because she would be the last in line. With her wound now dressed, I asked the woman in the mall office to page the girl's brother and have him meet his sister at Kids Foot Locker. When we arrived at the store, I told the manager who I was and what had just happened. I asked him to allow us to cut to the front of the line so this young girl would not miss out on buying a pair of Jordans. Alarmed at the sight of a sobbing kid with gauze and tape on her chin, the manager instead went into the stockroom and came back with a pair of Jordans in this young girl's size. The girl's eyes widened, and I gave the manager my credit card. The girl then offered me a handful of crumpled up cash, which she pulled from her pocket. I, of course, refused. A few minutes later, her brother arrived, relieved to see his sister but panicked just the same. He hugged her and took her by the hand, and they both left the mall. As they were walking away, the girl turned around and mouthed the words "thank you."

By the way, during their separation, the brother may have lost his sister, but he obviously didn't lose his focus, as he somehow found the time to score his own pair of Jordans.

It took my breath away to see Michael Jordan in a mall, watching a little boy gaze up at him in awe. Yet I found myself gasping for air when I saw a young girl face-down on a mall floor, sobbing and bleeding. I asked myself, Was this all worth it?

———

Beige against a tan wall.

Without realizing it, that's the way you begin to appear to others when you have been at the same brand for a long time. Before you know it, you are blending in with the wallpaper. And one thing is certain. You will be the last to know.

When you work for a company for a long time, it's easy to trick yourself into believing that you are legacy. After all, you've lived through good times and bad; you've dodged the layoffs and downsizings, and you got your annual 2 percent raise, which, despite being lower than the cost of living, you've somehow convinced yourself was a reward for a job well done. But is there such a thing as legacy anymore? Or are you really just a relic?

At this point, I had been at Nike for nearly twenty-one years. From driving all over the state of Florida in the early eighties to spending Saturday mornings in the early aughts at some Foot Locker, watching the throngs clamor for the latest Air Jordan release, I had amassed a ton of experiences. But I didn't really have any experience. Being in the same place for a long time is called tenure, like a college professor. Working within an industry and at several different companies gives you experience.

Even though I was a loyal company man, I had always been restless and never complacent, as for my whole life I've chosen to heed no compass but my own. But at the age of forty-seven and with four kids nearing college age, I had a burning desire to know if I was any good. Or was my value determined simply by working for an iconic and powerful brand? The looming question for me was, am I real or am I Memorex?

In the spring of 2003, I received a call from a friend and former colleague asking me if I was open to venturing away from Nike. I surprised myself when I immediately said yes, as this would put the looming question to test. A week later, I took a clandestine trip to Boston to meet with the new president of Reebok.

Martin Coles had been a highly regarded executive at Nike in the nineties before he left to join a dot-com start up in the UK. Welsh by birth and with a larger-than-life personality, Martin bore a bit of a resemblance to the actor Sean Connery. After his short-lived dot-com venture went bust, like many other internet startups at the time, Martin wanted to return to Nike, but there were no open arms for the return of a wayward son. Instead, Martin joined Nike's public enemy, Reebok, as its president, an appointment as blasphemous as when Rob Strasser left Nike for Adidas in the late eighties.

Since I was a known quantity to Martin, my visit to see him in Boston was more about when I would join Reebok than if I would join. I met some other senior leaders, and we had a wonderful and rousing dinner, and before I knew it, I was on a flight back to Portland with my head spinning. This was moving very fast, and much like earlier in my career, this wasn't just a job change; this was going to be a life change.

After clearing my head, I insisted on having another face-to-face in Boston, as now I had a litany of questions. I met with Bill Holmes, the head of HR and a quintessential Boston guy. After Bill answered my questions and quelled my concerns, I then met with Keith Wexelblatt, Reebok's legal counsel. Also at that meeting was an outside attorney by the name of Steve Manchel. Initially, I was a little perplexed as to why I was meeting with lawyers, but these two gentlemen were explaining to me in detail what possibly could happen to me, legally, if I were to accept an offer from Reebok. Being a little bit cavalier and very naïve, I thanked them for the advice, but I was certain that if I were to resign from Nike, I would receive a proper farewell, since I had dutifully served there for almost twenty-one years.

Nonetheless, Manchel gave me explicit instructions: On a designated Wednesday evening, at the end of my workday, I was to discretely remove any personal effects from my office. The next afternoon, around two o'clock, I would formally resign in person to my boss, Larry Miller, while handing him a brief letter stating as much. I would then inform Larry that I was leaving Nike to join Reebok while also mentioning how grateful I was to have served Nike. According to Manchel, Larry would promptly call HR to come to his office. HR would then summon security to walk me out of the building. Manchel concluded his instructions by offering one very special piece of advice: he told me that, as I was being escorted to my car, I should make sure that I stopped and turned around to take one long last look at the campus and all its majestic buildings, as I was leaving for the very last time and would never be there ever again. He went on to tell me that years later, this moment would be special for me, as it would be a reminder of all my experiences that I had over two decades and, most importantly, the friends I made along the way.

Everything Manchel instructed me to do, I did with letter perfection. I took my few personal effects from my office out to my car the evening prior. My resignation to Larry Miller was short but genuine, although it did catch him completely by surprise. He most certainly did call HR, as within minutes a very gracious and empathetic Oscar Cardona met with me and walked me to my car while security locked my office. This, of course, alarmed my team and others seated nearby. Manchel's strategy of resigning at two o'clock on a Thursday was to ensure that the gossip and rumor mill around my departure would only have a few hours to swell before the workday was done. That left only Friday, which would allow the dust to settle before the weekend came, and hopefully everything would blow over. However, the advice to stop, turn around, and get one last look at the campus proved fruitful for me, and not just in that moment, but it would become a ritual that I would follow a few more times during my career. I've also shared Manchel's advice dozens of times with many other people during their transitions.

Yet there was one thing that I predicted that would come to fruition. Sort of…

As a show of gratitude and thanks for my two decades of service and loyalty, Nike gave me a going-away present.

A trip to Federal Court and an all-expenses-paid, year-long vacation.

———

Noncompete clauses have become standard in employment contracts throughout many business sectors across America. Originally crafted to protect intellectual property, trade secrets, and proprietary information, noncompete contracts have, over time, become bloated and ambiguous, mostly because there is little legislation to cut a clear path toward governance. The guy who knows the secret formula for Coca-Cola should have an enforceable noncompete so he can't cross the street and join Pepsi or go off and start his own soft-drink brand. On the other hand, is it necessary for the kid who makes sandwiches at Jimmy John's to be prohibited from slicing turkey at Jersey Mike's simply because it's located a mile away?

Noncompetes are commonly used in media, financial services, manufacturing, and information technology, and many times the agreement doesn't necessarily involve disclosing trade secrets. They are typically bound by time or geography; if enforced, you may be relegated to sitting out for a period of usually six to twelve months, or you may be prohibited from working in a certain sales territory, for example. Whether you are terminated or resigned, noncompetes are still enforceable. The original premise of a noncompete clause was to ensure that a company would keep its status and standing in the marketplace while not being damaged when an employee left a company's ranks. It gives the employer control (read: power) over specific actions of an employee even after the relationship ends.

A few days after I left Nike, I received a letter in the mail that reminded me that I had a noncompete agreement with the company. The letter didn't mention anything about enforcement; it was just reminding me that I had a signed agreement. I took a few weeks off between leaving Nike and joining Reebok, certainly to prepare my family for a cross-country relocation but also to cleanse my palate so I could have a fresh perspective on working for a new employer for the first time in over twenty years.

When I finally joined Reebok, I had yet another bout of culture shock. Unlike when I stepped off the plane in Gainesville to move to the rural South, this culture shock was about brand rather than geography. When I eventually arrived at Reebok's campus, Nike by then had clearly been the market leader for well over a decade. Immediately, I felt a different vibe. Reebok back then was a bit like Avis Rental Cars ("We Try Harder"), while Nike was more like Hertz; we're number one, and damn straight, you're not. As the well-known venture capitalist Marc Andreessen once said, "The distinct advantage that a number-one company has over its competitors is being number one."

Less than a week into my new role as SVP of merchandising, I was in a product session, seated next to my new boss, Martin Coles. Suddenly, a young woman from the legal department came by and asked both of us to step out of the room. With a look of anguish on her face, she nervously explained that I had been served a cease-and-desist order that stated I had violated my contractual obligation to my former employer and that I must end my employment with Reebok effective immediately. Numb to what had just happened, I dutifully went to my office to collect my belongings before being escorted by security out of the building. I didn't take Manchel's advice this time to stop and turn to memorize the campus. I was too busy trying to remember where I parked my car. Martin Coles, on the other hand, had a fierce look in his eyes that said, "Game on, boys!"

Up until this point in my life, I had no real experience with legal issues or courtrooms. The only courthouse that I was familiar with was the Bronx County Courthouse, which I walked by each day from the subway to my high school. Aside from that, I relied on TV shows like *Law & Order* to shape my view of the legal system. The case, which was filed as *Nike, Inc. v. McCarthy*, was originally scheduled to be heard in Oregon State Court. However, Chris Carson, a Portland-based attorney who was working alongside Boston-based Steve Manchel, noticed that the Ninth Circuit Federal Court in Portland opened each morning a half hour earlier than the State Court. Taking advantage of this minor technicality, Carson filed a motion for a change of venue to federal court based on the premise that I might not get a fair trial if an Oregon court was presiding over a case that involved an Oregon company. The motion was granted, so off we went to federal court.

The presiding judge was the Honorable Malcolm F. Marsh, who received his federal judicial appointment from President Ronald Reagan. He had ruled on many notable cases, including the 1995 trial of several followers of the Bhagwan Shree Rajneesh, the Indian spiritual teacher who transformed sixty-five thousand acres in a remote part of Oregon into a small city for his devotees. Often at odds with the local community in Wasco County, Oregon, this cult was involved in poison attacks and murder plots with local officials, with whom they clashed. Judge Marsh sentenced several members to prison after their failed assassination attempt of a U.S. attorney who was investigating the Rajneeshees and their activities in a bioterrorist attack where over seven hundred people suffered food poisoning at local salad bars.

To be clear, I wanted nothing at all to do with any of this. My simple view was that I had worked hard for the last twenty-one years, and now I wanted only to move on and broaden my horizon. As I would later explain to Judge Marsh, I was just a lucky kid from the Bronx who grew up in a hardworking family. I didn't want this fight; I just wanted to go to work. Instead, both Nike and Reebok were digging in their heels and readying for a public battle. Suddenly, I found myself smack-dab in the middle of a real-life "sneaker war."

Preparation for the trial was incredibly intense, which included everything from rehearsing my lines over and over again for the eleven-hour deposition to being coached on what to wear in the courtroom. In late September 2003, and just two months after I drove off the Reebok campus, judgment day arrived. The trial was held in the Mark O. Hatfield United States Courthouse, a relatively new building at the time; Judge Marsh himself consulted on its design.

During my career, I had been on many stages and had given many speeches, as I was always comfortable with public speaking. In 2009, I was one of the guest speakers at Earth Day, which was held on the National Mall in Washington, D.C. Being introduced by Chevy Chase and having to speak in front of tens of thousands of people didn't faze me one bit. By contrast, I was so nervous in Judge Marsh's courtroom that I couldn't lift a cup of water to my lips due to my trembling hands. The trial had its moments of intensity, to the point that Judge Marsh sternly reminded everyone in the courtroom that this wasn't a tennis court but was rather a court of law. Someone who was in the courtroom that day mentioned to me a few weeks later that early in the trial, it became abundantly clear that this wasn't so much about contract law as it was about two companies that hated each other. It felt like when a wife asks her dog, "Fido, did Daddy walk you today?" Obviously, the dog isn't going to answer. It's just a way for the wife to talk to her husband through the dog. On that late September day, I felt like I was the dog in the middle. When the ruling finally came in, it favored Nike, and cheers broke out in the courtroom. Judge Marsh acknowledged to me that while he understood my desire to go to work, he told me that I was going to "sit on the beach" and that I would like it. The case did eventually go before the Federal Appellate Court, where, after an unusually long period of deliberation, the ruling was upheld.

———

After my Nike noncompete expired, I was finally able to join Reebok in August 2004. There were three rather important events that occurred at Reebok while I sat on Judge Marsh's beach. First, Martin Coles was no longer the president. The chairman, Paul Fireman, was famous for taking extended golf vacations while leaving the company in the somewhat trusted hands of its president. Yet always close by and with peeled ears was Fireman's designated hall monitor, Ken Watchmaker, the company's flamboyant CFO. Upon one of Fireman's illustrious returns to the office, while I was working on my tan, Paul changed his mind and was no longer in love with Martin Coles. My champion was soon replaced with a guy named Jay Margolis, whose background was in women's fashion apparel. While he was quite gregarious, Jay was also very direct and had no problem conveying his message. Because of this, I liked Jay right away, but I also liked that he wasn't from the sneaker industry. If you are standing at the front door of the Empire State Building, you really can't see it. But if you are in New Jersey, you have a great view of it. Something I learned is that fresh eyes are often much needed, particularly if a brand is in flux or stuck in the mud. With Jay coming in from the more cutthroat fashion industry, he was able to see what might have been hidden to others in plain sight, just like a good view from New Jersey. The second big event that happened during my year-long vacation was that my job changed. When I originally joined Reebok in the summer of 2003, I was the SVP of merchandising. When I rejoined a year later, I was the SVP of footwear, essentially responsible for all product creation from design to delivery.

The third thing that happened still stands as one of the most stunning events in the annals of the athletic footwear industry. As I was rejoining

Reebok in August 2004, there was a monumental secret handshake that took place that summer at the Olympic Games in Athens, Greece; Paul Fireman agreed in spirit to sell Reebok to its German competitor, Adidas. Herbert Hainer, who then was the CEO of the Adidas Group, believed that the best way to rival Nike on the fertile soil of North America was to buy its way in. So acquiring Reebok was a convenient way of doing that.

At the time, Reebok had the exclusive rights to outfit all the teams in the NFL as well as to sell all the fan merchandise. What better way to get to the pulse of America than through its most popular professional sport? Hainer reasoned. As well, Reebok had a deal with the NBA, and not long after, the Reebok vector logo was replaced on the team's uniforms with the Adidas three stripes. But what makes this all so sensational was how long the secret was kept, not only from a gossip craving industry but also from the employees of both companies.

For reasons that were certainly not clear at the time, our Reebok leadership team was given hard orders to drive off-the-chart sales. So we all began to "stuff the turkey." In 2005, Reebok grew its annual revenue to a whopping $3.77 billion, well above the year prior. When the secret handshake became a signed contract in 2006, Adidas paid $3.8 billion to acquire Reebok in its quest to crack the code in America.

By 2020, under the heavy hand of Adidas, Reebok reported an annual revenue of $1.7 billion, a decline of nearly $2 billion over a fifteen-year time span. In 2022, Jamie Salter and his Authentic Brands Group acquired Reebok from Adidas for $2.5 billion against a reported 2021 revenue of $2.3 billion. Adding $600 million in revenue is miraculous growth in just one year, especially during the once-in-a-century COVID pandemic.

Pass the gravy.

———

Just like at Nike, I had signed a noncompete at Reebok when I first joined.

When Adidas finally took over Reebok, I was let go. No ex-Nike people wanted here. My naïve streak continued, and I was surprised when it was enforced immediately upon my departure. This is when I learned firsthand that noncompetes can be enforced whether you walk out the door or are shown the door. This was the second of what would be four noncompetes exercised by four different brands during my career.

Now, sitting at home while collecting a paycheck may sound like a luxury, but it also had its trappings. If you didn't manage your time, a home vacation could quickly begin to feel more like being under house arrest. There were stages that I was going through that I instinctively started to rebel against, but over time I learned to surrender and let these stages run their course.

The first stage was waking up in the morning with the harsh realization that I had nowhere to go. Everyone in the house had their routine and was in their groove, ready to run out the door and make a mad dash toward their day. But not me. My mind was functioning the same as it always had; my only problem was that I didn't have a destination. I was all revved up with no place to go. This was much harder to manage than it sounds. To moderate this, I began to rise at the same time every morning and kept a routine of a healthy breakfast and exercise. I would then pack a bag with my computer and a notebook and set up shop for a few hours in a Starbucks. I treated this space as my makeshift office, and I used the time to stay informed of the industry so that hopefully, I wouldn't lose a step.

The second stage was all about managing stress. I never realized how much stress I carried until it ever so slowly began to exit my mind and body. My decision-making still seemed sharp, but the process I was now using became less rushed and more orderly. Less stress coupled with the advantage of more time can do that to you.

The third stage was a dangerous one. Eventually, I found myself getting used to a life of considerable leisure. To remedy this, I would try several times a week to meet with or speak to someone who was still active in the industry. This was like a smelling salt for me; it would snap me out of any complacency that might be setting in.

The last stage is a very potent one. It's when I realized that I was rested, grounded, and ready to get back after it while confident that the time off had refreshed and renewed my perspective. This is when you realize that a noncompete is really a birth certificate in disguise.

New day. New job. New Gene.

———

My very first job in the footwear industry was in July of 1978, at the original Athletic Attic store, where I sold running shoes. My last day in the industry would be on February 11, 2019. Excluding my eighteen-month detour to Pitney Bowes, I spent just over thirty-nine years in the world of shoes, boots, and sneakers. But to be totally accurate, the time that I worked in the industry was thirty-six years and seven months. This means that I was *of* the footwear industry, but for two and a half years, I wasn't actually *in* the industry.

I sat on the beach four times for a grand total of twenty-two thousand hours. Or…912 days. Or…two years, six months.

All of this spread over a span of twelve years.

This was hard on a kid who had always wanted to work and be in the thick of it since he was ten years old. For my former employers, this was nothing more than a waste of my time and their money.

I had the good fortune of being paid 100 percent of my salary each time I sat out on a noncompete. I also was blessed that a new job was waiting for me after each noncompete period expired. Many aspiring young people in the athletic footwear industry are almost forced to sign a noncompete as a condition of employment. I would even argue that some noncompetes are being signed under duress. Further, many noncompetes now only guarantee a portion of your salary, usually 60 percent. Now, what young person, potentially with a young family, can afford a 40 percent pay cut for six months while they wait to join a new company? Also, how many companies are willing to wait six months for new talent to arrive? I've even heard of designers having to sign noncompetes for two years. To what avail? Just to prohibit another company from having their own cool sneaker to sell?

While the original spirit of a noncompete contract was to protect a company and its position in a marketplace, in the athletic footwear industry, noncompetes have morphed into a way to suppress competition. And who really gets burned? The transitioning employee. If noncompetes were such a great idea, then why don't they use them in professional sports leagues?

In 2023, the Federal Trade Commission announced that they wanted to eliminate noncompetes as a way to raise wages and increase competition. In that same year, President Joe Biden went so far, in his State of the Union Address, to declare that noncompetes should be banned.

Until someone convinces me otherwise, I believe that noncompete contracts are purely punitive and are used as nothing more than hand grenades in the silly "sneaker wars."

PART THREE

THE REST OF THE PIE

CHAPTER THIRTEEN

BOOTIE CALL

I t's been said that in the city, the smart eat the dumb. That may be one way to describe the dynamics of the athletic footwear industry. It has also been said that in the great outdoors, the big eat the small. However, that is not a way I would describe the outdoor industry, where it's more like the big and the small comingle and live happily ever after. To me, the outdoor industry has lots of great brands, but it never felt very competitive, at least when compared to the sneaker industry. Even when you went to an outdoor trade show, the atmosphere felt chummy and fraternal. In the athletic industry, it would be considered treason if you hung out with the competition.

In the spring of 2006, after my six-month noncompete with Reebok expired, I joined the Timberland company. This was a huge career shift for me because at that point, I had been a sneaker guy for nearly a quarter of a century. What also made this a big move was that I am from the Bronx, and I am a seasoned card-carrying crime-and-pollution aficionado. I personally didn't really have any perspective on the great outdoors beyond my time in the urban jungle. I had spent a great deal of time outside, but not in the outdoors. I had never been camping or on a hike in my life. My idea of adventure was to show up at a Holiday Inn without a reservation. Heck, I don't even like trail mix.

I also wasn't a boot guy. I had limited personal experience with boots, beginning with the pair I was wearing as a kid in a frigid Yankees Stadium that my brother dumped his hot chocolate in. Over the years, my personal boot strategy was that if the weather required that I wear boots, then I would most often just stay indoors. While many people think that boots are fashionable, I prefer to regard them as merely popular. I associate fashion with being attractive, and I find nothing attractive about a pair of UGG boots. Yet as I learned from Jay Margolis while I was at Reebok, having fresh eyes on a business might initially cause disruption within, but it may help bring a brand to a feng shui it didn't realize it was missing.

When I joined Timberland, it was well before they were acquired by Denver-based VF Corporation. While it was a publicly traded company when I was there, it still felt like and was run like a family business.

Founded in 1952 in Haymarket, New Hampshire, the company was originally called the Abington Shoe Company. A young immigrant named Nathan Swartz worked his way up from being an apprentice to eventually buying out his partner before he brought his sons in to be a part of the business. In 1973, the company introduced its first waterproof boot named the "Timberland," and it proved so popular that in 1978, they renamed the company after its groundbreaking boot.

When I joined the brand, its chairman of the board was Sidney Swartz, one of Nathan's two sons. The CEO was Sidney's son and Nathan's grandson, Jeffrey. Originally, I was brought in as an SVP of merchandising, but after spending a considerable amount of time with Jeff and his longtime right hand, Ken Pucker, it became clear that the brand was in danger of stagnating. Timberland, at the time, had a boot simply called by its stock number, the 10061. Not very sexy, but neither was the boot. Every year from October through February, Timberland would sell tons of this one style, particularly to retailers in major urban centers. While sneakers were the official footwear of the cool city kid, they were impractical to wear in the winter months. Legend has it that during one harsh winter, some kids in New York City stumbled across the 10061 in an Army-Navy store, where its shelf appeal lent itself to warm and dry, something sneakers weren't known for. By the early nineties, the yellow boot was a staple of hip-hop style and ultimately became iconic. The problem for Timberland was that the original audience for this boot was the hard-working blue collar New Englander, so to have it adopted as a form of urban style was foreign to Jeff Swartz, and it made him extremely uncomfortable, to say the least. Additionally, street fashion had always been known to be fickle, so today's peacock could easily become tomorrow's feather duster. And while the yellow boot was wildly popular, it also accounted for a great portion of the brand's annual revenue and profit. So in the spirit of "fixing the roof on a sunny day," Jeff decided to create a division in the company and call it Authentic Youth, which loosely translated to "keep it real" (authentic) while "not being dad's footwear" (youth). This moniker made sense to the newly assembled team that would work on this initiative, but it was awkward, quirky, and confusing on a business card and when mentioned to the world outside of Timberland. Nonetheless, to lead this effort, Jeff appointed me as its president.

This certainly was a milestone moment in my life. I had led teams and managed business units in my career, but being a president carried a different responsibility. Privately, I found being named a president quite daunting yet very humbling. And just like I did when I won a big race or set a personal best in my running career, I celebrated, if only for just a moment, before I put my head down, not just to prepare for the task ahead of me but also to contemplate how I would posture and present myself in this important new role. To do this, I disappeared for a few days (not in the outdoors) to find some peace and a quiet place to clear my head so I could mentally, emotionally, and spiritually prepare for my next race.

I immediately reflected upon the lessons I learned along the way from both my working life and my running career. I recalled some profound moments to draw from, such as what I learned from Marty Liquori during my two years dedicated to chasing four. As well, I considered what I gleaned from all the bosses I had in my life, from Bernie at the drugstore in the Bronx to Fordham's beloved captain, Bobby Byrnes, and all the way to John Petersen at Nike. I also wanted to know what not to do, so I scoured my brain hard for what mistakes I had made throughout my life, whether errors in judgment or my failures to act.

During this quiet time of reflection, I also thought about my dad, who had passed away peacefully just about a year earlier. Like many sons, I spent a lot of time in my life trying to prove myself to my father. I had a flurry of memories of the times we'd spent together, some which were heartwarming while others were heartbreaking. I will never forget my near victory lap and standing ovation at Madison Square Garden and how proud that made him. I still can see his face in the crowd at the Penn Relays, a stopwatch in one hand and a thumbs-down on the other, when I missed making my dream come true by one second. Yet my most vivid recurring memory of my dad was the tired and often defeated look he wore as he trudged his way to work each day, just trying to feed his family. While I guess he would have been proud to see his oldest son be named a president, I think all he ever really wanted for me was to be unencumbered. I would eventually wish the same for each of my kids.

Being the president of anything, from your high school class to the leader of the free world, has a lot less leverage than many people think. *Merriam-Webster* defines "president" two ways:

1. "The chief officer of an organization (such as a corporation or institution) usually entrusted with the direction and administration of its policies."

2. "An elected official as both chief of state and chief political executive in a republic."

There is also a conventional notion that being president simply means you have power. As I would learn quickly through fault, failure, and the occasional hard-fought victory, the real meaning of "president" was having the power...to serve.

Soon after I joined Timberland, it seemed its main dilemma was that of an identity crisis. Who the brand served was completely different than who it sought to serve. Timberland's most loyal consumer was an urban kid who lived in a metropolitan city and was grounded in hip-hop music and its lifestyle. The brand, on the other hand, saw its target consumer as a middle-aged white male who religiously wore its signature boat shoes along with khakis and a button-down plaid shirt. While that made perfect sense when you considered the origins of the brand, this consumer was aging, and he had more of an allegiance to a boat-shoe silhouette than to its brand name. And he was purchasing less frequently as he got older. More importantly, this boring "dad look" was on the verge of extinction. On the other hand, the kids in the city were so fiercely loyal to Timberland that they essentially hijacked the brand and even christened certain boots with their own street names. The brand became known to the kids in the city as "Tims;" the 10061 became the yellow boot (even thought it was a shade of tan), while two other mid-cut boots were called "mac and cheese" and "beef and broccoli" based on their respective yellowish and brown/green colorways. Even a record producer named Tim Mosley, whose street handle and eventual stage name was Timbaland, once approached me to thank me for not suing him for his variation on the Timberland name.

My task as the president of the Authentic Youth division was to target and cultivate a broader young audience for the brand, since the aging boat-shoe wearer just wasn't getting any younger, and he was acting older than his chronological age. At the same time, my charge was to broaden the brand's reach as a hedge against the hot today, cold tomorrow inner-city business. For the next ten years, a variation of helping brands become more youthful would become a recurring theme in my career.

With a brilliant young creative director named Chris Pawlus driving a design vision, the Authentic Youth team launched a small capsule of outdoor inspired shoes called the Abington Collection, a nod to the company's original name. Also, there was the resurrection of a shelved project called the Timberland Boot Company, which was a premium-level collection made with the finest leathers. The target consumer was slightly older than the cool city kid, who sought a street-smart look to complement his young-professional lifestyle.

I sent a hungry young sales team out on the road for the better part of a year with the singular objective of gaining traction with these two sub-brands, in what was known as "high-end boutique distribution." They bulldozed their way through the marketplace and got the job done, and soon Timberland had a presence in previously untouchable premium retailers such as Bergdorf Goodman and Barneys.

Timberland's other struggle with identity was that it was walking the very thin line between being an outdoor brand or sliding into the murky abyss of becoming a casual brown-shoe company. While this identity conflict raged on, as it still does today for many brands in the outdoor industry, Jeff Swartz was absolutely sure about one thing; his brand was not going to be defined by its phenomenal success in urban America. In 1993, *The New York Times* ran a story about outdoor clothing brands and their crossover appeal to Black and Hispanic inner-city youth. In the article, Jeff shrugged off the importance of the urban youth market as a part of Timberland's success, saying it was "not sustainable." He went further, declaring that Timberland's focus was on "honest working people," a comment, to say the least, that was not very well received. After a backlash that included many prominent Black artists boycotting the brand, Jeff went on a redemption tour and met with Black cultural leaders, and in a subsequent editorial written by Jeff in *The Amsterdam News*, he vehemently denied any charges of racism. In the years leading up to my joining Timberland, the company did a great job of embracing the kids who helped this brand catapult past the mystical billion-dollar mark.

Jeff even went to greater extents, including a restructuring of the board of directors to make it truly diverse. While the board for a publicly traded company has certain responsibilities and accountabilities, one overarching goal is to guide and sometimes govern the CEO on behalf of the shareholders and investors. One noteworthy addition to the board was a guy named Ken Lombard, who had made a name for himself as Magic Johnson's partner in the former NBA legend's development company. Eventually, Ken would join Starbucks to launch its venture into music retailing. Ken was a towering presence who used his strong voice to constantly remind Jeff of that city kid who helped put Timberland on the map, not just with sales revenue but by elevating the brand to become a powerful cultural force.

During one board meeting, our marketing team presented some work it had done with an outside ad agency. Now, it's important to note that any agency's creative is only as good as the brief it receives from the client. After viewing a thirty-second TV spot, Jeff beamed with pride, while there was little reaction from any member of the board. After one long pregnant pause, Ken bellowed, "All I saw was a white man with white hair, skiing on a white mountain." Ken was pretty sure that this commercial was not going to resonate with the kids in the city, but marketing to the urban consumer was always a risky proposition anyway because any effort could be viewed as pandering or just make your brand look like it was trying too hard. The kids in the city don't want to be sold; they want to be respected.

Still, that poor choice of words in *The Times* clung to the brand several years later, like a stubborn piece of lint on an expensive suit.

Jeff Swartz was a highly educated and devoutly religious man who was often very hard on himself. While he was the grandson of the founder, Jeff's father, Sidney, was the real shoe dog in the family. Jeff never inherited that magic, but he was young, smart, and a great orator, so he was named CEO of Timberland. Yet he struggled with the idea that his lineage earned him that title rather than his merit, and he often suggested as much publicly. To his credit, Jeff was a true believer that "doing well while doing good" were not mutually exclusive ideas. Timberland was where I was first introduced to this thinking, although I would see varying iterations of it throughout my career. While some companies like Timberland truly embrace this, many other brands merely check the box, or they have some slick, saccharine approach to giving back. Timberland required that every employee performed forty hours of community service per year, with your bonus hanging in the balance if you didn't. It also generously supported Habitat for Humanity before it was fashionable to do so. As well, it was a sponsor for City Year, which was a youth volunteer program that was a Peace Corps of sorts for the underserved in American urban centers. While Jeff's intentions were noble, one couldn't help wondering if a part of this initiative was driven by an inner tug-of-war that he may have personally harbored by being born into privilege and the guilt that possibly could come with that.

Not long after the launch of Authentic Youth, Jeff decided to shift the power of leadership within the entire company so that he may be more effective as the board chair after his father had retired. Jeff would still maintain his CEO title, but he now would appoint a global brand president. While I had heard rumblings about this, there was no formal messaging to me, and quite possibly not to any other leaders in the company.

When Jeff asked to have a meeting with me, I was a bit anxious because I never knew where our conversations were headed. Jeff was inherently an introvert, which seems counterintuitive for a CEO of a publicly traded company, but this was something that I would personally identify with years later. Jeff certainly was a powerful public speaker, with a personal conviction toward doing good and giving back, but as our CFO once said, "Jeff loves humanity. It's human beings that he doesn't like."

In this meeting, Jeff took his favorite seat in my office, which was on the floor and resting against a wall, his ever-present Blackberry secure in both of his hands. I shimmied over near him on one of the black leather sofas adjacent to my desk. After exchanging pleasantries and small talk (one of God's worst inventions), Jeff asked me to be the president of Timberland. This was easily the most thrilling moment of my career. While many people may dream or aspire to being the president of a famous company, if you're like me, you never really believe it may ever come true. Here's a kid from the Bronx who, once upon a time, delivered dry-cleaning and then sold postage meters out of a Volkswagen Beetle being asked to hold a very prestigious position in a well-known worldwide brand that had annual revenues of well over a billion dollars. I was overcome with emotion, yet I maintained my composure and, graciously and without delay, thanked Jeff and accepted his offer to serve the company in this very distinguished role. Jeff also seemed moved by the moment, and after we both exhaled and collected ourselves, he added one little wrinkle. This is when he told me that a colleague and wonderful guy, a Brit named Mike Harrison, was also going to be president. So in about thirty seconds, I went from being *the* president of Timberland to being *a* president. While I was confused, so were many of the brand's employees. Upon hearing the news, creative director Chris Pawlus mused, "If God wanted us to have a car with two steering wheels, he would have created one."

Now, having co-presidents is certainly not unusual. World-famous brands like SAP, J.M. Smucker, Chipotle, and Whole Foods have had two leaders at the helm. The duality can work if each leader possesses a different skill set and background that complements the other. This would be beneficial when the co-presidents are building strategies and charting a holistic course for a brand's future. It's also effective in the day-to-day running of a company, as each leader can focus on certain competencies rather than being spread too thin over the entirety of an organization. For example, one co-president would lead the front end, the consumer-facing side of the business, while the other focused on the back end, the less sexy but vital operational functions. When Phil Knight stepped aside at Nike in 2001, he appointed Charlie Denson and Mark Parker to co-lead the Nike brand. Having had the privilege of knowing both guys quite well, it was easy to see how it would work. Denson was a tried-and-true salesman, while Parker was the steward of Nike's creativity. Yet what really made this cohesive was the chemistry and mutual respect that Charlie and Mark had for each other. They also had a powerful tiebreaker in case of a deadlock with Nike's chairman, Phil Knight.

At Timberland, our duties were split, with me overseeing the commercial side of the business while Mike Harrison was responsible for product creation and marketing. There was a rub with this alliance. Does the product team listen to the sales team and create product for the market's needs and trends? Or does the sales team dutifully sell whatever the product team cooks up? At a powerful brand like Nike, it's a little of both. Timberland was a popular global brand, but because of the company's reliance on a volatile yet lucrative urban boot business, the product team should have deferred a little more to the sales team to check the temperature and gauge the appetite of the market. For me, this didn't happen often enough, especially in America. Instead, the product team was more comfortable catering to the European market, where the Timberland brand had a completely different complexion than in America. In Europe, and especially in the UK, Timberland was viewed at the time by the consumer as a quintessential American brand, much like Ralph Lauren. There was a huge boat-shoe market in Europe despite the fact that many of those consumers had never been on a boat in their lives. The yellow boot was perceived in London as something construction workers wore. In the U.S. it was completely the opposite. The yellow boot was a symbol of street cred and style, while no self-respecting American kid would ever be caught dead wearing a boat shoe. Whether intentional or not, the product team found it easier to cater to a large market with a simple and predictable taste than to pay attention to a larger market that had a complex and demanding consumer.

As co-presidents, we had to find a resolution since at the end of each quarter, the measure of success would strictly be defined by revenue and profit, not who won the softball game at the company picnic. Success would only be defined by who showed up at the bank to make a deposit. That's when a classic and age-old conflict that is legendary for suffocating many a brand pervaded Timberland. The sales team said they missed their revenue target because they didn't have the right product to sell. The product team countered that they missed their goal because in their opinion, the sales team didn't sell the product line that was delivered to them. Just like Miller

Brewing's "Tastes great! Less filling!" both teams were right, sort of. But being right for the sake of being right wasn't going to drive the business. To solve this, Jeff Swartz needed to take off his ever-present Red Sox cap, put on his CEO hat, and give both presidents clear direction. Jeff, by nature, was conflict-averse, so he sent two presidents with two different perspectives on how to serve the market back to the drawing table.

The hardest part for Mike and me wasn't finding compromise but rather how long it took to get there. The deliberation was slow, more sundial than stopwatch, which wasn't unusual because the pace in outdoor brands is markedly slower than the more aggressive athletic industry. Meanwhile, on the floors below the executive level in our Stratham, New Hampshire, headquarters, the product and sales teams were digging in their heels, which caused a cultural divide among the people who did all the hard work. They were getting ready for a tug-of-war but without a flag on the rope. As I've said, this type of conflict wasn't exclusive to Timberland, as it was also prevalent at some of the other brands that I would eventually belong to, and which, by the way, did not have to suffer the quirkiness of having co-presidents. Still, the only way to remedy this was to have a clear and powerful mandate from the person who ultimately was in charge, and as quickly as possible.

In situations like this, the time lost can be very expensive. The failure to act can often end up as a withdrawal from the brand bank. Because of this indecision at Timberland, the business struggled, and worse, the brand's culture began to strain, revealing cracks in its veneer. Despite this past leadership logjam, Timberland today enjoys being a very powerful and revered brand.

With one president.

———

A little bit later in my career, in 2013, I was named president for another outdoor brand called Merrell. For a guy who was terminally unenthusiastic about the outdoors, it's fair to wonder why I would sign up for another tour of duty in the world of brown shoes. Well, for starters, I had just gotten off the roller-coaster ride called Under Armour, and yes, after sitting out noncompete number three. Second, it was becoming vividly clear to me at this stage of my career that who I worked with was tantamount to which brand I worked for. At Merrell, I was really impressed by the guy who recruited me. His name was Jim Zwiers, and he was a longtime executive at Wolverine Worldwide, the parent company of the Merrell brand. A lawyer by trade, Jim was incredibly intelligent, yet more important, he was a gentleman in every sense of the word. During the courting process, Jim and I would speak at length about our personal business philosophies as well as our individual styles. This really impressed me, so when Jim asked me to join, it was hard to say no.

As with almost every company or brand, the addition of a new president was either to pick up where your predecessor left off or to fix something that was broken, or maybe was about to break. This is when I realized that I was more comfortable as a wartime business leader than a peacetime executive. Joining a brand that needed a facelift or required heavy lifting seemed to come more naturally to me than just trying to further a brand on its same comfortable course. In other words, building a brand was way more appealing to me than running a brand.

Wolverine is a stalwart of the footwear industry. The company was established in 1883 and is based in Rockford, Michigan, a suburb of Grand Rapids, which is home to tons of small independent breweries as well as a global corporate giant called Amway.

Wolverine originally was a domestic manufacturer of leather shoes and boots, but in the twenty-first century, the company evolved into managing a portfolio of brands such as Sperry Top-Sider, Stride Rite, Keds, Hush Puppies, and Saucony, along with Merrell as well as its namesake, Wolverine boots.

Wolverine's goal for its new Merrell president was to eclipse the billion-dollar mark. As I've mentioned before, hitting a number wasn't a goal; it was a result. Of course, I needed to examine why this brand seemed stuck at around $800 million as well as try to figure out why my predecessor had trouble achieving this. But first, I had to make friends and influence people.

The Boston attorney Steve Manchel once said to me, "You're the type of guy that can walk into a room of twenty people, and nineteen will want to hear what you have to say. Beware, however, of the one person who lurks in the shadows." This advice was a little bit more of a polished version of one of my lifelong personal tenets, know who is friend or foe before the subway doors close, so it was always top of mind for me in any new environment. Fortunately, all the people at Wolverine were really nice. I would come to find out that this was a Michigan thing. As I acquainted myself with Grand Rapids, I initially found it unsettling when total strangers would pass me on the street and greet me with a random happy hello. Where I came from, that never happened, and when it did, it was usually a distraction before a pickpocket blindsided you.

As I dug in, Merrell had a deep-rooted problem that was greater than just stagnant annual revenue. The brand's core consumer was female, which was a great advantage, as she not only loved shoes, but she also influenced all the household footwear purchases for Johnny, Suzie, hubby, and boyfriend. However, the Merrell consumer was maturing (while the male consumer at Timberland was aging), and she was buying shoes less frequently than she used to. But Merrell also had another problem that cursed a lot of outdoor companies. The shoes were made too well, and therefore they didn't need to be replaced as often as athletic shoes. Even more, the older a pair of Merrell shoes or boots got, the more beautiful they seemed to appear to their owner.

Also, just like at Timberland, Merrell had one legendary style in its range that it leaned on too much, called the Jungle Moc. Originally introduced in 1998, the Jungle Moc was the brainchild of a shoe dog named Clark Matis. His idea was to create a shoe that you could wear at the campsite after a hike. This clog-like shoe became an instant hit with hikers and beyond, and at one time, the Jungle Moc was the unofficial official shoe in the blood-and-grease sector (a caustic term used to describe workers in both the healthcare and restaurant industries). While the Jungle Moc was incredibly comfortable, it certainly was nothing you should be wearing in your profile picture on a dating website.

To me, getting Merrell to the fabled billion-dollar mark could only happen if we made the brand, its products, and its consumers a little younger, faster, and fresher.

This, of course, proved to be a formidable task, as the Merrell team, like the shoes they created, were all about comfort. The formula they followed had been working, so why change it? Sure, we didn't hit a billion this year, but we didn't go backward either. Besides, there was always next year. This malaise wasn't exclusive to Merrell. I found it a recurring theme throughout the outdoor industry. During the same time, the sneaker industry was hardly stagnant and was rapidly encroaching upon the fashion industry. This collision of two very different planets was tumultuous while also very exciting. Sneakers were becoming fashion, not just fashionable, and the fashion brands didn't like it one bit. Meanwhile, some outdoor brands were becoming complacent, and instead of climbing up the mountain, they were chilling at the base camp. Before they knew it, they could find themselves sliding backward into the safety net of the footwear industry's version of comfort food, in a channel of distribution boringly yet aptly labeled as the "brown shoe" business.

Now, I admit that I will always have a soft spot in my heart for this network of shoe stores that serves the comfort and casual consumer. After all, it was stores like these where my mom dragged us to buy our back-to-school shoes. Whenever I would see one of these sit-and-fit stores in my travels, I would immediately become nostalgic, not because of the shoes but rather because of the people on the selling floor. The shoe store salesman was often bespectacled, donning a bow tie while wearing a pair of shoes that screamed comfort rather than style. Most importantly, he measured your foot with a Brannock Device, just as he did for your mother when she was a little girl.

Just like at Timberland, I believed that the remedy for Merrell was to inject energy into marketing and to be bold and daring with our shoe and boot design. When you walked into a sneaker store, even with an untrained eye, you could see style and brand differentiation. When you walked into an outdoor retailer, all the styles looked similar, and branding was something you discovered rather than noticed. Yet one of the most perplexing things about the outdoor industry was that the official color for all shoes, boots, and sandals was brown. It seemed that every single style in a store was colored brown, with a hint of brown and a brown accent (maybe a tan accent to be daring, or a dash of orange if you wanted to be edgy). And every style was sporting a clunky black lug outsole inspired, obviously, by monster trucks.

Even more mystifying to me was that plaid was the official master pattern for all outdoor clothing. Every season, all the brands tried their best to un-plaid plaid, but with little luck. Call me crazy, but to me, plaid was the opposite of camouflage, which seemed to be a color scheme that allowed you to blend in and become one with the outdoors. Plaid, on the other hand, sent up a flare to the grizzly bears and every other critter in the outdoors to please devour me because I'm wearing a jacket that looks like a picnic tablecloth.

While I had a great partnership with my creative director, Martin Dean, trying to wake up a dozing industry with provocative products proved to be too tall a task. As well, Merrell accounted for a great amount of the revenue and profit for the entire Wolverine portfolio, which at the time boasted more than a dozen brands, so every ninety days, we found ourselves chasing the quarter rather than advancing the brand.

I didn't realize it at the time, but the pace of the athletic industry was ingrained in me. Combine this with being a former competitive athlete and a native New Yorker, and I guess I was never cut out to be in the outdoor industry. Jeff Swartz once told me that I had "the diamond-hard look of a cobra," a line from a Bruce Springsteen song. Since we were both rabid fans of the Boss, I took this as a compliment. But I didn't miss his point. To try to smooth my city-boy edges, Timberland commissioned an executive coach to help align the leadership team and find a common ground of communication. After a few weeks, I had a one-on-one session with the coach in which she gingerly informed me that the other leaders would like it if I talked just a little bit slower. I acknowledged to her that I was somewhat aware of my rapid-fire delivery, but I quickly responded by asking her if it was at all possible for the other leaders to listen just a little bit faster?

The sports brands I belonged to in my career served consumers who sought vigor, energy, accomplishment, and fun. While there are many brands in the outdoor industry that serve a similar consumer, my time in this industry was with two brands whose consumers were more about chill than thrill. Still, what I learned on the trails while at Timberland and Merrell served me well when I eventually returned to the fast track.

CHAPTER FOURTEEN

OVER UNDER

H ard work.
      To each of us it has a personal definition. What one person may view as hard work could be another person's walk in the park. The same may be said about a hard job. The slight difference, though, is that a job can be made hard because of extenuating circumstances. Mowing a lawn in a thunderstorm, for example, can make the job hard.

Throughout my career, I'd like to believe that I worked hard. But I've also had my share of hard jobs. Whether it was the business climate, fierce competition, lack of resources, or just plain old office politics, hard jobs can break you more often than they can make you.

In between leaving Reebok and joining Timberland, I received a call from Under Armour. At the time, the brand was just turning ten years old, but it had become a powerhouse in the industry despite its age and size. Like in sports, momentum plays a big role in winning and losing. In 2005, Under Armour had momentum. Originally, the big brands ignored UA, treating it as if it were just an annoying noise, like a mysterious rattle in a '68 Volkswagen Beetle. Besides, UA was an apparel brand, so how much of a threat could they really be? Just like Adidas had ignored Nike in the early '70s, the big brands barely opened one eye when UA began in 1996, and then they went back to sleep.

I flew to Baltimore to meet with UA's founder and CEO, Kevin Plank. From the moment I shook his hand, I could feel the gravitational pull into his personal energy field. An entrepreneur in every sense of the word, Kevin got a taste for the hard work equals reward idea when he sold flowers at concerts while he was in college. His tireless hustle was best displayed when he walked on without a scholarship to the University of Maryland's football team.

I met with Kevin in his waterfront office that overlooked Baltimore's mucky Inner Harbor. Initially, the UA campus was a little distracting for me. In contrast to Nike, where the headquarters was like the Emerald City of Oz, or even Reebok, with its sprawling and glamorous campus just outside of Boston, UA had a series of old historic buildings right next to an active Domino Sugar refinery. Despite the charm of exposed brick, the hallways were narrow and dimly lit, with cubicles crammed in just about everywhere. And maybe it was just my imagination, but it seemed that every employee was handsome and beautiful, and they looked like they had just graduated from college a week before. There was one unsettling thing I noticed; all the young guys were wearing golf shirts and khakis, which was not only a certified dad uniform but a major departure from the jeans and T-shirts that the rest of the athletic industry seemed to be wearing. Years later, I would ask Kevin about this dress code. He told me that if he allowed the employees (or "teammates," as they were called) to wear jeans and T-shirts, he was afraid that they would feel like they were on spring break rather than at work. The dress code quickly loosened up, though, when some talented designers passed up job opportunities at UA simply because they had to wear khakis. No self-respecting creative type would ever be caught dead in a pair of Dockers.

Kevin explained to me that he wanted UA to become a footwear brand. He felt that in order to compete with the industry's best as well as to serve his rabidly loyal consumer, footwear had to be a part of the equation. So after a lively discussion, the task at hand was clear. This wasn't a job running a footwear team like I did at Reebok. It was being a part of a very small team that was to create an entire business from scratch. Anyone who knows Kevin or even has just met him once will notice that his drive, ambition, and enthusiasm are intoxicating. So here I was, being presented with an opportunity that, on paper, was hard to turn down. But still, I did.

I met with one other guy on that visit, who would be running the footwear show, and frankly, I found him to be a foe, not a friend, when his office door closed. Just another Nike hater who saw my background as intimidating rather than inspiring. Yet there was a bigger reason I turned down the job.

A little over a year earlier, our family had relocated to Cohasset, Massachusetts, on the south shore, just outside of Boston. We chose this town primarily because it had a midsize high school, as our youngest son, Patrick, was going to be a freshman just as I was starting my job at Reebok. I had a family rule. I promised each of our four kids that I would do everything not to let a career move disrupt their ever-important high school years. We were able to do this for Anthony and Ashlee, but a move back to Portland for the Jordan job meant that Christopher would have his senior year in a new school. While Chris handled it really well, it always troubled me, as I feared that I failed him. Still, Chris went on to play Division III basketball alongside his brother Anthony at Muhlenberg College in Allentown, Pennsylvania, and now both have high-level roles in the footwear industry, which they earned completely on their own and with no help from me. I guess they learned a lot at the dinner table, as their mom also had a ten-year career at Nike in the early years.

If I were to take the job of a lifetime at UA, it would mean a move to Maryland, which I felt would have been really hard on Patrick. So after deep contemplation, I flew back down to Baltimore on my own dime, and with a heavy heart, I told Kevin Plank of my decision. Both of us were disappointed, and we wished each other well. It was then that I took the Timberland role largely due to its proximity, since it was located just over the Massachusetts state line, in neighboring New Hampshire. The drive from Cohasset to Stratham was about ninety minutes, but only if you had the good fortune to be following a speeding ambulance in the HOV lane at three in the morning; otherwise the commute was often closer to two and a half hours. Because of this, I would often spend several nights a week at the Sheraton, in the quaint town of Portsmouth. Traveling for your job was one thing. Being away from home while doing your job was something different all together.

Shortly after leaving Timberland, I received another phone call from Under Armour. Nearly three and a half years after sitting with Kevin Plank in his office, I was asked once again to come down to Baltimore and meet with a few members of Kevin's leadership team. Unlike my first visit to UA, where I freely roamed the hallways, this visit turned out to be very clandestine.

When I had flown into Baltimore the evening before, I had the pleasure of being picked up at the airport by Kevin's delightful personal driver, Dana Dolvin. As I sat with him in the front of his impeccably clean SUV, we chatted casually about Baltimore, since I had lived just outside the city twenty years earlier, when I had my first sales job with Nike. We drove around the Inner Harbor before Dana dropped me off at the Waterfront Marriott and wished me a restful night while mentioning that he would pick me up the next morning.

Bright and early, I walked out of the Marriott and saw Dana, who was dutifully waiting for me. As I opened the front passenger door, Dana firmly shook his head no and motioned for me to get in the back seat. A little confused, I told Dana that I didn't need any special treatment. He then told me that my visit that day was top secret and that sitting in the backseat was preferred because of the tinted windows. As we approached the UA campus, Dana stunned me when he pulled out a walkie-talkie and informed someone that we had arrived, some sort of "the eagle has landed" moment. We drove up to an obscure doorway where a young woman briskly led me up one flight of stairs and then into what seemed to be an out-of-the-way conference room, where the windows were covered with brown paper. The woman told me that she was from HR, and she gave me a schedule of who I would be meeting with that day. She then placed a sticky note with her office extension number on a nearby phone and told me that if I needed to use the restroom to please call her first, and she would escort me. This felt more like a stealth military operation than a job interview. It turns out that the shroud of secrecy was for two reasons. First, UA now had quite a few new teammates who I had worked with at various other brands throughout my career, and second, the job I was interviewing for had an incumbent who didn't know that he was going to be replaced.

This obviously was a very different UA than the one I visited just a few years earlier. Some of the execs I met with were relatively new to the brand and had impressive backgrounds. Also, it seemed like there were a lot more handsome and beautiful people than I saw on my first visit. Yet the most important change was that the company had a less than successful launch of footwear since my original discussion with Kevin Plank. So in 2005, the job was to build a business. In 2009, the task now was to fix a business.

After a long and intense day, my exit was choreographed much like my entrance; I was rushed down the secret stairway and jumped into the back of Dana's SUV. Once safely off the UA campus grounds, I exhaled and powered on my mobile phone, which was turned off for the entire day. Suddenly, I had a flood of text messages, many from former colleagues who, in a variety of ways, asked the same question. Was I going to join UA? As it turns out, despite all the witness-protection measures put in place for my visit that day, there happened to be a sign outside the conference room where I was sequestered that read, "Reserved for Gene McCarthy." Oh well. The best-laid plans…

———

It was late spring and just over three years into my tenure at Timberland when I was out and about with our son, Patrick, who was days away from graduating high school. Only hours earlier, I had received a call from Josette Sayers, a well-known international executive recruiter from Ireland whom I had been working with. She gleefully told me that on Monday, I would be presented with a formal offer to be the SVP of footwear product creation for Puma at its huge center in Boston. I had always been a fan of the brand, as it neatly straddled the two varying worlds of sport and fashion. Plus, at the time it was a sleeping giant, so I saw a lot of upside. While this was great news, and I was certainly flattered, for some reason I found myself more relieved than excited. Sure, it was goodbye boots, hello sneakers, but during the courting process, I felt uncomfortable with one certain leader from Puma's headquarters in Germany. During my interview with him, I felt a bit antagonized, and I got the impression that my Nike background was an impediment rather than an advantage. I had become used to Nike haters along the way, but I wondered if, once I joined Puma, would this all dissolve or progressively get worse?

As Patrick and I ran errands that Saturday, I got another phone call. Even though it said Unknown Number, I did something I would never do today. I answered it.

"Gene? Hello, it's Kevin Plank."

Naturally, I was caught off guard since it was a Saturday, but here was Kevin calling me from Colorado, where he was attending the wedding of one of his original partners. We exchanged pleasantries, and then he quickly shifted gears.

"Are you ready to join Under Armour?"

Patrick was standing very close to me, trying to read what he couldn't hear. He always seemed a bit overprotective of me, and he knew that while my joining Timberland wasn't in my sweet spot, he appreciated that my time there gave him four straight years in one school, where he went from being a young teen to become an amazing young man. During the call, Patrick instinctively squeezed my hand as I was reminding Kevin of the reason why I couldn't join UA a few years earlier. "Sometimes, timing in life is everything," Kevin said.

That Sunday, I was sitting at an outdoor restaurant with my family, enjoying great food and a beautiful view of Cohasset Harbor. I had an interesting dilemma, since the very next day I would have to make two phone calls. One would be pleasant and the other, not so much.

On Monday morning, I called Josette Sayers to tell her that while I was honored and grateful for the generous offer to join Puma, I was unfortunately going to politely decline. Josette was initially perplexed yet very nice at the same time. Still, I was pretty sure that after that call, I was no longer on Josette's Christmas card list. After informing the powers that be at Puma, Josette called me back and asked if I would take a call from the one executive whose prior interview with me gave me pause. Reluctantly, I agreed. Once on the phone, the executive did his best to be gracious, yet he couldn't resist telling me that UA would never make it, so I should try to enjoy the ride for the short time that it would last.

————

The athletic industry has always been exciting and fun, yet its pace is relentless. Nike had declared decades earlier, "There Is No Finish Line." This ad slogan would eventually define the pace of the entire industry. And unlike the outdoor industry, the athletic community isn't very friendly, and it certainly doesn't roll out a welcome mat for new brands. As well, the footwear side of the industry always had a provincial and condescending view toward apparel brands, and sometimes even toward its own apparel divisions. Yet when it came to any upstart footwear brand, there was clearly a "no vacancy" sign on the industry door. Now, there is some validity to this. Whenever you walk into a sneaker store, you will notice that all the shoe shelves are filled with shoes. There is no small grouping of empty shoe shelves outlined with yellow police tape and a sign that says, "Reserved for the Next Big Idea." So if you were a new brand with the latest and greatest new sneaker, you needed to have an audience before you could successfully knock a few of the other brand's shoes off the wall. The good news was that at the time, UA clearly had a captive audience with a ferocious appetite.

For many business leaders who join brands that need a course correction, it can often feel like fixing a flat tire while you're driving a car on the freeway at fifty-five miles per hour. This was certainly the case at UA, and there was no time to stop for gas. If someone were to ask me what I needed in my first six months at UA, I would've said twelve months.

On my first day, I was reacquainted with a guy named Gavin Ivester. I knew Gavin from my time at Nike, but he also had Apple and Puma on his résumé. Prior to my joining, Gavin was hired as a consultant, and before I could find out where the bathrooms were, he immediately gave me his unfiltered view of what needed to be done "to complete the sentence below the ankles." UA had solutions for its fiercely loyal brand fans all the way from head to toe, but it stumbled greatly in its first attempt to make something to wear over its popular moisture-wicking socks. Since the brand had roots in football, the first attempt by UA to introduce footwear was in cleats. The results were less than spectacular, as the styling was drab (yes, even football players want pretty shoes), and worse, there were quality issues. To compound the problem, UA was about to introduce its first collection of running shoes. Like Gavin, I was underwhelmed with the offering, as there were three styles at the center of the collection, each one created for three different types of a runner's foot strike. I had several concerns; first, they all looked similar to one another. Second, the colors and styling didn't have the energy that consumers came to expect from UA. And third, the shoes were too expensive, as the price-to-value ratio for each style was way off. To me, this was a missed opportunity, since UA had a powerful brand with a captive audience. And second chances at a first try to break into the athletic footwear industry were rarely successful. This wasn't a playground. No do-overs allowed. Even though retailers always struggled to find new open-to-buy dollars, the good news was that the consumer always had an open-to-listen if you had a compelling idea. However, by the time I joined UA, the bull was already out of the gate, as this new collection was booked way in advance by the best retailers in America and was soon to be in stores everywhere.

Gavin believed, as did I, that the brand needed a lot of things, but nothing more urgently than design help. So we recruited a former Nike guy who was at Puma at the time, Dave Dombrow. Recruiting for the ranks at UA was always very difficult for two reasons. The industry's best talent was usually mature and deeply rooted, both professionally and personally. The best of the best had solid careers, and their families were established in their schools and communities. So for top talent, it was more a matter of not wanting to leave rather than wanting to go. And while it didn't help that Baltimore wasn't a garden spot, that wasn't the lone reason we struggled to attract talent. Many if not all the industry's best stars had noncompete contracts that would force them to sit out for at least six months, and with the possibility of being compensated with only a portion of their annual salary. Dombrow, though, was difficult to recruit for yet another reason. He was skeptical, just like I originally was, that a company that made T-shirts and shorts would be committed to performance footwear. He also wondered if UA footwear could survive in this very cutthroat industry. To this day, I have always espoused the view that making performance apparel was like making a paper airplane. You fold it and crease it perfectly, and then it takes flight. If something goes wrong, the damage is usually limited to a dent in the nose of the paper plane. Performance footwear, on the other hand, is more like building a Boeing 747; it's designed to safely carry people from one place to another. But if it crashes, it could be catastrophic, not to mention that the airline's own brand could be irreparably damaged.

After a lot of soul-searching and contemplation, Dombrow eventually agreed to join UA. One important thing that connected Dave and me was that we both believed that sometimes in life, you have to choose to do something where the stakes are high while the odds may be low. Knowing this, both of us chose to focus all our energy on the thrill of victory rather than cower to the agony of potential defeat.

While Dombrow worked hard to create a design language that was visually compelling and unique to Under Armour's DNA, he also had to lead and reinspire the design team. One thing that I had to do to help him was to build a moat around the footwear team. In the early days, it was common for many UA execs to roam the halls of the footwear division and offer unfiltered views on the product as it was being created. Many don't realize that a shoe in progress is often unattractive. A beast precedes a beauty. And it takes a footwear eye to see its potential. Besides the footwear designers and developers, there weren't many UA employees at the time with a footwear eye. This unbridled drive-by criticism would often have young designers retreating back to the drawing board to protect their jobs rather than pushing forward to protect their designs. To thwart this, I arranged formal product-viewing sessions so that the powers that be could see the product at certain junctures during the creation process, which hopefully would satisfy them and eliminate their random visits, which often would impede progress. Over time, as the footwear team expanded, we were able to move into a beautiful space on the UA campus, which also had a secure entry and required approved access. This wasn't so much to keep people out as it was to keep the energy in.

As many in the industry would know, the footwear community has its own unique culture. A lot of it is rooted in a time when working with your hands was considered truly artisanal. At the beginning of the twentieth century, if you were a shoemaker, you were rewarded with high praise. It was an honorable profession, one that was handed down from generation to generation, much like someone who becomes a cop or a fireman because their parents and grandparents were. Over time, footwear became a revered society with its own secret handshake. There are nuances, habits, and a vernacular that are only common to those who design, develop, sell, and market the stuff. If you are an outsider, you will surely find this quirky, as you can only know about it if you know about it. The hard part for me was how to nurture and preserve this unique culture while ensuring it meshed with UA's own culture, which for sure had its own flavor.

Since it was originally founded as an apparel brand, UA certainly had a *garmento* mentality, which is natural and essential for a company that makes clothing. Like shoe dogs, *garmentos* have their own unique dialect, but overall, footwear and apparel creators have little in common. Still, the governing culture at UA was something different. Nike's culture, for example, has a lot to do with the fact that it was founded by a runner. UA's culture is noticeably different, as it was founded by a football player. Runners are known to work hard. So are football players. Runners wants to win. Football players also want to win. A runner's unform is merely a mesh singlet and a pair of nylon shorts. Football players wear dense pads and helmets. Runners run as fast as they can. Football players hit as hard as they can.

At UA, I was a runner working with football players.

The pressure for footwear to grow at UA was beyond intense. The apparel business was growing nearly 20 percent each quarter, so the internal expectation for footwear was to run at the same rate. Wall Street was intoxicated with UA's explosive growth, and often the quarterly analyst calls focused more on footwear than apparel. UA footwear had two previous launches, one in football cleats and the other in running shoes, both receiving mixed reviews. The retailers were still trying to cleanse their palates, yet they were rooting for UA because there were only two or three powerful sneaker brands that dominated the industry, so retailers naturally wanted more diversity for their consumers. So this third footwear launch had to be a charm in "Charm City."

But the overriding tension that pervaded in UA footwear was the pressure to drive top-line revenue at all costs. If getting an order required offering a big discount, then do it. If getting an order meant taking back unsold inventory, then do it. In other words, in the holy name of top-line revenue, be transactional. This, of course, was against my religion, as I had come from the church of praising revenue but worshipping profit. My stubborn stance on this point would ultimately cause friction with my peers as we all looked at the two different sides of the same coin. Or as Yogi Berra once said, "We agree different." So ultimately a flare went up from the mother ship on the Inner Harbor, and it became clear that it was time for me to leave.

During my four years at Under Armour, I had the privilege of working closely with a tenacious entrepreneur, the honor of assembling a talented team, and the pleasure of having a front-row seat as the brand doubled its revenue in a mere four years. Often, but not always, being a part of this was nothing short of exhilarating. But also in those four years, the UA alumni association was growing at a faster rate than the brand's rocket-ship revenue. UA loved the top talent it brought in from its competitors, but it fell out of love quickly and frequently.

On the day it was decided to announce my departure, *The Wall Street Journal* ran a headline, "Under Armour Footwear Executive Exit Sends Shares Lower." This certainly wasn't about me, but more of a response to UA's revolving door of leadership.

Later that day, I received an email from Marty Liquori. With a nod to his words of wisdom to me after my last competitive race thirty-three years earlier, it said: "Gene, I read about you in the news today. Enough is enough."

CHAPTER FIFTEEN

TIGER TALE

I n the spring of 1971, following my *Sports Illustrated* epiphany moment, I took the subway down to Union Square in Manhattan to buy a proper pair of running shoes from Paragon Sports. Up until that point, I had labored through successful high school freshman cross-country and indoor track seasons while wearing a pair of Lico running shoes that I bought from a sporting goods store in the Bronx. They were made of a harsh leather that caused abrasions and blisters, but I thought that was a normal part of the break-in process. Still, the shoes looked fast to me, so that's all that mattered. Plus, they were on sale for $12.99.

Paragon had a small section of track shoes, yet my eyes were trained on only one style. Sleek and slender, with a nylon upper and, most important, in a vibrant royal blue to match my school colors, they also had a very cool name: Tiger. There was no deliberation necessary. I had to have them. No other shoe on the wall mattered. After I told the salesclerk my size, I waited anxiously for him to return from the stockroom, hoping he would not come back empty-handed. When he emerged with a shoebox in his hand, I refused to be elated until I opened the box to make sure these were the Tigers I wanted and not a salesclerk substitute. When I tried them on, I was less concerned with how they fit and more obsessed with how they looked. After all, if I could run well in a pair of bloodstained leather Licos, then I was sure that I could withstand any discomfort that may be hidden inside of a pair of cool blue nylon Tigers. Instantly, I was certain that these shoes would catapult me to being one of the top runners in New York, if not one of the coolest.

The Tiger brand, first established in 1949, was founded in a war-torn Japan by Kihachiro Onitsuka. The original premise for starting the company was his concern that Japan's youth had lost hope for the future. Onitsuka believed that by his promoting an active lifestyle, the younger generation would be uplifted. The first shoe that Onitsuka Tiger produced was a basketball shoe with a sticky outsole, designed after the company studied the many starts and stops that a basketball player would make on the court. It wasn't until the mid-fifties that the company designed a running shoe, after collaborating with a Japanese marathoner named Toru Terasawa. In 1957, Onitsuka Tiger convinced a world-class Ethiopian runner named Abebe Bikila to wear a pair of its new running shoes. This was amazing at the time, since Bikila became one of the fastest distance runners in the world…while running barefoot. The Tiger brand had a pinnacle moment in 1976 at the Montreal Olympics, when Finnish distance runner Lasse Virén won gold medals in both the 5,000- and 10,000-meter races. A now-iconic photo emerged at the time showing Virén taking a victory lap while jubilantly holding his Tiger shoes above his head. Many saw this as an unabashed endorsement of a footwear brand by an amateur athlete, which at the time was unheard of. Arguably, this may have been a pivotal moment in the advent of modern-day sports marketing.

In 1977, Onitsuka Tiger and its other holdings merged into a new company and was renamed ASICS, which is an acronym for a Latin phrase, *Anima Sana In Corpore Sano*, which translates into "A sound mind in a healthy body."

In the spring of 2015, while I was the president of Merrell, I received a call from an executive recruiter at Korn Ferry, one of the world's most prominent search firms. The call was somewhat cryptic, as initial calls from recruiters usually are until they determine your level of interest and before you sign a nondisclosure agreement. The recruiter mentioned that there was a confidential search for a president and CEO position for a "global athletic brand located in Southern California." She continued, "Gene, I'm sure by now you know who it is, but I can't confirm or deny until you sign an NDA." Even though at that point I had been in the industry for quite some time, the only company that came to mind was Skechers, and they were certainly global but hardly athletic. When I expressed my interest in the role, if only because I was intrigued as to which brand it was, I agreed to sign the NDA. It was then that the recruiter told me that the brand was ASICS. Of course, as an industry veteran, I was completely aware of ASICS, as they were a staple for serious runners, not to mention they were my brand of choice as a schoolboy runner. Where this Japanese company was based in America never really occurred to me, as ASICS was the type of brand that was always just there. Never known to be compelling marketers or to be big and splashy, ASICS had a core collection of shoes that it seemed to update every so often to appeal to its fiercely loyal consumers, who largely were middle-aged marathon runners. For the other brands that I'd worked for, ASICS was never really considered a competitive threat, but rather, a highly respected fixture in the industry.

Once I was designated as a candidate for this prestigious role, I was asked to visit the Korn Ferry offices in New York City to meet the team assigned to the ASICS search. Before I sat with the team, I was greeted by Sandra Kozlowski, a principal at Korn Ferry and one of its rising stars. After a warm welcome, Sandra said, "Gene, please tell us about yourself, but don't read us your résumé, as your accomplishments are already duly noted." Once again, credence is paid to my notion that a résumé may get you the interview, but it's your character that ultimately gets you the job. After nearly two hours of being listened to and observed, I left Korn Ferry feeling optimistic. Then it dawned on me that the art and science of interviewing had come a long way since my Pitney Bowes interview in Denny's.

———

Twice in my career, I was subject to psychometric testing, which was used by some companies to evaluate skills and personality traits to determine a candidate's suitability for an executive position. For one role where I was a candidate, the psychometric testing was done over two full days. I had been sent some materials to review in advance about a fictitious company, where I would be role-playing as its leader. When I arrived at the designated location, I was immediately escorted to an office where I sat alone and was somewhat bemused, when I suddenly realized that at that very moment, I was the leader of this fictitious company. A bit unsettled, I quietly sat behind the desk, and you got it, I began gazing out the window…reflecting and wondering, What had I gotten myself into? Suddenly, the office door burst open, and a guy glided in like Kramer on *Seinfeld* and identified himself as the head of marketing. On his heels was another guy who said he was the head of sales. Obviously, they were both actors, yet much more obvious was that I was not up for any of this one single bit. When the actors (who were a long way off from receiving their Screen Actors Guild cards) took a break, I was given a series of written tests. I was tremendously unenthused since I had never been a good test taker. Still, I dug in. Each test had a time limit, but at one point, I just got up from behind the desk and gazed out the window, trying to decide if I should remove myself from consideration for this job. I found the role-playing very cheesy, and I thought the written tests were personally invasive. But in my mind flashed the moment when I quit my final race in college, so I returned to the desk and resumed the tedious test taking.

A few weeks later, I was offered the job. Shortly after I joined this brand, I had a meeting with a representative from the psychometric testing company. She shared with me an assessment of my personality traits, noting that it was unusual for an executive who had high social engagement and verbal skills to be scored as an introvert. I felt that was spot on, and I took it as a compliment. She then became a little uneasy, fidgeting in her chair before she asked me, "Mr. McCarthy, have you ever been diagnosed with a learning disability?" She pointed out an unusually low score on one of the cognitive tests. Perplexed and offended, I replied that I had never been diagnosed with a learning disability, adding that since I was in my fifties, it seemed a little late for that assessment. Later, it dawned on me why I had this low score. When I briefly stepped away from the desk to look out the window to consider throwing in the towel, I returned to the test, and on one section I just randomly penciled in the little circles without reading the questions.

———————

After several interviews with various ASICS executives, both in California and in Japan, I was asked to be the president and CEO of ASICS America. I've had a few powerful moments in my life, from being inspired by the cover of a sports magazine all the way to getting my first job in an industry where I would eventually enjoy a four-decade career. Yet here was something that seemed extraordinary to me. I was now being asked to lead a brand whose magical royal-blue shoes had helped me launch my running career nearly fifty years earlier. This moment felt as if my life had come full circle.

After sitting out yet another six months on my fourth noncompete, I joined ASICS in October 2015. When I arrived at the beautiful offices in Irvine, California, I received a warm welcome from Jackie Sakurada, who was to be my executive assistant. I've had the honor of working with some amazing assistants in my career, but Jackie would turn out to be the GOAT. As she showed me to my new office, I was struck by two things. On one wall was a floor-to-ceiling black-and-white photograph, the iconic image of Lasse Virén holding his Tiger shoes above his head after winning gold in Montreal. The other big surprise was a massive bouquet of flowers. The card read, "Gene, all the best in your new role." Signed by the sender, Kevin Plank.

As with any new leadership role, the first day is all bright lights and niceties. The second day is when you begin to realize what you've signed up for. It's when you hear all the stuff they didn't tell you in the interview, maybe because they feared it would scare you away. Just a few weeks prior to my first day, I had flown to Japan to meet with ASICS's longstanding chairman, Motoi Oyama. After tea and the exchange of pleasantries, we discussed Oyama-San's vision for the future of ASICS America, which at the time was the company's largest region, as it comprised all of North and South America. Just prior to my joining the brand, this region had hit a billion dollars in revenue. Oyama-San told me that his expectation was to double that number over the next five years. My immediate thought was that there were two options for me to achieve this. We could somehow convince ASICS's current loyal consumers to buy twice as much, or we could start introducing the brand to new consumers.

In my first few weeks, I had much to accomplish, yet there was nothing more important than meeting the ASICS employees whom I was about to serve. After an all-hands meeting in the spacious gym, we enjoyed refreshments outdoors in the beautiful California sunshine. I always found it interesting to mingle with the team because there was so much you could learn about the culture of a brand from random conversations. As my dad would say, "The first thing the captain should do is look at the ship through the eyes of the crew."

Soon after, I had a meeting with my newly inherited leadership team. I asked them to come prepared to answer one simple question: "What keeps you up at night?" I've always found this to be quite revealing, as you will learn everything from individual ambitions to team synergies or lack thereof. Joining me from day one as a consigliere was a guy named Ron Pietersen, a long time ASICS employee whom I had the pleasure of meeting during the interview process. Ron, who was from the Netherlands, held a variety of roles during his long tenure with ASICS, and now he was joining me as my chief operating officer. Ron had been at the ASICS Irvine office for a short while before I joined, and he was seen by the leadership team as somewhat of a grim reaper. I found Ron hardly to be the hatchet guy, and he was a lot more fun than how the self-preservationists had viewed him. For me, Ron was the perfect partner in a not so perfect situation.

When any brand brings in new leadership, there can be a variety of reasons as to why. At ASICS, it initially wasn't quite clear to me since the brand had enjoyed explosive revenue growth during the three years prior to my arrival. So Ron briefed me on what he was aware of, but he also urged me to spend my first few months just looking under the hood. We decided that he would look at all things operational, the backroom, so to speak, while I would focus on the front end of the business. We then would get together every evening and compare the day's discoveries. Sometimes those evening sit-downs would be eye-opening, much like when you lift up that rock in your backyard garden and all those little black bugs scurry about. One thing, though, was very clear to me from the beginning; just like at Under Armour, whatever it took to get this brand to the first billion dollars in revenue will not be how we would get to the second billion.

Unlike footwear behemoths like Nike and Adidas, ASICS wasn't really a multi-category brand. While it had dominant market share in niche sports like volleyball and wrestling, ASICS had no noticeable presence in soccer, the biggest sport in the world, or in basketball, which was hugely popular in the U.S. Because of this, one of the scurrying little black bugs we squished was a million-dollar contract that ASICS had with two guys from Los Angeles whose company specialized in making connections with elite basketball programs, camps, and players. This might have been a nice thing to have if only we made basketball shoes.

ASICS, though, did have a few notable athlete endorsers. One was the amazing Kerri Walsh Jennings, the beach volleyball legend who won gold in three different Olympics. She was charismatic and brilliant on and off the sand, which briefly distracted me from the fact that beach volleyball players wore very little apparel and no shoes.

Sometime during my first few weeks, I flew to Baton Rouge to have dinner with another athlete we supported. Her name was Lolo Jones. A four-time World Champion hurdler, Lolo also had the unique distinction to have competed in both the Summer and the Winter Olympics, where she was a bobsledder. In addition, Lolo had a very dynamic online presence, with nearly a million followers. But dinner was a little more than just a meet-and-greet, so I was a bit nervous.

A week earlier, a young guy in our sports marketing department had written a long email coldly outlining why we shouldn't renew Lolo's contract. There was one little wrinkle…when the young guy hit send, the email went to Lolo. A bonehead mistake and a not-so-small detail.

I had lunch with Lolo's agent in New York and profusely apologized while taking my lumps. I then told him that I wanted to meet her in person to apologize. He felt that a phone call would suffice, but I insisted on flying to see her, something I think Lolo appreciated. We decided to continue with her contract, not just because she was a decorated athlete but also because off the track, she had star power. To this day, I enjoy a friendship with Lolo despite the circumstances of our first meeting.

Kerri and Lolo added great credibility to ASICS and reinforced to our longstanding and fervid consumers that ASICS was a premium performance brand. If our shoes were good enough for Olympians, then they certainly could help someone break four hours in a marathon. But in order to double the business, we had to build relationships with new consumers. In essence, we had to start talking to strangers.

Courting or converting consumers is a hard and time-consuming process, not too different from trying to meet someone at happy hour.

You enter a crowded bar filled with a lot of people looking to persuade and a smaller group who are open to being persuaded. If you're lucky, after a few hours, you might just lock eyes with someone who is willing to lock eyes back. You then muster up the moxie to go over and say hello. Small talk ensues (did I mention that this was one of God's worst inventions?), and hopefully this lasts long enough to buy this stranger a drink so that the small talk may evolve into big talk. The measure of success of this venture is to exchange phone numbers. For ASICS to grow the business, it needed to get off the treadmill and go to a few happy hours.

The most successful brands always have a hardcore audience that aspires to the brand's promise. But they also have the pleasure to serve a secondary, and usually larger, audience who just likes the idea of the brand. ASICS was a well-known entity to the fifty thousand participants in the New York City Marathon, for example, but it had very little if any traction with the 2 million spectators who lined the racecourse throughout the five boroughs.

To solve for this, I partnered with United Entertainment Group, a top-shelf public relations firm that helped brands to define their position at the intersection of culture, sports, and entertainment. After several intense days spent with UEG's president, Mary Scott, and her team, they presented to me a daring solution to expand ASICS's voice to a new consumer, who likely had never heard about our brand.

Steve Aoki was one of the most popular electronic dance music DJs in the world. He was known for his wild performances where, near the end of each concert, he would throw a massive sheet cake into a rabid audience, who felt blessed if they should be hit by it. Steve also had a huge presence on social media, 12 million followers on Instagram alone.

While it's common, if not overkill, for all the sneaker brands to have relationships with music artists, I felt that if ASICS were to follow the same cookie-cutter formula, we could possibly look like we were trying too hard to be "just like Mike." But Aoki was a good fit for several reasons. Steve was born in Miami but raised in Newport Beach, California, and his parents were Japanese. His father, Rocky Aoki, was a former wrestler who founded the restaurant chain Benihana. While Steve's heritage blended nicely with our Japanese brand, there was another element that made this partnership feel organic. Steve was incredibly athletic and religious about his fitness, and his stage presence clearly showed this off. Yet as I'd witnessed many times throughout my career, being a great athlete or a well-known celebrity didn't always mean that you were a good person, so I insisted on meeting Steve to see if his values meshed with the values of our brand.

In August of 2017, I was in London for the IAAF World Championships of track and field. I was there to cater to our athletes who were competing as well as to entertain some of our best retail partners. One late afternoon, I snuck away and caught a flight to the south of France, where I was going to meet with Steve Aoki. The metaphor was not lost on me, that I was leaving one of the world's most prestigious sports events to go meet with a guy who was equally as prestigious, but to a completely different audience.

I joined Steve and a few members of his team at a quiet and quaint outdoor restaurant, where we dined on fresh-caught fish, before Steve and I had an intimate chat. I learned of his rigorous touring schedule, his obsession for fitness, and his love of sneakers, including the ASICS Tigers he wore as a kid. I also learned of his sense of humility and his love of family, including his team, which seemed more like a brotherhood than a staff that one evening. So after a late dinner on the French Riviera, and worlds away from a track meet in London, I was convinced that Steve Aoki could be a powerful friend to our brand on every level. But Steve also expected the same from me.

Later, when I visited him at his home in Las Vegas, I had to pass an initiation test. Steve had in his home a massive gym he called Aoki's Playhouse. If trust were to go both ways, then I had to jump from a platform three stories high into a foam pit. Reluctantly, I did, but I drew the line at jumping off Steve's rooftop patio into his pool below, which he did several times with the grace of an Olympic diver.

———

Ron and I continued to find little black bugs that sometimes led us to big black bugs. When Ron asked me if I had ever seen these little black bugs before in my career, I told him yes, but not all in the same place and not all at the same time. While the task at Under Armour was like fixing a flat tire while driving on a freeway, ASICS was more like taking apart a car's engine, with all the parts spread on the floor, and not having enough time to put it back together again.

During my time at Nike, we had the pleasure of hearing from many prominent guest speakers. One such speaker was Michael Jordan's longtime personal trainer, Tim Grover. In his talk, Tim spoke of being asked to work with Michael's teammate, Scottie Pippen, who apparently was struggling with his outside shot. During Tim's talk, there was a photo on the screen of Scottie from the waist up. As Tim highlighted Scottie's ripped arms and torso, he noted how this physique had helped Scottie to become one of the best shooters in the NBA. Then Tim broadened the photo to show Scottie's full body. Tim pointed out that Scottie's legs were underdeveloped in comparison to his upper body. Tim had determined that for Scottie Pippen to get his shot back, he had to focus on his leg strength.

ASICS, to me, had a billion-dollar upper body, but in order to maintain it and keep it strong, we had work to do on its lower body. The brand had always focused on being a leading performance running brand, and probably will continue to do so, as it is their DNA. There is absolutely nothing wrong with that, since the running category accounts for a large majority of all shoes that are sold in the athletic footwear industry. But if your brand has lofty revenue goals along with the ambition to compete with giants like Nike and Adidas, you had better sell boatloads of running shoes, not to mention apparel, which was never a core competency at ASICS. To do that, you had to have strong legs. So for ASICS to have a powerful lower body, we had to do a lot of heavy lifting.

In the first eighteen months, we had to do reconstructive surgery on just about every element of the organization. We first assembled a twelve-person leadership team from scratch, where every member was new to the brand except for our beloved incumbent CFO, Kenji Sakai. The U.S. sales force was overhauled, including its compensation program, and the geographies the sales team managed were recalibrated. Every one of our third-party distributors was replaced with wholly owned subsidiaries in Colombia, Peru, Chile, Argentina, and Canada. As well, we made leadership changes in Mexico and Brazil. All of this was time-consuming, yet it also was delicate, as we were saying hello and goodbye to a lot of good people. The toughest task of all, though, was relocating the product-creation and marketing teams from California to Boston.

Early on in my tenure, Chairman Oyama-San told me that he didn't like that the ASICS America headquarters were in Irvine. He believed that California and Florida were places where Americans went to rest rather than to work. He wasn't entirely wrong. While he didn't have any particular city in mind, he did mention Portland, for the obvious reason that Nike and Adidas were headquartered there. I was always opposed to that idea, even while I was at Under Armour, when they, for some reason, opened a Portland outpost. While the city was loaded with amazing talent, it wasn't necessarily a talent pool. As I saw it, all the good ones were already taken. Also, my experience, along with my biased snobbery, always had me believe that the work ethic on the East Coast was always about hustle, while on the West Coast there was more of an ardent striving to chill. Even the popular television show *Portlandia* proudly and aptly boasted that "Portland was where thirty-five-year-olds go to retire." So instead, I chose Boston.

Home to a lot of the great challenger brands, including New Balance, Reebok, Puma, Saucony, and Converse, the Boston area was also home to more than forty colleges and universities, so there was a combination of industry experience and fresh-faced talent to draw from. Also, Boston, unlike Portland, was a bona fide sports town, as it was home to legendary franchises like the Red Sox, Celtics, Patriots, and Bruins. Almost as legendary were Boston's sports fans, who not only loved their teams but were also afficionados of the sports their teams played. Loving your hometown team is one thing. Having a deep knowledge of the games they play is a level above.

Yet an overarching reason I chose Boston was its deep tradition of shoe-making. Over a century earlier, there were shoe factories all throughout New England. Remarkably, a few are still active today. I believed that the heritage of those factories, as well as the spirit of its cobblers, would give our team a sense of authenticity and pride to be building great running shoes in a town so rich with history. Overall, I believed that being in Boston created an ethereal standard for our product and marketing teams to aspire to.

After creating this beautiful workplace in the heart of Boston, which won awards for its design and architecture, we received a warm welcome from the city's then-mayor, Marty Walsh. Despite this, the transition from California was hands down the most challenging and grueling endeavor of my entire career. As I told the mayor, we were bringing a lot of jobs to the city but not a lot of people, since virtually no one from the Irvine office, especially some leadership team members, wanted anything to do with working or living in Boston. So the task at hand wasn't just a relocation, but instead, it was a combination of winding down two revenue-generating and consumer-facing teams while starting up two brand new teams at the very same time. And all the while trying to keep the business moving, hopefully without disruption.

This colossal operation, while vital to strengthening ASICS's legs, made me unpopular among the ranks, especially with the native Californians. They loved where they lived way more than where they worked, and to some degree, I guess that's okay. But this was the painful price to pay to strengthen the brand's infrastructure and give it a strong and sustainable foundation for the future. The big conundrum for me, though, was to deliver on the directive from the chairman of the board, which was in the best interest of the brand, while preserving the trust and morale of a California Dreamin' workforce. Most members of the leadership team embraced the Boston move, as they knew it was for the greater good, while a handful dissented simply because they didn't want to move. However, it only takes a few to disrupt an entire team, and a divided team is not a team at all. And a divided team always has a hard time winning games. When that happens, the front office has to make a change, and usually that means the leader is the sacrificial lamb. Just like the manager of a major league baseball team, a CEO is merely hired to only eventually be fired.

Such is the life.

This didn't sneak up on me like Mark Belger did, when he passed me on the inside lane in Madison Square Garden. During this arduous project, I was acutely aware that my tank was running on fumes, and my get up and go just got up and went. And for the first time in my life of work and play, it showed no sign of returning. Unlike when I was the rabbit in the Astrodome in 1980, I didn't step off the track when the other runners didn't follow me. And unlike my final college race, I refused to quit. Except now it seemed that my working life was quitting on me.

———

As I stood waiting for the elevator, I felt a warm, almost Zen energy enveloping me. When the elevator finally arrived, I slowly stepped in, minding the gap and fixing my eyes on the doors to make sure they were shut. As I descended from the twelfth floor to the lobby, I closed my eyes and felt this sensation as if every cell in my body had just woken up from a long winter's nap.

When the doors opened, I strolled through the lobby and rolled through the revolving door, out onto the busy street already claimed by the rush hour commuters. Oblivious to the frigid winter air, I hardly even remember my feet touching the ground during the short walk to my apartment. I had been on countless walks on my journey, but this one was transcendent.

Just a few hours earlier, I had arrived at an upscale downtown hotel for a "strategic alignment meeting," which was a not too protected code for "we're getting rid of you." As I entered the dimly lit conference room, I felt a peace and a calm...which contrasted with the assembled firing squad.

On one side of the table was the shiny attorney in his bespoke suit and pomaded hair. Next to him was the Human Resource person, with her piercing, steely eyes and her trademark Cheshire Cat grin. I recognized that grin from working closely with this person, as I knew that she perversely lived for moments like this. She was a pariah in the world of HR, as separating with employees seemed to give her way more satisfaction than welcoming them. I was then immediately drawn to my side of the table, where my European counterpart nervously fidgeted, hating why he was there in the first place. Still, he was working really hard to be his jovial best, but at a time when jovial just wasn't on the menu.

Several months earlier, that same HR professional had unknowingly tipped me off and inadvertently prepared me for this inevitable moment. Casually sauntering into my office one day, this HR person told me that she just happened to be reviewing my contract, because that's what the heads of HR normally do, just randomly look at the CEO's contract while sipping their morning coffee. She happened to notice during her light morning reading that the company owed me money based on an obligation it failed to meet. This wasn't the first time I noticed her Cheshire Cat grin, but it was the first time I noticed that it was directed at me.

Knowing this, I arrived at the "strategic alignment meeting" with my computer, mobile phone, and access card all ready to surrender. When I left my office for the short walk to the hotel, I had already taken one long last look around this space I created to be the North American outpost for this global brand. I had to memorize the office, since I knew that I would never be there ever again. The painful part, though, was looking at all the young faces who would find out the next day that when I said goodnight to them, it was instead goodbye.

After nearly four decades, Marty Liquori was finally right. Enough was enough. It was now someone else's turn, and it was time for me to slip off my track spikes without unlacing them for the very last time.

I will always wonder if the play part of my life, my boyhood dream of chasing four, may have ended too soon. But I will sleep well knowing that my work life ended right on time.

PART FOUR

AS I SEE IT

CHAPTER SIXTEEN

GAMES OF WAR

One of the most enduring sports leagues on the planet is World Wrestling Entertainment (WWE). Originally founded in 1953 as the Capitol Wrestling Corporation, WWE thrives to this day, can be seen on television sets in more than 1 billion homes, and is broadcasted in thirty languages worldwide. In 2002, when it was called the World Wrestling Federation, its CEO, Vince McMahon, changed its name after losing a trademark battle with the World Wildlife Fund. Yet as early as 1989, McMahon acknowledged that WWE was less sport and more theater, essentially telling everyone what they already knew.

The primary component of WWE's formula for success is best described with one very simple word:

Versus.

As old as the world is, so is the concept of versus. WWE may even have taken a page out of the good book, the Bible, where versus played out with Good vs. Evil, Cain vs. Abel, and David vs. Goliath, not to mention the biblical 1988 cage match between Hulk Hogan and André the Giant. To this day, who doesn't love a good rivalry?

This idea of versus was also a go-to formula for several Madison Avenue advertising agencies in the seventies and the eighties, when Coke and Pepsi duked it out with competing television commercials in what famously became known as the "Cola Wars." Even Miller Brewing got into it by having Miller Lite battle with itself when they launched "Tastes Great! Less Filling!" These soft drink battles and internally conflicted beer companies have one very important thing in common with WWE.

It's all made up. It's fake. It's merely for our entertainment.

Then, of course, we have sports, or should I say real sports, where versus has played out for centuries. In modern times there are storied rivalries that begin with teams but then extend to cities and fans. Yankees vs. Red Sox, Celtics vs. Lakers, and even Ali vs. Frazier. And unlike WWE, there is no fake blood, sweat, and tears here.

The athletic footwear industry certainly has its own version of versus, famously known as and sometimes facetiously called the "sneaker wars." And just like WWE, some of these wars are fake and some are real, like pro sports, while other feuds are sibling rivalries, like Miller Lite.

One of the earliest if not the most brutal sneaker rivalries in history happened between two brothers. In 1919, Adolf and Rudolf Dassler founded a shoe company in Herzogenaurach, Germany, and called it Geda. Despite the political climate at the time, Geda proved to be quite successful in making athletic shoes. Years later, at the 1936 Berlin Olympics, the great American sprinter Jesse Owens was triumphant while wearing Geda shoes.

After nearly three decades of working together, the brothers' relationship began to fracture. Legend has it that it was a bitter battle between the brothers' wives that caused the fissure. Or maybe, as the story goes, it was because Rudolf believed that Adolf was behind his conscription into the army, leading to his eventual capture and imprisonment by the Allies. In any case, in 1948, the brothers shut down Geda and then each started their own shoe brands. Rudy called his Ruda before eventually changing its name to Puma. A year later, Adi opened his shoe factory and paid homage to himself by naming his company Adidas. The brothers, their families, and now their shoe brands became the most vicious of rivals. While still working and living in the same town, the families, as well as each company's employees, were forbidden to speak to each other. But this very first "sneaker war" formally commenced on soccer fields across Europe, and eventually around the world, as both Puma and Adidas sponsored the best football clubs and teams. The hatred and contempt the two families and their companies had for each other would continue for decades, even after the brothers passed away. Rudi and Adi were both buried in the same cemetery, albeit at opposite ends.

By the early aughts, this hard line had softened quite a bit. In 2022, Adidas rehired a defector named Björn Gulden to return and be its top executive after a successful run as Puma's CEO. While Gulden was not a member of the Dassler family, twenty years ago a move like this would have been considered treasonous. Since Gulden had been praised for the recent resurgence of Puma, you must wonder if his hiring was a shot across the bow, or perhaps…if you can't beat 'em, join 'em.

————

Years later, while this German version of the Hatfield and McCoy feud was still at fever pitch, Nike burst onto the scene. Cofounder Phil Knight started the brand with two premises: his love of running and his hatred for Adidas. What's ironic here is that Phil, whose passion was track and field, knew all too well that it's a sport where when a race was over, the first thing you would do is shake the hand of your opponents, win or lose. Even Steve Prefontaine, Nike's most famous endorser at the time, understood this. While Pre was as fierce a competitor as they come, he still had respect for his opponents. However, for Knight and Nike, this wasn't a race. It was a war. And Adidas wasn't a rival or an opponent; it was an enemy. What became unhealthy, though, was that this hatred and vitriol was being justified as a natural element of being plain old competitive. This was a tone and an attitude that would unfortunately become somewhat of a standard practice throughout the athletic industry for a long time.

In the fall of 1986, when I had moved to Portland, Nike had outgrown its two building on Murray Boulevard and was now located in an industrial park called Nimbus. Like many Nike employees at the time, I was drawn to a guy named Rob Strasser. Rob was originally an attorney for the brand, but by this time he was the head of marketing, fresh off his success and genius with something called Air Jordan. A big guy in size and larger in stature, Rob was loud, brash, and irreverent. Still, he always seemed to find some humor in even the most intense moments. Phil Knight had relied on Strasser so much that he once said that if Rob were a five-star general, he would follow him into battle. While they weren't blood brothers like the Dasslers, they were close.

In 1987, Rob abruptly left Nike, and along with Peter Moore, the designer of the original Air Jordan, he started his own sports consulting company and gave it the unclever name of Sports Inc. The resentment and betrayal that Knight felt would only become worse when, in 1989, Strasser and Moore would take on a client that had lost its way in the U.S. market. The client was Adidas.

This was a brand in dire need of a new energy and vision, so Rob ultimately took the reins at Adidas. He even had the audacity to relocate its American headquarters to right there in Portland. Here was a city in the Pacific Northwest, too small of a market to have more than one professional sports team, yet now, in an instant, it was home to two footwear giants, only separated by the murky Willamette River.

The hatred that Knight had for Adidas would never diminish over time, no matter how successful Nike would become. Yet this disdain took on a boundless intensity when Strasser joined Adidas, as he now became public enemy number one. Sadly, a few years later, Rob Strasser became ill before passing away suddenly at the all too young age of forty-six.

Phil Knight did not go to Rob's funeral, and it was suggested that no Nike employee should attend either. War was one thing, but betrayal was something else. Later, when Rob's wife, Julie Strasser, who, along with Laurie Becklund, wrote a book called *Swoosh: The Unauthorized Story of Nike and the Men Who Played There*, no Nike employee would admit to owning the book, as it may cost you your job. Many employees, including me, read it at night, under the covers, with a flashlight.

———

In the mid-eighties, when the "running boom" stopped booming, it was Reebok, not Nike or Adidas, that caught the aerobics wave. Originally, Nike dismissed this as a fad, and it wasn't until Reebok passed Nike in annual revenue that Reebok became public enemy number two. Nike's original efforts to make a shoe that could go up against the Reebok Freestyle largely failed. So now the war resorted to public insults, like when someone in Nike's upper ranks remarked that "Reebok's idea of research and development was a Xerox machine." (A surprising comment, since Nike's first running shoe, the Cortez, was a knockoff of a Tiger shoe, which Knight's Blue Ribbon Sports distributed in America).

Nike, to this day, in its ardent striving for world domination, always thought there was not enough room in the athletic industry for one competitor, never mind two. Over time, Reebok would have its highs and lows, yet most often, the Boston-based brand would prove to be its own worst enemy. Adidas, who was still the lumbering giant, would eventually acquire Reebok in its attempt to battle Nike on its home turf. Then, in the mid-nineties, along came Under Armour.

While footwear was always the primary focus and the core of the athletic industry, Under Armour instead was an apparel brand. Peddling workout gear that promised to keep you cool and dry was UA's focus, and hardly a new concept. It was the brand's narrative, however, that gave it momentum. The "hard work gets you to the top" message was originally aimed at high school football players, and it was a huge hit. Nike was initially dismissive of UA, just like it had been of Reebok, until UA became the new sweetheart at big-box retailers like Dick's Sporting Goods and The Sports Authority, a channel of distribution that Nike once considered second class. Yet seeing the seemingly overnight success of an apparel brand, only then did Nike take notice.

UA began to string together a few years of 20 percent year-on-year growth, a rate not seen in the industry for quite some time, so adding talent and experience was vital for UA to bolster and sustain this growth. Founder Kevin Plank personally loved to see résumés from people who worked at his biggest competitors, as he saw it as validation for his brand. And there was no shortage of talent from the big brands secretly coming to interview at UA.

When I was at UA, I was occasionally asked to interview some of these candidates. One day, I received a call from Kevin Plank's assistant, Fran, who asked me last-minute to interview this guy from one of the big brands. "Sure," I said, "send me his résumé." At this point of the day, the guy had already interviewed with several UA executives. When I looked at the résumé, I recognized the guy's name, but I was a little bit surprised that his title was chief information officer. My recollection of the guy was, let's just say, that he was several pay grades below a CIO. When he arrived at my office, I immediately recognized him, and he was shocked to see me, as I wasn't on the list of interviewers. Obviously, this was someone on a surveillance mission, not a job search. I excused myself and told HR what was happening. Moments later, and just before security arrived, he told me that he couldn't believe how he was able to roam the halls unescorted. As he said this, he now had his escort...off the campus.

"Sneaker wars" indeed.

Sports agents and professional athletes also got in the fray, as they saw the land mines as gold mines in the "sneaker wars." While I was at UA, some marquee NBA players would come to visit with no intention of signing a shoe deal with us, no matter how much money we offered. The intent was to get an offer only so they could go back to Nike or Adidas and simply raise the stakes.

I also believe that there were defensive moves from the bigger brands to block out the challenger brands. One could argue that in 2012, when Nike outbid UA for the NFL deal, it was probably more to keep UA off the field than to put the near-ubiquitous Swoosh on it.

———

I've always said that good things are contagious and bad things are infectious. Being truly competitive, of course, is a good thing, and that spirit can positively influence a brand's culture. But when you regard your competitor as an enemy, that bad energy can spread like a disease throughout the ranks.

During a sales management meeting earlier in my career, a sales director had to give a brief on Foot Action, which at the time was a Texas-based retail chain that he and his team sold to and managed. When he was asked what his strategy was for Foot Action for the upcoming year, he enthusiastically replied, "To put Foot Locker out of business!" Now, in the broader scope, to wish for the demise of your brand's largest worldwide customer was nothing short of insane. Who then would make up the nearly billion dollars in revenue? Foot Action? Still, that was the culture. Kill the other guy by any means necessary and take pleasure in it. Ironically, a few years later, Foot Action would crumble into pieces, and Foot Locker would eventually acquire the scraps on the cheap.

While the idea of "sneaker wars" got a little old and tired for a lot of people in the industry, it was still a sexy theme on Wall Street. Egged on by overzealous analysts, UA started to become intoxicated with the idea of becoming bigger than Nike. UA's voice for being a champion for the hard-working young athlete gave way to a David vs. Goliath narrative. This fascination even played out during one major sports event.

In January 2011, Auburn University, which was sponsored by UA, beat the Nike-endorsed University of Oregon in the BCS Football Championship in Arizona. It was a particularly poignant moment for me because at the time, I was UA's footwear chief, so I couldn't help but reflect to when I was with Nike, when it was the upstart challenger brand. As I sat in a skybox with other UA executives, relishing this great win, we were suddenly stunned to see Kevin Plank racing across the field toward the Oregon sideline, where he beelined for Phil Knight. Kevin was definitely not going to congratulate the Nike founder on a game well played and then offer to take him out for a beer. Luckily, one of our guys, Matt Mirchin, intercepted Kevin, and the scud missile was disengaged. Knowing both men, I can only imagine what that exchange would have been like.

There comes a time in all growth companies when you naturally slow a bit, reach a plateau, and then rest before charging up to the next base camp on your way to the summit. UA, and especially Kevin, wouldn't settle for this. There was no rest for the weary. For UA to beat Nike, Kevin continued to push the team for 20 percent growth year after year after year. This turned to be calamitous for a few reasons. First, just do the math. UA at the time was in the vicinity of $5 billion in annual revenue and had a lot of growing to do to catch a strong Nike, which was nearly ten times bigger. Without a population explosion or a Nike implosion, catching them was nearly impossible. Second, it was taking a toll on all the UA teammates. If the brand grew 10 percent, it was deemed a failure. Attrition suddenly was high, and morale was at an all-time low. But the third reason was the most important. Aside from short-sighted analysts on Wall Street, nobody really cared. A kid may like Nike, and another kid may like UA, but she or he probably didn't factor in a brand's top-line revenue in their purchasing decisions. After all, who buys a Lexus because they have a higher annual revenue than Infiniti? So here was a "sneaker war" that was fake, but unfortunately, it drew real blood.

In his excellent book *Essentialism*, Greg McKeown writes, "There is a difference between losing and being beaten. Beaten means they are better than you. Losing means you lost your focus."

By shifting the energy from empowering hard-working young athletes to just trying to beat Nike, Under Armour lost its focus and, for a time, squandered its voice.

CHAPTER SEVENTEEN

CONFLUENCE

For many young people, getting a job in the athletic footwear industry would be a dream come true. One reason is that there is a romantic notion that a typical day at a sneaker brand is like an endless loop of an ESPN commercial: You're in your cubicle, feet up on your desk, watching *SportsCenter* on your computer while checking your fantasy football league on your phone, when you casually look up and just happen to see former Yankee catcher Jorge Posada strolling through the hallway. You stand up and join your fellow slouches in a chorus of "Hip-hip Jorge!" Then you go back to work, waiting for the next sports star to breeze by. This may be a typical day at *Barstool Sports*, but definitely not at any of the major sneaker brands. Sorry, kids.

One thing is true…anyone's rabid desire to be in this industry is rooted in their younger years, when sneakers became a huge part of your existence. Sneakers were your constant companion, from when you were a little kid playing with your friends in the park to your glory days in high school sports, then all the way to young adulthood, when sneakers defined your personal style and established your street cred.

As many will attest, life was much simpler years ago, and so was the sneaker industry. Back when kids actually went outside to play a game like tag or

Ringolevio (a New York original), sneakers were just a matter of function and practicality. You wore sneakers so that you didn't mess up your school shoes. During those times, your sneaker choices weren't very complicated. Most kids wore Keds or another brand that promised that you could run faster and jump higher, PF Flyers. If you were deemed a basketball protégé, then there was a more expensive option. For the ungodly amount of $9.95, you could own a pair of Converse, or Cons, as they were known. They were available in low-cut or high-top, the latter being preferred because there was a circular patch on the ankle collar, surrounded by the words "Converse All-Star." Embedded in the middle of the patch was a blue star with a signature by Chuck Taylor, who in the 1920s was a player and manager for a team called the Converse All-Stars. But all that mattered back then was that you were wearing the same shoe the pros wore, and it said All-Star, which was all you aspired to be.

Another measure of simpler times was the color selection: white or black. The more popular color was white, as that was the choice of most NBA teams. The trick was keeping them clean, which meant that you only wore your Cons in the gym and, God forbid, never on the playground. If some kid showed up in the park wearing his white game shoes, he was certified crazy. Moms, of course, preferred black sneakers, as they took a page out of Red Auerbach's book. His Boston Celtics famously wore black Converse, not to be menacing or intimidating but because they didn't show the dirt, so the team didn't have to replace them as frequently. Who would have thought that being cheap was a key to winning eleven world championships, which the Celtics did between 1957 and 1969?

For me, the sneaker business, or should I say the athletic footwear industry, had several defining moments in its history that propelled this simple thing called a sneaker into becoming a vital staple in popular culture. From womb to tomb, sneakers are a part of just about everyone's lives. Today, all the sneaker heads, as well as the tenured professors of sneakerology, love to banter, debate, and rap philosophically about the most popular sneakers of the past fifty years. But it's important to know that some of the most legendary kicks weren't just shot out of a cannon and into the stratosphere. In my view, there was almost always a confluence of social, political, and global events that not only factored into the success of some iconic sneakers but also, I believe, helped shape the course of the footwear industry as well.

———

One of the first notable moments of confluence happened in the mid-sixties, when sports were becoming more widely broadcast on television. Every young kid back then loved to follow their hometown teams. But when color television became more affordable, this gave a new life to watching a game or match. Unlike black-and-white broadcasts, seeing sports in color somehow made you feel like you were there. But it was the Summer Olympics of 1964 when television had a big influence on athletic footwear.

It was hard for a TV viewer not to notice that most of the track and field athletes at the Tokyo Games were wearing Adidas shoes. You just couldn't miss the distinctive three stripes, which were prominent not just during the competition but also on the medal stand.

Also in Tokyo, Adidas included in the equipment kit for the basketball teams of the countries it sponsored, a training shoe of sorts called the Olympiade. This sneaker was certainly intriguing, especially to the athletes of the nations that were wearing Converse. The Olympiade challenged the notion of a canvas basketball shoe, like Converse, where the main technical feature was that a high-top could potentially reduce the severity of an ankle sprain. The Olympiade, on the other hand, was constructed with a supple yet more supportive leather and had a sole that gripped the court much better than a pair of Cons. Most distinguishing, though, were those three stripes, which not only showed up really well on television but also were a vivid contrast to what suddenly became the tired and dated Converse All-Stars.

———

As a kid, you knew that summer was just about over when your mom dragged you to shop for school shoes. The reason this hurt so much was not just that you were about to be fitted in a pair of stiff black oxfords to comply with the strict Catholic school uniform policy, but because there was always some public-school kid sitting next to you in the store, gleefully picking out a pair of sneakers as part of his school uniform. This was absolute torture.

Back then, there were two rival shoe stores in New York that sold the dreaded black lace-up dress shoes. One was called Kinney Shoes, and the other was Thom McAn. Both stores were stocked with similar, if not the exact same shoes for the family. There were lace-ups and penny loafers in black and brown for dad and the boys, while there was a little more variety for mom and the girls, such as saddle shoes and black patent leather Mary Janes, which were strictly banned in Catholic schools. As legend has it, a mischievous boy could look down at a girl's shiny patent leather shoes and see a reflection under her skirt! Somehow, though, maybe through a divine intervention, an exception was made for girls making their First Communion, probably because there was less glare from white Mary Janes.

Over time, both Kinney Shoes and Thom McAn increased their selection of sneakers. I seem to have a vivid memory of one school shopping trip to Kinney where, in the corner of the store, there was a gym locker with a display of white leather sneakers, which looked suspiciously like the Adidas shoes that were now all the rage after the Tokyo Games. The one difference, though, was that there were four stripes on the Kinney model, rather than Adidas's trademark three stripes. A small detail. Almost immediately, Thom McAn began carrying their version of "four stripes."

Seemingly overnight, sneakers were squeezing out dress shoes on the display wall in many traditional shoe stores. Interestingly, the corner locker display at Kinney eventually became the store itself, morphing in the seventies into the now iconic Foot Locker empire. This was an era when traditional sporting goods stores sold baseball bats, football helmets, referee whistles, and tennis racquets. Athletic shoes were an afterthought, usually relegated to a small section on the back wall of the store and mainly focused on football cleats, baseball spikes, and coaching shoes. Foot Locker completely changed the game by putting athletic shoes in the front, the back, the center, and on both sides of the store. If they could, they would have put them on the ceiling too. One big distinction was that the kid who shopped at the local sporting goods store played sports, whereas the kid who frequented Foot Locker when it burst on the scene watched sports and loved sneakers.

———

The first time that the Olympic Games were broadcast on television was in 1936, but at the time, it could only be seen in public viewing rooms. It wasn't until 1948, in London, when the Games could be broadcast into your living room. Track and field had always been popular with viewers since it was a sport based on three simple ideas: running, jumping, and throwing. Yet outside of this once-every-four-years event, the sport was reserved for its enthusiasts, while the rest of the world resumed its focus on professional soccer, football, baseball, and basketball. This changed, though, in the seventies.

Munich in 1972 had at the time the largest worldwide television audience for any Olympic Games. Sadly, a lot of those viewers were tuned in not just to watch U.S. swimmer Mark Spitz win seven gold medals but also because there had been a terrorist attack on the Olympic Village. A Palestinian group called Black September took some Israeli athletes hostage while demanding the release of Palestinians held in Israeli jails. This drama unfolded live on television and played out to a horrific ending, with more than a dozen dead, including eleven Israeli athletes and coaches. The Games were postponed for one day before the Olympic Committee President, Avery Brundage, declared that the Games must go on, if only to prove that terrorism shall never win.

While competition is certainly central to the Olympic Games, so is patriotism. People all over the world tune in to witness magnificent athletic performances, but also so they may cheer proudly for their country. Five days after this horrible tragedy, seventy-four runners lined up for the last event of the Games, the men's marathon. A good portion of the race was televised, but it was the distinct image of an American runner, Frank Shorter, that left an indelible impression on viewers all over the world, most especially at home in the U.S. The laser-focused Shorter, with his prominent mustache and his bright yellow Adidas shoes, crossed the finish line to win the gold, becoming the first American to do so in sixty-four years.

To me, this stunning victory and its dramatic television coverage gave way to a broader public interest in something called…running. Up until this point, running was merely an action, not an activity. Back then, you were running late or running to catch the bus. There was no such thing as going out for a run. That just wasn't a part of the vernacular. Unless of course, you were training for the Olympics.

A few years later, in 1977, a guy named Jim Fixx wrote a blockbuster bestselling book called *The Complete Book of Running*. Soon after, the "running boom" was christened. Running was no longer just reserved for the world's fastest humans or for high school kids chasing four. It was now for anyone and everyone. This was not to be some come-and-go fad. Running, or more accurately, jogging, became a cultural movement. This gave birth to fun runs and 5K and 10K races, where the goal of enjoying yourself was tantamount to clocking your best time. Celebrating after a fun run with your fellow joggers also became a thing.

Up until the explosion of the jogging craze, Nike was uniquely focused on track and field. Sure, they made shoes for long-distance runners who trained mainly on the roads. But shoes for joggers? Unheard of. Yet whether they wanted to or not, Nike became a "running boom" brand literally overnight. Once a brand with a targeted niche audience, Nike was instantly transformed into a brand for the masses.

I'm pretty sure that Nike will never acknowledge this, but I do believe they owe a huge debt of gratitude to Jim Fixx, who died of a heart attack at the early age of fifty-six, ironically while he was running. They should also be eternally grateful to Frank Shorter, regardless of what shoe brand he wore in Munich. But no matter how big your lungs are, don't hold your breath and go into oxygen debt waiting for that to happen.

Nonetheless, the confluence of these unlikely events didn't just change an industry; it created one.

———

In the eighties, because of social tumult and a technology revolution, there were two movements that proved transformational for the athletic footwear industry.

In 1980, a movie was released called *9 to 5*. Starring Jane Fonda, Lily Tomlin, and Dolly Parton, the movie was based on three working women who live out their fantasies to overthrow their sexist, egotistical boss, played by Dabney Coleman. The movie was inspired by a real-life group of Boston secretaries who, in the early seventies, had a few simple goals: better pay, more advancement opportunities, and the end of workplace harassment. When their demands fell on deaf ears, the women had no choice but to publicly shame their CEO to get what they rightfully deserved. Despite being a comedy, the film was a huge hit, largely because it struck a nerve with working women everywhere.

Two years later, one of the film's stars put her movie career on hold and began making and starring in exercise videos. *Jane Fonda's Workout*, which was released in 1982, not only brought fitness into the privacy of your own home but also helped propel the idea of "for women, by women." Sales of her VHS tape stayed at number one for forty-one weeks and then were stuck at number two for another seventy-five weeks.

In the early eighties, the "running boom" was still booming, yet it still skewed very masculine. Most of the running gear, especially footwear, was built for men. In order to satisfy the demands of the women who took up running, the sneaker brands did little more than "shrink and pink," industry jargon for taking men's shoes and disguising them as women's models. Just like in the workplace, women began to demand equality in all things health and fitness, and most particularly in their gear. Even though the JogBra was patented in 1978, it was disparagingly referred to as the jockbra.

———

In 1958, an Englishman named Joe Foster, along with his older brother, Jeff, formed a company called Mercury Sports Footwear. Their pedigree came from their grandfather, who founded and operated J.W. Foster and Sons, and who is credited with pioneering the spiked track shoe. When they realized that the Mercury name was already registered to another company, the brothers sought to change it. They liked the sound of the name of a South African antelope, so they decided to name their company Reebok.

After years of toiling on building their business, Joe realized that in order to be successful, they needed to have a stronghold in America. So in 1979, Joe attended a sporting goods trade show in Chicago and set up a modest booth to showcase his shoes. This is when he met a journeyman sales guy named Paul Fireman, who liked what he saw and heard from Joe. After a lot of back and forth, Paul eventually arranged financing so he could license the Reebok brand in America.

If the "running boom" was a movement, then the fitness, or "aerobics boom," was a revolution, for two very important and game-changing reasons. First, Reebok introduced a shoe called the Freestyle, an aerobics model that was designed specifically for women. Second, this created a Reese's Peanut Butter Cup moment where two unlikely forces started flirting with each other, sports and fashion. Looking good in a fitness studio, all of a sudden, was just as important as feeling good.

At one point, the ridiculously popular Freestyle, which was available in what seemed like dozens of colors, accounted for nearly half of Reebok's annual revenue. Just like Nike snuck up on the sleeping giant, Adidas, Reebok went end around on Nike, and for a time was the champion for women and fitness.

Still, there was one more example of confluence that would not just change the athletic footwear industry but the world of sports as well.

———

In autumn of 1984, a promising young rookie basketball player arrived in Chicago. Fresh from winning a gold medal at the Los Angeles Olympics, Michael Jordan joined the NBA's Chicago Bulls. While he had a notable college career at the University of North Carolina, it's important to note that while he was extremely gifted, he wasn't quite yet the human highlight film the world would eventually come to know. During his unmatchable NBA career, there was a running joke as to who was the last person to hold Michael Jordan to under twenty points in a game. The answer: Dean Smith, Jordan's coach at North Carolina.

Michael was selected by the Bulls with the third overall pick in the NBA draft. The Houston Rockets used their number-one pick on the future MVP and two-time world champion Hakeem Olajuwon. The second player selected was Sam Bowie, by the Portland Trail Blazers, in Nike's home market. To this day, many people in Portland lament the legendary blunder, where they could've had a future GOAT in their own backyard if they had chosen Jordan instead of Bowie. Yet in hindsight, a big part of the Jordan success equation was for him to play in a major sports market, which Portland wasn't. Another part of the equation was that Jordan played in a time zone where the sports-crazed East Coast didn't have to stay up all night to watch him dazzle.

The brilliant marketing of Air Jordan began in the fall of 1984, even though Michael's first namesake shoe wouldn't be released for sale until

April of 1985. The NBA, just like my Catholic grammar school, had a strict uniform code back then. The policy mandated that a player's shoes must be mostly white, and any secondary colors had to be the same as the team's uniform. Nike had Jordan wear a black-and-red shoe, knowing quite well that this violated the uniform code and would result in a $5,000 per game fine by the league. Thanks to the genius of marketing chief Rob Strasser, Nike willingly paid the fines on Michael's behalf, looking at it as a shrewd marketing investment, not an expense.

Sacrilegious as it is for me to say, the design of the original Air Jordan was nothing revolutionary. But when it's in NBA-banned colors, adorned with a logo that mimics an airplane pilot's wings, and it's named after a colorful young rookie…that's when a sneaker was no longer a sneaker. It was a statement.

As I see it, there were three other things going on in the mid-eighties that were critical to the success of Air Jordan, which eventually created another dimension in the athletic footwear industry.

Michael Jordan's new workplace, the NBA, was a mess. For several years, the league showed no sign of being the NBA we know and love today. For starters, most of the league's franchises were losing money, while the fans were losing interest. Often, arenas were more than half empty, and television viewership was in a steep decline. There was also a drug problem that ran rampant with players throughout the league. Still, the NBA was plagued with another problem that also divided the country.

While racism was embedded at the time into the fabric of society, and sadly still is today, it also played out symbolically on the basketball court. The league's two biggest stars, Magic Johnson and Larry Bird, couldn't have been more unlike each other, and way beyond the color of their skin. Bird played in the hard-working blue-collar town of Boston, while Magic was in the hype of Hollywood, and both players' styles on the court reflected this. Magic was the consummate showman, always wearing a big, bright smile, while Larry was the fundamental player, with a perpetual scowl on his face.

In addition, both teams, the Lakers and Celtics, hated each other, and so did both cities' fans. These two teams weren't opponents but rather were enemies, just like in the "sneaker wars." Still, it's important to note that while they were fierce competitors, Magic Johnson and Larry Bird had a profound respect for each other, unlike in the "sneaker wars."

Michael Jordan could prove to be the perfect antidote for this tension, and maybe he was just what the league needed at that moment in time. Michael had a game that combined the skills of both Magic and Larry, as his personality on the court had a little bit of party going on, like Magic, yet he could be all-business, like Larry. Just like Bruce Springsteen saved us from disco, maybe Michael Jordan could revive the NBA and rescue it from extinction.

While he went through the rigors and hazing just like any rookie, Michael also received some player-hating because of all the hype, which was mostly created by Nike. Though it may not have been appreciated at the time, the Jordan and Nike partnership would eventually prove lucrative for lots of other future players in the league, as his Nike signing would revolutionize the world of sneaker endorsements. But aside from the emergence of a very exciting player who wore banned shoes that every kid in America just had to have, there was an important medium in the eighties that helped fuel Air Jordan on its rocket ship ride. It was called cable television.

I know, hard to believe today, but back then people actually watched television on an actual television set. Channels were abundant; the color and picture were becoming more vivid and almost lifelike, while the screens were getting bigger and bigger. Some were so large that the delivery guy had a hard time squeezing them through your front door. Once upon a time, you were defined by the car you drove. Now your social status was predicated on how big your home-entertainment system was. Living rooms all across America became more like theaters, and to resolve the household conflict of who got to watch whatever they wanted, a television was now in every bedroom of the house.

Two of the most game-changing cable networks were ESPN and MTV, both providing programming that was new and fresh in concept. ESPN, which launched in the fall of 1979, would eventually have around-the-clock highlights and commentary about the day's sports events. Before then, you got your sports news from the back page of your newspaper or a two-minute snippet at the end of the six o'clock news.

Arguably, MTV was more revolutionary than ESPN. First broadcast in 1981, this was a medium where you could not only hear music but also see it. MTV originally started with an album-oriented rock (AOR) format, but in 1984 it shifted to being more like Top 40 radio. Both networks quickly went on to dominate and define pop culture for years to come. MTV created a new way for us to access music, while ESPN changed the way we followed and enjoyed sports. And don't forget that the "E" in ESPN stands for "entertainment," which made them somewhat of a bedfellow, if not a soulmate, to MTV.

It was a time when MTV could break a new artist literally overnight with a new music video. And it was a time when ESPN's *SportsCenter* could create a new star with a two-minute highlight reel. It was a time when athletes and rock stars wanted to trade places. A time when John McEnroe swapped tennis lessons for guitar lessons with Carlos Santana. And it was an era where people viewed television commercials as an art form. ESPN and MTV became massive canvases for Nike's ad agency, Wieden+Kennedy, and Spike Lee to paint their masterpieces of Michael Jordan.

There is absolutely no doubt that Michael Jordan was destined to become one the greatest players of all time. However, without a struggling NBA in need of a savior, and without the pop culture collision of ESPN and MTV, I'm not so sure that there would be the legend of Air Jordan, both as a player and a brand, as we've come to know it today.

CHAPTER EIGHTEEN

COMPANY MAN, BRAND GUY

John Steinbeck once said, "We don't take a trip. A trip takes us."

For any executive, travel is a vital part of the job, and for some it's nothing more than a necessary evil. Even when all goes well, traveling is nothing less than a grind. And when it doesn't go well, it becomes a prison sentence.

Since I took my first flight when I was seventeen, I've had a unique perspective on what used to be called "the friendly skies." In his book *A Pirate Looks at Fifty*, the late Jimmy Buffett waxes philosophical about being on a plane, musing that we should treat the time differently, as we are technically off the planet. For the better part of a half century, I've heeded this advice. Unless it was absolutely necessary, I refuse to do anything work-related while in the air. At thirty-five thousand feet, I surrender all control to the pilots, the crew, and my thoughts. When people tell me to "have a safe flight," my response always is, "I will tell the pilot." Sure, I may occasionally read a book or watch a movie, but no matter the length of the flight, I always take the time to look out the window…and reflect.

In my early twenties, I was on an Eastern Airlines flight when I had the pleasure of sitting next to an off-duty flight attendant. She dazzled me with her stories of turbulence (both inside and outside the cabin), emergency landings, and near misses, like some passengers' failed attempts at joining the Mile High Club. She also told me that any disdain she may have had toward passengers was because of things that usually happened in the front of the plane, in first class and business class.

At that time in my life, I was a regular in a middle seat in the back of the plane, so I was eager to learn from this flight attendant everything to do and not to do, should someday I be fortunate enough to fly in the front. To punctuate her point, she told me that she had a nightshirt that said, "My Job Is to Save Your Ass, Not Kiss It."

The privilege, and sometimes fleeting pleasure, of flying in business class came years later for me, when it was a perk connected to a job title. Anything good about being seated in the front of the plane, though, can be quickly dashed by that guy who oozes entitlement and self-importance. The stereotype of the traveling salesman, with the name of his company embroidered above the pocket on his light-blue button down, is a real thing in business class. When he boards the plane, he's usually on his phone and louder than necessary, seeming to believe that his conversation needs to be heard in both cabins. He tries to squeeze in two drinks before takeoff while attempting to chat with his usually unwilling seatmate. The tutorial I received from the off-duty flight attendant always stayed with me, and to this day I pay full attention to the flight attendants' instructions before takeoff, even though I've heard them a thousand times, and even while a soap-on-a-rope salesman is yapping in my ear. It is forever ingrained in me, as my flight attendant teacher pointed out, that it shouldn't be called business class; it should just be called business, since some of those passengers don't have any class.

In my quest to ensure that my time off the planet is used in a special way, I try to immediately identify friend or foe before the boarding door closes. I will open a book and pretend I'm reading, even if the book is upside down. Or I will put on my headphones, even if they're not connected, just to send a not too subtle message that I'm flying in privacy class today. Usually it works, but once in a while, it's not going to stop that guy.

Let me tell you a sad story.

On a flight from New York to Los Angeles, my seatmate was that guy. Despite any effort I made to thwart a conversation just short of wrapping myself in camouflage, that guy was destined to make me his plane pal. I feigned interest in his business exploits for a bit before he asked me the dreaded question. "So, what do you do?"

I've never been fond of talking about what I do, especially with strangers on airplanes, because the only escape route is the emergency exit, and parachutes are not handy. Beginning with my EKIN days at Nike, most people had become instantly fascinated when you mentioned that you can make a living in the world of sports without being a star athlete. It sounds way sexier than selling postage meters, or soap-on-a-rope, for that matter. And this fascination leads to tons of questions, which inevitably ends with a request for your business card.

"I work in the sports industry," was my measured and vague response.

"Wow! Have you ever been to the Super Bowl?! I've always wanted to go to the Super Bowl!" was that guy's enthusiastic reply. Looking to deflate his balloon without popping it, I played down my answer.

"Yes, I've been to a Super Bowl, but let me honestly tell you that the best seat in the house for the Super Bowl, or any sports event, is two feet from the fridge and four feet from the toilet. The beer is colder and cheaper, the restroom is cleaner, and the line is shorter."

Unimpressed and undeterred, he continued. "Have you ever met any famous sports stars?" After a big exhale and a long pause, I said, "You know, athletes are just regular people who put their pants on just like we do."

"Hmm..." was his grunted reply. After a glance out the window and a swirl of his bourbon and ice, he shifted in his seat and said, "So, what company do you work for?"

"ASICS," I reluctantly muttered. After another quick glance toward the window and a slurp of his drink, he turned to me and said, "ASICS?... Never heard of it."

As he said this, I lowered my eyes only to notice that the guy was wearing a pair of ASICS shoes.

That's why it's a sad story.

But this didn't surprise me. At the time, Nike was fiercely battling ubiquity, Reebok was stuck in the quicksand of nostalgia, and Under Armour was impaired with blurry vision from staring into the sun, while ASICS was a perpetual feast-and-famine brand; there were those who fiercely loved ASICS, and there were those who never heard of it or recognized it even if it was on their feet.

If I were to walk into a room with five or even five hundred people, it's a pretty good bet that every person in the room had at one time or another owned a pair of sneakers or boots from at least one of the brands that I had the pleasure of belonging to. But it's also a good bet that not everyone in the room has heard of some of these brands, much like that guy in business class. I would bet that the Pope has heard of Nike, but it's doubtful he's heard of Merrell, even though he would be in their core consumer set.

A lot goes into becoming a great brand, with luck and perseverance being two of the necessary ingredients. Yet the most important ingredient is possessing the instinct to know when to toggle between being a company and a brand.

A company is defined as "an entity created in a trade purpose of producing goods or services for the market, which may be a source of profit or other financial gain for its owner."

What distinguishes one company from another is usually the product or service it offers. If there are several companies offering a similar product, the main point of differentiation is usually price.

A brand, however, has broader dimensions than a company. Whether it's a name, slogan, or color scheme, a brand tries to differentiate from its competitors beyond price. A good brand will try to market itself as having a unique purpose. A great brand will create an emotional connection with its consumers, rendering its products and services as vital rather than just necessary. But in order to be a great brand, a good company must be embedded within. And to lead a great brand, there needs to be a constant toggling between the fundamental attributes of a company and the brand's core principles. Because of this, during my career in leadership roles, I needed to be both a company man and a brand guy.

At all hours of the night, the brand guy is notoriously strategic and fiercely protective about his brand's reputation, and he is always striving for its durability. But during business hours, the company man must focus on the seamless execution of tactics while driving growth and obsessing over the bottom line, with a keen eye on the checking account. This then allows the brand guy to make steady deposits into the savings account so the brand can enjoy a robust future.

The brand guy is intent on making and keeping a promise to his loyal consumers. He constantly toils to create wonderful concepts and crafts stories that bring them to life. The company man lives up to this promise by introducing these great products and providing unmatched service. He then brings them to the bank by getting an order.

The brand guy will strive to create a price-to-value ratio that is always more lucrative than the simple cost to manufacture. The company man then ensures this by tightly managing costs and being diligent about profitability. And while the brand guy must be a steward of the brand's core values, the company man will always stay allegiant to industry standards.

The brand guy will constantly invest in marketing. The company man must manage that expense for a valuable return. The brand guy will religiously attract attention to the brand. The company man must be relentless about retention.

The company man must be vigilant about credibility, while the brand guy must always push the brand to be incredible. The company man must stay disciplined and get things done right now. But the brand guy must ensure that things get done right and that it always feels right.

The brand guy will constantly ask, Why not? The company man needs to be the alter ego that always challenges the brand guy and asks, Why?

The company man should always see history as a precedent. The brand guy will only use history as context. The company man must innately be a museum keeper, while the brand guy should always be a master gardener. And all the while never forgetting that you work at the company but for the brand.

———

In late fall of 2000, the Jordan marketing team received an interesting phone call from the management team for NSYNC, whose lead singer was Justin Timberlake. At the time, the popularity of this boy band was off the charts. So it was no wonder they were asked to headline the halftime show at Super Bowl XXXV, to be held on January 28, 2001, in Tampa.

The request was for each member of the group to wear Air Jordans during the show, where they were to share the stage with Aerosmith, Mary J. Blige, Nelly, and Britney Spears for this twelve-minute extravaganza. This caused an intense debate within our management team, who were firmly divided into two camps on the request. The company men played data-driven hardball, since over 80 million viewers would be intently tuned in. The brand guys were absolutely certain, on the other hand, that the fanatical Jordan kid would consider this treason and would never forgive the brand. Both the company men and the brand guys were not wrong. But only one could be right.

NSYNC's request was swiftly yet graciously turned down.

———

I've never had the pleasure of working for Adidas, but I've had the herculean task of being its competitor. A giant global brand with universal name recognition, Adidas has always fiercely protected its iconic three stripes. If any company should use a variation of the three stripes, Adidas will see you in court. But protecting your logo is different than protecting your brand.

In 2022, Adidas made front-page news when one of its contracted endorsers, Kanye West, or Ye, as he's ordained himself, went public with a rash of antisemitic statements. Ultimately, Adidas severed ties with Ye and then suffered financially, since the Yeezy brand generated nearly $2 billion in annual revenue. But it also suffered immeasurable brand damage, as Adidas was ruthlessly criticized for how long it took to end the controversial relationship.

If you over-index on being a company, you may be protecting your bottom line, but only for the short term. However, obsessing only about brand will not always pay the bills. The constant toggling between company and brand is essential, and while I see it as a lot of art and science, it also must be governed by a strong moral conviction.

———

Another pop quiz I like to give when I speak at universities is to ask the students, "How many brands are on an NFL jersey?" More often than not, no one gets the correct answer.

There are four brands on an NFL jersey. Here they are, and in order of importance:

The Team. It's fair to say that most of the eighty-two thousand people in Met Life Stadium on a fall Sunday afternoon will be wearing a New York Giants jersey, and that was the primary if not sole reason they purchased it.

The Player. A subset of those jerseys worn in the stadium bears the name and number of various star players.

The League. The NFL logo sits smack in the center chest of the jersey, authenticating to its wearer that this is the same jersey that the Giants are wearing on the field.

The Manufacturer. The fans don't buy the jersey because of who made it. Russell and Reebok, for example, sold a ton of NFL jerseys, just like Nike, when they had the league license.

Similarly, when a runner attends the expo at the New York or London Marathon, she is likely to buy a hat, T-shirt, or jacket because the race logo adorns it, not because they like the color. The quality and price of the garment is considered, yet it's only a small part of the purchase decision. However, if the garment is of poor quality, it definitely will reflect on the integrity of the brand that made it while putting a big chink in that brand's armor. While a brand will never get credit for a marathon's logo on a jacket, it is certain to get blame for poor quality.

There was a time when it was important to consumers which brands sponsored which schools or teams. It was almost like a sport. Nowadays, if you obsess over brand sponsorship, you either work in our industry, or you have too much time on your hands. Or both.

———

Brands are hardly static objects. A brand's recognition, power, and prestige will constantly ebb and flow. There are many winds of change that can affect a brand's popularity, from political and cultural influence all the way to the unpredictable shifts in consumer taste and preference. The best brands in the world were built with a strong company embedded within as its rock-solid foundation, which then serves as the secure base for the brand's four tentpoles.

Tentpoles, if they are properly planted, will offer sturdy support while being pliant, able to move with a strong wind and hold ground with a roof overhead. As I see it, here are the four tentpoles for any aspiring brand creators.

The first is…A Name.

What's in a name? Who would we be without our names? Would we just be assigned a number? When I was born, my birth certificate read Eugene Raymond McCarthy. Within minutes, and without my approval, I was known as Gene Raymond. By the time I reached first grade, I insisted on being Eugene, as Gene sounded like a girl's name. By high school, the Irish

Christian Brothers decided, and without debate, that my name was Gene. In college, thanks to my coach Tommy Byrne, I became Geno, a name I deplore to this day. And in the current day, I've been relinquished to the letter "G," which doesn't even qualify as an acronym. Yet every variation was rooted in my birth name, which was handed down from my father and grandfather, tradition be damned. Today, we name pets after people and people after pets, and if you're a rocket-launching billionaire, you might just name your child after the symbol of a chemical compound.

Some people were given names at birth that decided their fate. Mickey Mantle and Derek Jeter were born with baseball-player names. Joe Montana's name gave him no choice but to be a quarterback with movie-star good looks. And with a name like Rocky Marciano, you belonged nowhere else but in a boxing ring. Other famous athletes weren't so lucky, like Ben Roethlisberger. But we solved that by calling him "Big Ben." Of course, with a name like Mick Jagger, you could only be a rock star, but Bruce Springsteen had to become "The Boss" to earn rock star cred. Even two of America's most iconic fashion brands are named after men that we probably wouldn't name our newborns after, Ralph and Calvin.

Years ago, businesses had names like Aardvark and Acme simply to get top listing in the Yellow Pages. Today, more and more companies have clever names, like a pet groomer called Hair Off The Dog. Elon Musk started The Boring Company, which drills tunnels to enable rapid point-to-point transportation. On the other hand, the chamber of commerce in Boring, Oregon, has its work cut out for it.

Being clever apparently wasn't an option in the early days of naming sporting goods stores. Herman's, Dick's, and The Athlete's Foot all have had great success despite their unfortunate monikers. And until the last minute, Nike was going to be called Dimension Six. Thank God for Jeff Johnson, Nike's first employee, who saw the name Nike in a dream. He approached Phil Knight just moments before he filed for a patent, and he reluctantly agreed to the new name, saying he wasn't crazy about it, but it just might grow on him. The cool-sounding Onitsuka Tiger changed its name in 1977 to the less sexy ASICS, but at least the acronym has a cool meaning.

Plenty of brands had names that morphed over time into acronyms, like when Kentucky Fried Chicken simply became KFC. Abercrombie & Fitch became A&F and then, once facing brand headwinds, became just plain old Abercrombie. This Can't Be Yogurt was originally born to compete with soft-serve ice cream. Then, when other frozen yogurt brands jumped in, they quickly and aptly changed their name to The Country's Best Yogurt before joining the acronym craze as TCBY. Hopefully, over time, Under Armour will earn acronym status, as the name is a little clumsy, if not counterintuitive to footwear, which is something that you wear over your socks and on your foot. I guess a case can be made for under the foot, but I'm reaching here. And if your brand climbs into the upper echelon, it can become a verb, like Uber, Google, and FedEx. Also, it's not a small point that the names of many of the best brands in the world have no more than two or three syllables.

Brand marks and logos also need to be thought about carefully. The Nike Swoosh reads movement, as does FedEx, where an arrow is embedded within its logo. Ralph Lauren's mark barely looks like a man on a horse with a stick, but rather, it suggests country club, preppy and Americana.

Like a Coke can, whose design has been slightly tweaked over time without losing its essence, some brands can benefit from a refresh. When I was at Timberland, I charged our creative director, Chris Pawlus, to bring a little energy to the brand's familiar "tree" logo. The subtle change made a big difference, but you probably wouldn't notice unless you compared the original mark and the refreshed mark side by side.

Reebok, on the other hand, stepped into "New Coke" territory when it created a new logo altogether. However, instead of giving the brand a refresh, it came dangerously close to an erasure of history, which for a time made this struggling brand unrecognizable. Fortunately, they returned to the original mark and thus rescued its heritage.

The next tentpole…What Are You Solving For?

In the world of goods and services, building a better mousetrap is an age-old formula. The Toyota Camry competes head-on with the Honda Accord. While both cars might not be identical, they are pretty darn close. They are similar in price and features, but each tries to outdo the other with small details such as a different shade of blue or the size of a cupholder. Both cars have been extremely popular and successful for decades, and they probably will always compete with each other based on continuous improvement. Should a new brand want to enter the auto industry, its success won't come from taking two giants head on and trying to beat them at their own game. Instead, a new brand must deliberately choose to be different while also being better.

Some of the best brands in the world burst onto the scene simply by solving a problem. Uber, which was originally called UberCab, began with the intention of disrupting the yellow-taxi industry. When it struggled with the headwinds of regulation and almost went out of business, it shifted its focus when it saw a problem to solve. As many young people didn't have the desire or the money to buy a car, they still needed to get from point A to point B. Uber then solved this problem by introducing us to ride-sharing. This not only created a new business concept but also rattled brands like Toyota and Honda, who were laser-focused, if not blindly, on automobile manufacturing. Uber on the other hand, was solving for transportation. Maybe BMW began making bicycles because they shifted their energy from building a better mousetrap to solving a problem.

Kevin Plank created Under Armour because he hated how the cotton T-shirt under his shoulder pads and football jersey would stick to his skin, drenched with sweat after a practice or game. While moisture-wicking garments were nothing new, building a company solely based on solving Kevin's cotton tee problem was unique at the time.

Hoka One One was founded by Nicolas Mermoud and Jean-Luc Diard as they sought to design a shoe that allowed them to run downhill faster. Running faster down a hill was nothing new, but building a shoe specifically for that purpose was. Hoka also had a compelling design where the mid-sole was exaggerated, therefore creating a visual cue that the industry had never seen before. It didn't take long for all the established running brands to mimic Hoka's oversized midsole, as it's an industry that has a history of getting stuck in the rut of imitating rather than innovating. Nonetheless, *Men's Health Magazine* declared that Hoka "was in a league of its own." All because it simply set out to solve a problem.

The third tentpole is arguably the most important…Nobody Cares About Your Brand Until They Know What Your Brand Cares About.

As I've mentioned, I believe that mindshare leads to market share. What consumers know about your brand is one thing. What they think about your brand, though, is the important thing. Any brand that desires relevance needs to ask itself, "If our brand ceased to exist today, would it matter?"

What brands care about comes in all sizes and shapes. Some brands put their money where their mouth is, while other brands spend money just to check a box. They view social responsibility merely as a budget line item, an act versus an action.

While boarding a flight in London, I noticed on the jetway a colorful, loud, and proud advertisement from a very large European bank. On the several placards along the way, the bank boasted about planting a million trees in the Amazon Rainforest. As impressive as it sounded, the effort totaled about a million euros, as the saplings cost about one euro each. The marketing cost for this campaign in airports all over Europe probably cost ten times that amount.

Each of the brands that I belonged to made very noble efforts through corporate social responsibility. Yet it was at Timberland where I learned the benchmark.

In 2006, we held our global sales meeting in New Orleans, a year after Hurricane Katrina devastated the city. As was sales meeting tradition, every employee spent the first day performing community service. Roughly two hundred of us spent six hours on a variety of tasks, from cleaning the streets to repairing and adding fresh paint to storm-battered homes. Before we began, New Orleans's mayor at the time, Ray Nagin, thanked everyone for being there, and our CEO, Jeff Swartz, told the mayor that we were proud to help rebuild his city. Mayor Nagin told Jeff that New Orleans didn't need to be rebuilt, but rather, it needed to be reimagined. True words of wisdom, not just for mayors but for brand builders everywhere.

In late afternoon, the two hundred of us, all sweaty and grimy and wearing our Timberland boots, climbed aboard the buses, each of us anxious for a shower and a meal. Unbeknownst to everyone, the buses didn't head straight back to the hotel, but instead took us to the Lower Ninth Ward, the section of New Orleans hit hardest by Katrina. Words could not describe what we saw. Aside from our team, there wasn't one other person in sight, only disaster, desolation, and the litter of strewn debris, the remnants of what once were people's homes. And sadly, this was one full year after the storm.

We all got off the buses and began to walk, not so much to see but to feel. After about twenty minutes, we began walking back to the buses. The silence was deafening. Along the way, there was a battered tent that served as a makeshift outpost where the residents of these long-gone homes could pick up a pamphlet with information for support and help. A young woman named Tammy Lowery just stood and stared at the tent. Without a word, she unlaced her Timberland boots and placed them near the tent, a small yet thoughtful gesture, like putting some coins in a red kettle during Christmas. Instinctively, every last one of us did the same, and then we walked quietly back to the buses in our stocking feet. The ride to the hotel was solemn. No one imagined for a second that a few hundred pairs of boots would make any difference. But the gesture itself was profound.

It is moments like these that demonstrate when a brand does indeed care.

The final tentpole must be the sturdiest.

Culture.

After giving a talk at Columbia Business School, I was asked by a student if I thought Adidas would ever beat Nike. It was certainly not the first time I'd been asked this, and it's not close to being my favorite topic. The "sneaker wars" thing was never really about the glory of victory as much as it was about gloating over killing the other guy. Still, I answered the question this way. "I don't know if Adidas will ever beat Nike, nor do I care. While I get why you are interested in that, it's irrelevant to the millions of fans that each brand has. But I will tell you what can beat, or even kill, both Nike and Adidas. It's something called culture."

Peter Thiel, the cofounder of PayPal, has said, "No company has a culture. A company is culture." Saying who you are and what you stand for only works if there's action that supports it. Reggie Jackson once said, "It ain't bragging if you can back it up." In other words, the audio has to synch perfectly with the video.

Culture can have many faces, and sometimes those faces can rear ugly heads.

There is a locker-room culture in many brands, and especially in the athletic footwear industry. One brand I worked for was infamously called "the thirteenth grade," where pranks and stunts prevailed not only in the hallways but sometimes in front of unsuspecting customers. Prior to a visit to a major account, everyone would agree on one word that each presenter should use during their pitch. Whoever used the word the most would be crowned champion at the airport bar on the way home. For example, if the word was "essential," you could be the champ if you said in your presentation: "Essentially, we are trying to sell new essential products to consumers who essentially don't know how essential they are." Yes, this essentially happened. Just a notch below calling Dr. Lipschitz from a pay phone at ten years old.

Then there is the culture of denial. Nike, as an example, originally shunned the idea of aerobics as a legitimate sports category, so they delayed their response while waiting for it to fizzle out. Another brand I worked for was terminally in denial about shifting or pivoting its position based on a new world order of running and fitness. Instead, they clung on to a quarter-century-old strategy, hoping to withstand the industry's gale forces of change. One member of my frustrated leadership team remarked in response to the flagrant denial by our parent company, "We have a headache, and we have cancer, but all we are doing is taking a baby aspirin."

The culture of comfort is a silent but deadly brand killer. I've been a member of several brands where the workforce loved where they lived rather than being enamored with where they worked. Now, it is true that you can't really love your job since your job can't hug you back. But you can really like it, and just as much as where you live. The danger of this culture is that many employees will stay in the steady center and keep their heads down with the intent of just keeping their jobs rather than being daring to challenge the status quo, to help advance the brand toward a greater good. The best brands have a culture where the team is comfortable being uncomfortable. And while it's certain to create a tension, aggravation really does cause the pearl. However, one brand that I served had a culture of no. Not "why?" or "why not?" Just plain old no.

Raf Simons was, at the time, the creative director at Calvin Klein. Prior, he held the same role at Christian Dior and later became co-creative director at Prada. Raf was a fan of our brand, and he expressed interest in working together.

Sir Richard Branson is heralded for many great business successes, from music stores to making airline and space travel fun. He approached us with the idea that sport and adventure should be fun and exciting, not just for the participant but for the spectators as well. He proposed that we would join forces to create sports festivals that had the feel and energy of rock concerts, where the performers and the audience had equal amounts of pleasure and fun.

Jennifer Aniston discovered this brand by accident. Literally. After she saw her doctor while complaining of hip pain from an injury she incurred while working out in the gym, he instructed her to immediately discard her current workout shoes of choice. He then recommended our brand to her, which Jen said she had never heard of. Another sad story. This time from world class rather than business class. Still, she was so impressed with how our shoes helped her to recover that she passionately wanted to become a brand ambassador.

Three different opportunities, all with amazing potential to advance the brand's reach. Yet each opportunity resulted in one resounding reply from our global parent company.

No. Simply because it was not part of the brand's success from a quarter of a century ago.

Steve Jobs, no stranger to brass rings and beds of fire, once succinctly said, "In weak companies, politics win. In strong companies, best ideas win."

CHAPTER NINETEEN

THE POWER OF THEY

Throughout my career I've been afforded the occasional opportunity to meet famous people, and often under unique circumstances. I've had the chance to spend time with a knighted British airline mogul to brainstorm about the power of sport. I was chided by a Beatle, who, after a spirited debate about each other's fitness regimens, proceeded to bust my chops about my slight physique. I got a one-on-one history lesson from a former U.S. president about the famed former senator from Minnesota also named Gene McCarthy. And I've also had America's sweetheart make me a cup of tea and sit on her sofa in her beautiful Bel Air mansion while we discussed all things worldly. I will always look back on experiences like these with a particular fondness, as they were incredibly motivating and inspiring for me. Yet to this day, the people I always value meeting and getting validation from are…They.

"They say that restaurant has the best burger in town."

"They say that the Yankees will win the pennant this year."

"They say we are going to have a lot of snow this winter."

They seem to know a lot…now, don't they?!

Near the end of my time as co-president of Timberland, I had lunch with Patti and our youngest, Patrick. I was telling them a story about a frustrating problem at work when Patti asked, "When are they going to do something about it?" Patrick then said, "Mom, he is they."

They certainly can have a voice of authority, but you don't necessarily have to be an expert or an executive to have valuable insights. Since my days of traveling all over Florida as a Nike tech rep, I have always been fascinated to hear the thoughts, ideas, and points of view of the people you meet in the course of an average day, except maybe on an airplane.

Over the years, I also relied upon the perspective that came from my executive assistants, who each had a great perch within each brand that I served to hear the dog whistles and to see under the radar. Each of them also had an unfiltered view of me, and they were quick to remind me of things that I may have missed or that were sneaking up from behind me. As a collective, the assistants in any brand could often be more powerful than their bosses. As I learned early on, from my Pitney Bowes days, they are power brokers with an unparalleled line of sight and a subtle but deadly form of power.

One of my favorite assistants was the vivacious Michelle Lund. While in her early twenties and in all her glory, she walked right up to me on my first day as president of Merrell and boldly pronounced, "You and I would make a great team!" Hired without a doubt and on the spot, she then spent most of her time deciding friend or foe for me from every corner of every room and made me laugh when laughter wasn't necessarily on the menu. She also was one of the few who looked at being an executive assistant as having access to power rather than just being an accessory.

I always looked forward to the streetwise wisdom I received from my car-service drivers, since the passengers they saw in their rearview mirrors and the conversations they happened to eavesdrop on offered a unique reflection of the world. For over twenty years, I made countless car reservations with Sharon from Continental Limousine. We know each other as well as anyone could know anyone, but we've never actually met in person. Continental's decades-long drivers Carlos, Beatrix, Oscar, and Felix (yes, their real names) all have, not surprisingly, figured me out in their rearview mirrors and probably know me better than I know myself. Because of that, they were never shy to offer their raw and unbridled points of view after listening to one of my phone calls while I was strapped into their back seats.

And while there are many hotels in New York City, I spent many years staying at the very same Hilton Garden Inn on 28th Street, as I was always inspired by the hard-working, sleep-deprived young women from the outer boroughs who worked there. For Damaris Sanchez and Johnmary Rosario and the other beautiful souls, the hotel may have been their full-time job, but really it was their side hustle, as they worked harder in their off hours while chasing their dreams. They were also a good reminder for me to never forget where I came from. I also enjoyed giving them fatherly curbside advice and then took a slight bit of pride as I watched them advance their lives and careers. They were a real-world reminder that working hard while chasing a dream does indeed pay off.

———

I certainly respect the value of data, but sometimes this is what data could sound like to me: 75 percent of the people in the country make up three-quarters of the population.

I believe that some leaders rely too heavily on data to qualify their decision-making. For me, data merely quantifies. Data is not a period at the end of a sentence, but rather, it should be a question mark. When data morphs into an insight, only then can it properly qualify a decision. One important path I followed to form data into an insight was to get validation from They.

While I was a sales rep at Nike, data told us that in late spring, there was a sharp spike in sales in the D.C. area of tennis skirts and baseball cleats. Only after talking to some girls in the district did we find out that rather than working on their backhand, the city girls were using tennis skirts as coverups over their bathing suits as they rode the Metro to splash parks.

And the boys bent the rules of the high school prom dress code, which only required their shoes to be black and leather. Now, baseball cleats might not make for great dancing shoes, but it let the city boys make an unusual fashion statement while wearing their beloved Nikes.

———

I was having lunch with a journalist, who asked me why some CEOs of athletic footwear brands seem to frequently mention that they are chasing the quarter. I told her that in my case, it was simply because we were making athletic shoes and then trying to sell them to people who weren't athletic. The financial pressures for a brand can sometimes contradict a brand's principles. At Jordan, we made the greatest shoe in the world for the greatest player ever to play the game, but we were uniquely aware that most of the shoes we sold would never make it to a basketball court. The reason we knew this was because we didn't own the Jordan Brand; the kids did. We just managed it for them.

Some brands focus on retailers more than consumers as their primary audience. Because of this, there is a tendency to view the marketplace as tiered, like a kingdom of stores. When a brand puts the consumer's perspective first, it's then seen more as a continuum. Because of my upbringing, both in the streets of the Bronx and my travails in the industry, I've always tended to view everything from a consumer perspective, from the outside looking in, seeing it as They see it. Sure, retailers are your customers, and that's how you get paid. But understanding your consumer and listening to They is the key to making money.

ASICS, as an example, has an attentive audience that I brilliantly call runners.

These are mature women and men who are very serious about their running, and their measure of success is determined by how many marathons they've run and what their best time is. This audience truly loves to run, and for many, it is their only form of exercise. In fact, many of them eschew other activities, like cycling, as inferior and trivial. And they are most certainly very particular about their running gear. They do tons of running-shoe research, and they will only shop in independent running specialty stores, where a sales associate studies their gait and foot strike on a treadmill or a 3-D scanner before giving them a college dissertation on the perfect shoe to buy. If you belong to this cult of serious runners, then you probably agonize more over selecting a running shoe than buying a house or a car.

We move then to a broader consumer group that I cleverly call people who run.

This is a gal and a guy who enjoy health and fitness, yet running may only be a part of their exercise regimen. They also would never purposely identify as a runner, as it's a little too geeky for their taste, and besides, running is just a part of their lives, not their sole reason to exist. The techie running brands have some traction with this consumer, but unlike with runners, brand loyalty can often be fleeting.

Then there is the largest part of the market, people who wear running shoes.

From eight months to eighty-eight years old, it seems that everybody in the world has a pair or two of running shoes in their closet. Now, this massive group of consumers is more likely to run an errand or get a run in their hosiery than to run a mile. They buy running shoes for the idea of them, surmising that if someone could wear a pair of shoes to run twenty-six miles, then they must be comfortable enough to do just about everything else in, besides running.

If these three segments were stacked as a pyramid rather than a continuum, obviously runners would be at the peak, albeit the smallest segment. People who run would occupy the more generous middle. And people who wear running shoes would make up the volume base. The top of the pyramid is where precious brand equity is built. Then, as you cascade down the pyramid, brand power can dilute while revenue grows, though staying profitable can become more challenging.

Good running brands innovate and invest in runners with the hope and expectation that the investment will trickle down. Great running brands, however, know that like in baseball, the infield may make a lot of plays, but they never forget that the outfield makes big plays too. The best brands obsess over the target consumer, but they are also shrewd and strategic about the consuming target.

———

Attention is a currency that every brand craves. In the nineties, kids spent their waking hours chasing sneaker brands. However, now we are faced with the hard truth that attention is one of the scarcest resources of the twenty-first century. Because of this, brands are now chasing kids. Today, the best brands spend a lot of time and money just hoping to get a sliver of a kid's attention. Once upon a time, kids were instantly cool when they laced up a pair of Air Jordans. Now, when kids wear Jordans, they believe they are making the brand cool, as if they are doing the Jordan Brand a favor.

We also live in a time where instant gratification takes too long. It wasn't too long ago when we hailed a cab and never knew when one would arrive, or even if one would stop. Today, we get upset when we have to wait six long minutes for an Uber. While there are new and endless challenges for every brand in the twenty-first century, understanding what they are is not enough anymore. Deciphering why is vital, and the best way to do this is to always seek the wisdom of They.

CHAPTER TWENTY

BY DESIGN

There has never been a shortage of colorful characters in the athletic industry. One of my favorites is a guy named Tom Shine. In the late sixties, Tom cofounded a company called Logo Athletic, which would become the largest sports-licensed apparel and headwear company in America, only to file for bankruptcy in 2000. Tom and I were both at Reebok in 2004, when I shared with him my frustration with the sales team and how they were pressuring my product teams. In my holier-than-thou view, the integrity of every last shoe we made would never be compromised. The sales team, on the other hand, cared way more about the price tag than the shoe that was attached to it. Tom then told me a story about a dog food company.

This well-known dog food company was having its weeklong national sales meeting when word spread that the CEO would address the attendees on the final night. This was big news because the CEO rarely attended sales meetings, and since he was known as a great orator, the sales team was buzzing with excitement.

When the final night arrived, all the men put on their best shirts, and the women wore their favorite dresses and assembled at the traditional cocktail party. About an hour later, the CEO took the stage to thunderous applause.

After the usual salutations, the CEO had the undivided attention of the sales team when he asked them:

"Who has the largest sales force in the dog food industry?" The audience shouts, "We do!" "Who has the best in-store displays in the dog food industry?" The crowd roars, "We do!" "Who has the largest marketing budget in the dog food industry?" "We do!" was the enthusiastic response.

The CEO pauses and then soberly asks, "Then why is it that we are in third place?" Suddenly, all the oxygen is out of the room, and you could hear a pin drop before one man in the back of the ballroom, leaning against the wall, dryly says, "Because the dogs don't like the food."

———

Certainly, product is at the center of any consumer goods brand. Afterall, without something to sell, a brand is just hot air. Yet one thing that distinguishes a great brand from a good brand is where product and design sit in the internal pecking order.

For a long time, Bill Gates's trusted right hand at Microsoft was Steve Ballmer. A sales guy by nature, Ballmer drove the company's growth by tripling its revenue and doubling its profit during his tenure as CEO. However, his legacy has received mixed reviews, since during his reign, Microsoft missed out on the biggest twenty-first century technology trends, such as smartphones. During roughly the same period of time, Steve Jobs's closest collaborator at Apple was Jony Ive, the now-iconic knighted British industrial designer. Without the creative freedom and support that Jobs gave to Ive, the world would be a very different place today. While both Microsoft and Apple have similar market caps in trillions of dollars, I see both brands with a distinct point of difference: Microsoft is all about technology, whereas Apple obsesses over innovation.

Technology can be something tangible, like the engine in an electric car. While innovation can also be a physical property, I think its definition is broader, as it can be how you do something. For example, if you lose a button on your shirt, you might be innovative if you were to restyle a paper clip to fasten it.

In the athletic footwear industry, the words technology and innovation are thrown around a lot, and sometimes they are confused for each other. In the world of sneakers, Nike Air and ASICS-Gel are technologies. They are also both decades old. Changing the durometer of a foam midsole is not necessarily a technology, but it is innovative. As I see it, technology is driven by science, whereas innovation is caused by design. Because of this distinction, companies that focus on technology will make instruments of utility, whereas brand that embrace innovation often create objects of desire. Steve Jobs believed that innovation distinguishes between a leader and a follower.

In all my leadership roles, I have always gravitated to the creative side of each brand I belonged to, not because I was creative but rather because I wasn't. Certainly, chasing the quarter and hitting the number is a priority for any leader, as it is the daily measure of success. But encouraging your team to be fiercely creative can ensure success for the future.

The pace of a CEO is often measured with a stopwatch. Marketers race against an hourglass. Product developers are governed by a calendar. Designers, however, don't usually adhere to the rigors of time, but if they did, their only measure might be a sundial. The Swiss designer Yves Béhar once said, "Good designers don't tend to retire. They tend to die at their desks."

Still, I find the best designers to be quite strategic. While their starting point may be on the International Space Station, the smart designers will eventually bring a good concept down into the earth's atmosphere, where it can enjoy some oxygen. And while it's likely that whoever invented the safety pin might not have initially known where to stick it, I'm pretty sure that she quickly figured out that art without commerce is nothing more than a hobby. A drawing only becomes art when it sells, as art is decided by money. Similarly, a great sneaker design only has intrinsic value when people put it on their feet. However, every sneaker in the history of the industry is magnificent…at least according to those who designed them. And while there are varying reasons for success or failure, a good designer will own up to the strikeouts just as much as to the home runs, since creativity blossoms when the good considers the bad.

One brand I belonged to continually confused product quality with great design. There was no doubt that their shoes were impeccably constructed, but if the overall design is not compelling, then it doesn't matter, because then the shoe ultimately won't sell. If people only bought things simply because they worked, then everyone would be driving a Hyundai. This certain brand's compulsion for manufacturing, and thus its insensitivity to design, ultimately forced the sales team to become the scapegoat if a particular shoe didn't sell. This is the same thing as a restaurant firing the waiter instead of the chef if the customers thought that the food didn't taste good.

———

Creative directors are an unusual breed. Their careers advance because of their successful designs, but having to lead people can go against the very nature and makeup of their being. They are not wired to manage people in the conventional sense, as they skew toward being more subjective than objective. Rare is it that you find a great creative director who is also a competent manager. And when you do, that's a good thing.

I first met Martin Dean when I was named president of Merrell. A talented young Brit, Martin had joined Wolverine when he sold them a casual brand that he founded called Cushe. Martin and I hit it off from the very start, and we spent a lot of time thinking about how to bring some heat to Merrell to make it cool. I loved the way he approached his creative briefs, as that would set the tone that would guide the designers. He wouldn't tell them specifically how to design, but he would give them context and a framework to design within. As an example, the brief for the creation of *The Jerry Springer Show* was "Give me something interesting to watch with the sound turned down." In a similar way, Martin would inspire rather than direct his designers with missives like "Design something that, when I see it on a wall, will make me want to take up trail running." Or "There is no such thing as bad weather. Just bad dressing." Certainly, a good design was in its details, but Martin had his designers start on the moon, and then he'd help them bring their designs down to planet earth.

While at Under Armour and on a trip to Asia, we visited a massive bra factory in Shenzhen, China, called Regina Miracle. My creative director, Dave Dombrow, and I were the only two footwear people traveling with Kevin Plank and several of our apparel counterparts. During the tour of the factory's campus, the CEO of Regina Miracle whisked Dave and me to a small standalone building, where he showed us a small production line that made footwear with the same molding technology used to make bras. At the time, this production method was fairly radical. What was most impressive was that the number of steps of assembly was dramatically less than what a traditional shoe factory would use. Said another way...less labor intensity, more profitability. The CEO swore us to secrecy, as even his executive team was unaware of the venture. Once back home, Dave partnered with Kevin Fallon to explore this opportunity, and to honor our commitment to secrecy, they cryptically named it the Apollo Project.

Back in 1969, in America's quest to put a man on the moon, one of the biggest problems was having a space suit that would be multifunctional on the moon's surface and in its atmosphere. After failed attempts by both the U.S. Army and Navy to build a spacesuit, it was a private company, ILC Industries, that solved the problem and crafted the innovative suit that allowed the astronauts to safely walk on the moon. ILC Dover, as it's now called, was a division of Playtex, a bra manufacturer. So our Apollo Project's launchpad was at a bra factory before we sent it to the moon.

———

There are few things more exciting than seeing a shoe designed by Tinker Hatfield. Known as the creator of Nike's Original Air Max as well as many legendary Air Jordans, Tinker is a master of the art and science of athletic footwear. But what made his work so compelling was how he used empathy to drive his design thinking. When he spent time with Michael Jordan before designing a shoe, he wanted to understand how Michael felt about all things, not just basketball. He would immerse himself in Michael's world and usually emerge with an idea or story that would serve as a north star for what he was about to create. My time with the Jordan Brand gave me more than a glimpse into how prolific Tinker was, since he was also a good and patient teacher for the next generation of designers.

While Tinker Hatfield was trained as an architect, some young designers today seem more like interior decorators; they start with an already constructed house, and then they add color and accents. Just like watching ESPN doesn't qualify you to be a basketball coach, or playing *Madden* on your Xbox doesn't make you a football player, neither does coloring by numbers make you a designer.

The footwear industry also suffers from collaboration overkill. There is too much reliance on partnering with another cool brand, celebrity, or influencer. Collabs are a shortcut and can sometimes be brand-dilutive rather than brand-enhancing. They are the lazy way to building brand relevance. The brands that consistently focus on innovation will ultimately win because the world doesn't need more things; it needs different things and better things.

———

While consumers always want something new, the athletic industry does have several shoes with a long heritage, like the Nike Pegasus, first introduced in 1983, and the ASICS Kayano, which hit the market ten years later. Both have legions of fans because these styles have evolved over the years without any dramatic change. Every twelve to eighteen months, these heritage styles would come into the market, easily recognized like an old friend, but now with a nice tan and a fresh haircut. Occasionally, there may have been a nip and tuck here or there, but not enough to scare you away. When I led the product creation teams during my career, I would remind those designers that were assigned to care for heritage shoes that there were only three things they could do to these legacy models: they could refresh them, refine them, or renew them. While it sounds simple, this delicate approach to design is surprisingly harder than creating a new shoe from scratch.

———

Over the years, I have been dazzled by the many footwear designers that I've had the pleasure to work with. I've learned many things from them, but there are four universal principles that always recur to me:

Good design makes elegance of simplicity. There is always the temptation to add elements to a design under the false pretense that you are adding value. Rather, you are probably just adding cost. Many young designers have a tendency toward overdesigning, particularly with running shoes. Sure, building a shoe requires certain structural elements to make it functional and supportive, but running is a simple activity, and its gear should be too.

The best performance footwear is absent of sensation. Contrary to a great marketing campaign from 1944, you cannot run faster and jump higher with PF Flyers. Unless, of course, your last pair of shoes were made of cement. The basic premise of exercise is to become fit, get healthy, and do your best. While you are working out, your senses should be aroused so you can focus on what you want to achieve. A quarterback wants to focus on throwing touchdowns rather than being concerned if his helmet fits. It's no different with athletic shoes. You shouldn't have to think about them while you're wearing them. They should become one with you, an extension of what you're doing, not an appendage on your lower limbs.

Color is the cheapest technology. The best designers don't color shoes, they use color as an accent to highlight a design line or a certain feature of the shoe as well as to create movement. If done right, color can add value to a shoe, and you can ultimately charge a higher price. Even the color name can add value. If a shoe is moderately priced, and one of its primary colors is purple, just change the color name to aubergine and add $20 to the price. However, if the application of color is overdone, then the shoe could have a tag on it after two weeks that says 50% Off.

The last 10 percent of building a shoe is more important than the first 90 percent. Footwear designers and car designers have had a long-standing fascination with each other. The final touches, whether in a car or on a sneaker, create an element of discovery for the user while allowing the designer a chance to sign their work. Viewed another way, without these final details, a shoe might be simple but probably not elegant.

CHAPTER TWENTY-ONE

ON BEING THE RABBIT

I f I were able to send letters of advice to my younger self, one may read like this:

Dear Eugene,

This is your much older self. I promised my whole life that I would never pry into your race to the finish with any curbside advice for your future. But there is one thing that I do want you to know.

There will be a time when you will love to go to bookstores. You will be drawn to many different sections in the store, though, spoiler alert, the fiction section will not be one of them. When you become a young professional, you will peruse books on leadership because thankfully, your life's ambition will not only be about chasing four. Now, reading leadership books is fine, and you will devour many, but just make sure that you also read books about leaders.

My advice to you is to try to understand these leaders. Read carefully about their early years and their upbringings. Learn what matters to them. Find out what shaped their values and what determined their integrities. Ponder the pivotal decisions in their lives and how they were formed, not necessarily how they were measured. And it's okay to be impressed with where leaders end up in life, but you will find it more intriguing to follow the trail of how they got there. Promise yourself not to mimic what they may have done, but rather, decide for yourself how you will choose to do things.

Because as Oscar Wilde once wrote, "Be yourself; everyone else is already taken."

Love,

Your much older self

———

In the last stretch of my career, I traveled quite a bit, and when I passed through New York, I would always meet Patrick in the city for a beer or dinner. At this point, Patrick had established himself as an excellent graphic designer who would soon work for a very cool brand called Vans. So our meetups were just as much about being peers as they were about being father and son. One evening, with his peer hat on, Patrick asked me with a not so slight touch of skepticism, "So. Dad, what does a CEO really do?" After a thoughtful moment, I said, "Pat, I only do four things. I look, I listen, I think, and then I decide." Based on my answer, Patrick instantly felt that he had the harder job of the two of us. Actually, my answer initially surprised me with its simplicity, but as I thought about it later, I'd come to realize that looking, listening, thinking, and deciding were pretty complex processes and are at the heart of any job, not just a CEO.

Look.

The English writer G.K. Chesterton once wrote, "One sees great things from the valley; only small things from the peak." Since I was a kid in the Bronx, I had always been looking and observing while careful never to stare. As the subway doors closed, I sought safety, yet once my checklist was complete, there was a lot to take in while riding the subway in New York. I developed an instant fascination with people, always wondering who they were, where they were going, and what their lives might be like. For my whole life, I have been a serial observer, and not just while I was working.

While you're looking, don't always believe what you see. I was in a women's clothing boutique when a little girl, maybe six years old, strolled in unaccompanied. While I was a little concerned, a very astute salesperson approached the little girl, bent down, and asked her if she needed help. The little girl casually answered, "No thank you. I'm just looking."

If you stand on the corner of 34th Street and 7th Avenue in Manhattan at any time on any weekday, you will notice lots of people. As a matter of fact, about six hundred thousand people stroll, stride, or power walk that corner every single day. On one side of the street is Macy's flagship store, known as the world's largest department store. It has been on that corner in Herald Square since 1902. If you were standing in front of Macy's and were to look across 7th Avenue, you would notice a bank. Which, shortly before, was a Modell's sporting goods store. Which, shortly before, was a Foot Locker. Which, shortly before, was a Foot Action store. Which, shortly before, was a bank. Not one of these stores was there for but a couple of years, never mind over 120 years, like Macy's. The reason is that the people on the Macy's side of the street are there for Macy's. Most of the people across the street are moving as fast as they can to catch a train at Penn Station, which is a half a block away. On paper, the foot traffic on that corner makes it seem like a great location for a bank or a sneaker store, but when you look at who those people are and what they're doing, you'll see that it's a great location to maybe start a railroad.

Under Armour had a rabid following of teen boys, so logically the next step should be to build cool apparel for teen girls. As expected, the girl's product they created was exciting and colorful, and in many stores, it sold out fast. If you were in UA's Inner Harbor headquarters, you might be celebrating while planning a marketing campaign focused on high school girls who played lacrosse or field hockey. And if you went to watch ten-year-olds play soccer on a Saturday morning, you would see lots of this colorful UA gear. On the moms.

If you visited a Dick's Sporting Goods store on a random weekday afternoon, you just might see a mom with her kids who just got out of school, shopping for Johnny and Suzie's soccer cleats. Then, while heading to the cash register, mom just happens to notice the cute and colorful UA workout gear, which would look great on mom at the bus stop, in the gym, and at Starbucks as well as at Johnny and Suzie's Saturday soccer game.

In the nineties, hot trends in athletic wear might have lasted for weeks or months. When kids in the city began wearing Starter jackets with an NFL team's logo on the back, it became a hot trend. By the time the kids in the suburbs caught on, the city kids were already on to something else. Over the years, I've learned that when you've seen it once, it could be an idea. When you've seen it twice, it might be a trend. But when you've seen it three times, it's probably over.

Since ice begins to melt on the periphery, I spent a lot of time looking at the market from the margins. I once met a financial analyst who told me that he spent long hours every day poring over data to inform his decisions. But he would occasionally eat dinner at an Applebee's restaurant on a Friday night, even though he was more of a French cuisine kind of guy. He believed that as long as families were flocking to affordable restaurants, this was a small indicator that the economy was probably in good shape. If on several Fridays he noticed a few empty tables rather than a packed house, he saw it as a reason to dive deeper into his data and look for any small warning that the economy may be on the verge of cooling off. He certainly didn't make any bets based on a dinner at Applebee's, but it was a tiny little measure that tweaked his radar. It's easy to draw a conclusion about the economy when there are vacant stores in a city center, but by then it's too late. But it also should raise an eyebrow if a Pier One Imports home-furnishing store goes out of business and is replaced with a dollar store.

You might think that Reebok or Under Armour are doing well when you see lots of their shoes on feet. But you might think otherwise if you knew that because of inventory issues, their shoes were heavily discounted, and that caused a spike in sales. What you look at and what you see can tell two very different stories.

————

"Believe nothing you hear and only one half of what you see."—Edgar Allan Poe

Listen.

There are tons of books written about the art of listening because most people don't. We live in an age of information overload, not to mention opinion overload. I'm not that crazy about opinions, as I'm more interested in points of view since they can initiate a discussion. An opinion might be that I don't like Mondays. It can become a point of view if I rephrase it by saying, I'm not sure I like Mondays, what do you think? Because the only way to listen is by talking to as many people as you can.

There was a time in the mid-nineties when white nylon track pants made by Adidas seemed to become a hit with city kids. Soon, Adidas started ramping up production, and industry experts (there are multitudes) wondered if Adidas was hot again. During one of my many market trips, I was on 125th street in Harlem visiting a Dr. Jay's store. As usual, the store was packed, and I began to chat with two kids, both wearing white track pants. After learning that I was with Nike, they became comfortable with me and also quite animated. I casually mentioned that it looked like Adidas was hot. Perplexed, they said that Nike was hot, not Adidas. When I pointed to their track pants as evidence, one kid laughed and told me that they wore the white nylon pants because you could see a silhouette of the very colorful Tommy Hilfiger boxer shorts they were wearing underneath. Turns out Tommy Hilfiger might have been the hot brand.

On another market trip, I went into a store where I was the lone shopper. I mentioned to the girl at the cash register how quiet the store was. She then said, "Oh my God, you should have been here yesterday; it was horrible. The store was packed all day long." Obviously, it never occurred to this girl that a packed store was better for business than an empty store. No employee of the month trophy here.

I'd like to believe that I'm a serial listener, but I'm also a work in progress. I'm guilty of sometimes calculating instead of listening, and I admit that I can confuse skepticism with cynicism. But being aware of these flaws is a step in the right direction. I also continue to remind myself to beware the loudest voice and the squeakiest wheel, because that's when you really have to listen between the lines. The immortal philosopher Jimi Hendrix told us, "Knowledge speaks, but wisdom listens."

But worse than hearing something wrong is not listening at all. Just imagine how different the athletic footwear industry would be if in the sixties, Onitsuka Tiger had listened to the product suggestions of its West Coast distributor, Phil Knight.

———

Think.

For decades I have been looking out the windows of bedrooms, class-rooms, dorm rooms, conference rooms, cars, subways, airplanes…and re-flecting. Also, for many years, I would wake up at four-thirty in the morning to find quiet so I could think. Quiet allows me to listen to the soft voice of my intuition. As Pablo Picasso said, "Without solitude, no serious work is possible." I also consider that early-morning time as a form of open-eyed meditation, where I allow my thoughts to wash over me. The simple rule is "don't just do something, sit there."

For the casual runner, a five-mile run can be a time to dissociate, to clear your mind. When I was a competitive runner, the ten-mile road workouts were spent visualizing the many race situations I might face. Thinking was all I did. After my running career was over, I was never one to listen to music while on a run, so I still used my workouts as a time to visualize and think. Facebook founder Mark Zuckerberg said he quit running because it gave him too much time to think. Running doesn't give me enough time to think. Pete Townsend, the legendary guitarist for The Who, once said that "Rock and roll will never make your problems go away, but it gives you a chance to dance all over them." Running allows me to organize my thoughts and my perspective so that when I go back to a quiet place to think, everything seems to be in order. A workout doesn't necessarily make you stronger; it's when you rest that you build muscle.

The important part of thinking, though, is to be able to face yourself, to possess an unfiltered view of who you are, so that thinking transitions to deciding.

"Knowing others is intelligence; knowing yourself is true wisdom. Mastering others is strength; mastering yourself is true power" said Lao Tzu

———

Decide.

I've had the privilege to work for several amazing brands, and despite all of them being in the same industry, each was considerably different from the others. And even though some of my job titles may have been similar throughout the years, the tasks at hand were always markedly different, with their own unique nuances, complexities, and desired outcomes. Yet one aspect that I always kept static from job to job was the layout of my office.

I have never been a desk guy. Maybe that's a remnant from my grammar school days, and definitely from my early Nike days. Nonetheless, I just don't like a desk. I see a desk as an obstruction to a good discussion with the person on the other side. I also don't like the false sense of power that a desk represents. Instead, I prefer a table with several chairs to be a great place to chat, like a kitchen table. I also like to have a sofa and some comfortable chairs in my office, as I find that to be disarming, particularly during uncomfortable discussions.

I seldom had personal effects in my offices, as I wanted to keep aspects of my life, well, personal. Plus, in the rare air of a president or CEO position, it was less to carry to the car when your number was up. But in each office that I had post-Nike, I always had two framed photographs on a bookcase or credenza to warm the room up a bit, but more so to serve as a vivid daily reminder for me.

The first photo is of me in 1999, sitting and smiling next to Michael Jordan, in a conference room on the Nike campus. It was the first time I had met him, as our team was presenting to him a refresh of his brand during the lull in business that followed his final retirement from the NBA. At first glance, the photo was often a conversation piece for visitors, but it's the second photo that tells a story.

In that photo, I'm explaining to Michael that the best way to jump-start his brand at retail was to cut our channel of distribution in half. As a man who was getting paid a royalty on the sales of certain styles, this was not good news, particularly since he was very excited about the product and marketing presentations that preceded my sales strategy. My plan to deprive the market to reinvigorate craving was, to say the least, not music to his ears, as he saw it as less money in his pocket. The photo perfectly captures the greatest player ever to play the game wearing a facial expression that says, This is the worst idea that I've ever heard in my life. I had just royally pissed off Michael Jordan. Three of my teammates, Ted Clarke, Erin Patton, and Pamela Neferkará, are also in the photo, and their grim expressions complete the picture.

Michael could be an intimidating presence even when things were good. Yet in this moment, he didn't like what he heard, and suddenly I didn't like where I was sitting. As I tried to explain to him the age-old concept of shorting supply to create demand, he wasn't buying it one bit. He asked me if I was sure that this would work. I instinctively asked him to trust me.

Fifteen years earlier, Dr. Cade had given me sage advice in the form of a story about how a football player spit out one of the final versions of his Gatorade, calling it piss. He didn't go back to the drawing board, intimidated by a 275-pound offensive lineman. He stuck to his guns because he knew he was right.

So did I.

———

Patrick McCarthy didn't follow in his father's footsteps and try to chase four, but he did accomplish something that I'd always dreamed about. He became a high school all-conference basketball player, a point guard no less, following in the footstep of his brothers, Anthony and Chris. Before you scratch your head, it's important to mention that Patrick is six feet tall. Not a small detail.

Patrick attended Cohasset High School, in a tony little town on the south shore of Massachusetts. Like his dad and his brothers, Patrick was a team captain for the Skippers, an unfortunate name, but a nod to the sailing heritage on Cohasset Harbor. At one home game during his senior year, Patrick caught the ball at the opening tip-off, but rather than heading up the court and running the offense, he just froze. He had the ball in his hands, but he didn't start to dribble, and his feet never moved. Both teams by now had set up their offensive and defensive positions but were a little bewildered, as was the gymnasium crowd. The referee walked over to Patrick to see if he was okay. They exchanged a few words before Patrick handed him the ball, and the referee blew his whistle.

Prior to the boys' game, the Cohasset girls' varsity had played. As it turned out, the ball used at tip-off in the boys' game was the girls' ball, which is an inch smaller in circumference and two ounces lighter than the ball that the boys use. Patrick instantly knew the minute the ball touched his hands that something wasn't right. He trusted his instinct. Running a play in a high school basketball game requires planning and preparation. So does making a decision. Any thought and consideration you put into a decision becomes more valuable when it's governed by your instincts.

In the mid-nineties I was the East Coast sales manager for Nike. One of our sales reps asked me to visit a potential account in Manhattan. The proprietor was a young guy named Udi Avshalom. As a young boy, Udi and his family emigrated from Israel with ninety-six dollars in their pockets. They tried to make ends meet by being unlicensed street vendors selling all kinds of tchotchkes, like Christmas ornaments in July. Later, Udi's dad opened a shoe store, but father and son had a falling out, so Udi opened his own sneaker store.

While his store sold Nikes, there was one small problem: Udi did not have an account with our brand so the shoes he was selling he acquired through a grey market. Since his financials were a little shaky, Nike had refused to give him a line of credit. After listening to Udi's animated plea, my head told me no, but my gut told me something else. I convinced the credit department to open Udi's account on a tight leash. Just a few years later, Udi would own a chain of stores throughout New York called Training Camp, and develop a reputation as a sneaker aficionado, who soon counted Jay-Z and other hip-hop moguls as his customers and friends. Later, Udi would become the COO for the Yeezy division of Adidas where he was the architect of that brand's success. I'm glad that I met Udi and I'm proud that I trusted my gut.

————

Seldom is decision-making black and white. Many decisions require taking one from column A and two from column B and adding more sauce while requesting vegan and gluten-free. So it's important to realize that decisions are choices.

In one of my president roles, I was exploring whether to continue employing a third-party design firm that specialized in color. We were paying a lot of money for this service, but in my opinion, we were receiving little benefit. I realized that this couldn't be an abrupt action, and I decided it would be best for both parties to wind down our relationship rather than just turn off the faucet.

I flew to Vermont to meet with the firm's CEO, as I concluded that it was best to end this long-term relationship in person and to jointly craft the best transition plan. I also met with several of the thirteen colorists to offer them a few more months of work. One colorist I met with had a difficult time making a decision, as she was perplexed by the options that were presented to her. Black and white can sometimes be daunting to creatives who live in a world of Technicolor, so I rephrased her options as choices and hoped that she would pick the best one for herself. She could continue to work for two more months, or she could go home and look for another job. To help her think a little more clearly, I told her that I had traveled a long way to visit her in Vermont. To return home, I had a few choices: I could fly, rent a car, take a bus or train, or I could even walk home. She told me that walking home would be ridiculous. I agreed with her, but I reminded her that it was still a choice. I believe that to inform a decision you have to consider every last option, not just a convenient few, to make the best choice.

One temptation of decision-making is to try and please everyone. If you believe your decision will make everyone happy, you've likely missed something, or you're trying too hard. A good decision will often mean everything to a critical few rather than having a little something for everybody. Most important, though, is that the best decisions will come to you much easier and can be more fulfilling when you rely on both your intellectual and moral compasses while respecting the fact that the power of decision is one of your few freedoms left in this world we live in.

———

Carlos Ghosn, the former chairman and CEO of Nissan, will live in infamy because of his dramatic escape from Japan in a wooden crate while under indictment for alleged corporate crimes, rather than being known for his remarkable turnaround of the giant Japanese automaker. In a lecture at Stanford University in 2014, Ghosn posited that no two CEOs were alike and that they shouldn't be. When asked by a student what it takes to be a CEO, he mentioned, "Be an interesting person and a good public speaker." Ghosn was certainly a very interesting person.

While I know that public speaking is not a comfort zone for many people, it is a vital tool for any leader. In every speech there is obviously a message to convey, but words are only a part of it. The tone and feel really matters; otherwise you might as well just send an email. A good speaker will not only inform her audience but also punctuate her key points with inflections and gestures that provoke her listeners not just to hear but also to think. And the success of any speech should be measured by how you made the audience feel.

I have relied on some basic principles of public speaking over the years that have worked for me, although maybe not for everybody.

Avoid podiums and handheld microphones.

Be animated and use stories to draw your listeners in.

Speak, don't read, even if you have notes.

Tell your audience what you're going to tell them, then tell them, and then tell them what you told them.

Don't tell your audience that water is wet.

And don't bore your audience with your adventures in skydiving…they already know the ending.

———

In 2023, the International Women's Day website posted this story:

One day, Winston Churchill and his wife, Clementine, were walking through a posh neighborhood in London. People greeted and exchanged words with the Prime Minister.

A street sweeper, on the other hand, greeted Mrs. Churchill in particular, and the two stayed aside for a while in a familiar conversation. Churchill then asked his wife what she had to discuss with a street sweeper for so long. "Ah…he was in love with me a long time ago," she said. Churchill smiled and said, "You see, if you had married him, you would be the wife of a street sweeper today."

Mrs. Churchill looked at her husband in amazement and said these now legendary words:

"But no, Darling, if I had married him, he would be Prime Minister today."

As Lainie Kazan's character, Maria, said in the movie *My Big Fat Greek Wedding*, "Let me tell you something. The man is the head of the house, but the woman is the neck. And she can turn the head any way she wants."

I've mentioned how over the years I've sought out wisdom, enlightenment, and grounding from They. Also, throughout my career, I've relied on She, although not nearly as much as I would have liked or wanted to.

The athletic footwear industry may be rooted in sport, but the culture was born in a locker room. The towel-snapping and frat-house mentality has softened its edges over time due to the pressures of social change, but more so due to the evolution of women in sport. In some sports, like U.S. soccer, women are way out in front of the men. A few notable brands in the industry have a lot of catching up to do because before they know it, instead of snapping towels, they might just be forced to throw them in. The power of women in sports is undeniable. And the power of women in the sports industry is evolving at the same pace. There are dozens of new fitness brands founded by women that are constantly stealing mindshare and market share while some of the big brands hardly bat an eye, maybe forgetting how Nike snuck up on Adidas, and Reebok on Nike, and then Under Armour on everybody. Aside from powerhouses like Athleta and Lululemon, Sally Bergesen introduced us to Oiselle, a beautiful women's running apparel brand, while a future star named Brooke Torres created Hilma, a shoe brand that offers a customizable sizing solution for the adventurous runner.

And these are just two of many.

While I was at Merrell, I was blessed to have Deirdre McDonnell and Sylvie d'Azemar not only to run our footwear and apparel product-creation engines, but they also had a profound influence on the dynamics of our many leadership team meetings. At ASICS, I was proud to watch a young star named Sarah Bishop quickly go from being our Canada marketer to overseeing all marketing for North and South America. Soon after, Sarah became a top executive at the NFL, where she was instrumental in getting flag football to become an Olympic sport in 2028. I also know that while at the NFL, Sarah will be a positive influence on the poster boys of locker-room towel-snapping. Mary Scott, now the former president of UEG, was my partner in all things public relations while I was at ASICS. She was not only comfortable in her own skin while entrenched in the boy's club, but she also had the magic to make the boys comfortable in their own skin too. And like most women in the sports industry, Mary was an exceptional listener, if only because she couldn't get a word in edgewise.

If the boys in the athletic industry are wise, they will take some cues from the trajectory of U.S. women's soccer and not only broaden the industry's scope but maybe also learn a thing or two about a new style of competing and winning.

———

It's often been said that men run for political office to make a name for themselves, while women run for political office to make a difference. It's no wonder, then, that many men in leadership love to posture and pontificate, while great women leaders will take a position and postulate. One of my favorite views of leadership comes from Jacinda Ardern, the former prime minister of New Zealand. In her final address to Parliament, she had this to say:

"You can be anxious, sensitive, kind, and wear your heart on your sleeve. You can be a mother, or not, an ex-Mormon, or not, a nerd, a crier, a hugger. You can be all of these things, and not only can you be here, but you can also lead."

———

As one ascends in a career, every new level is certain to bring with it new devils. Just after my co-president appointment at Timberland, I brought my mom and Patrick to the New Hampshire headquarters for a late Friday afternoon visit. My eager and charming assistant, Marie Croteau, insisted on giving Cassie and Patrick a tour while introducing them to as many employees as she could. Nearly an hour later, they returned to my office before we were to leave for the weekend. On the way to my car, Cassie put her arm through Patrick's and said, "Come on, Pat. Let's go home and have a drink. Aren't you tired from getting your ass kissed?" Both Cassie and Patrick found a little humor in the way they were received at the office, but they were wary of the saccharine praise and hoped that I would be too.

One of the lifelong gifts I received when I moved to Gainesville to chase four was learning how to build my own personal version of confidence but also how to keep it in check. I learned how to take a hard, honest, and realistic look at the skills I may have had, along with a deep dive into who I was at my core, not who I wanted to be or who others expected me to be. I'm sure, to this day, that any of my modest running accomplishments were fueled by my confidence as much as my workouts. But confidence and cockiness tread a very fine line.

In 2023, on a pilgrimage to Gainesville, I was having a very introspective conversation with Marty as we both reflected on our lives and our careers. Marty mused about how other runners saw him as arrogant, something he felt was never intended. I mentioned to him that what I learned from my post-track experiences in leadership roles was that the people who find you arrogant are usually threatened by you, whereas those who see you as confident are challenged by you and are eager to raise their game. Whether you are the best runner in the world or the leader of a brand, you are relentlessly subjected to how others see you, something you cannot control. But you have complete control over how you see yourself.

———

Early on in my life as a leader, I developed a few working principles that were unique to my personal brand of leadership. Inspiration didn't come from any one person, place, or experience, nor did it come from a book, as I don't believe that a leadership style should be cookie-cutter. It should be deeply personal and unique. I will admit to having been inspired by different role models over the years, but I will stop short of considering myself of having ever been under their influence. My principles were informed by my life's work and then shaped by my innate values. It's my secret sauce, and it works for me, yet I doubt it could work for anyone else, nor should it. And while these principles have evolved over time, there are four that I lived by with more earnestness as the years went on:

Nothing changes…if nothing changes.

Try to spend less time on perfect and more time on brave.

It's okay to make mistakes as long as they are the right mistakes.

And secure good footing, as the wind blows strongest on the top of the mountain.

———

As you surely must know by now, I tend to view things in fours, like a mile run—four laps, four quarters, four minutes—and inspired, of course, by a four-leaf clover.

The first quarter of a lifetime is dedicated to formal education. In grade school, we are trained to memorize. In high school, we are encouraged to learn. Then, in college, we are challenged to think. In the second and third quarters, which is our working life, we are demanded to produce, something there wasn't much focus on in the good old college curriculum. So that's why I've chosen to spend the fourth quarter of my life sharing with young people what I have learned in quarters two and three.

As an aspiring young cross-country runner, I quickly learned that I was more comfortable when I was in the lead. Even at that young age, I felt that my senses and instincts were much sharper when I was in the front. I could clearly see what was ahead of me, and I liked that much better than looking at another runner's back, because then I could focus on conquering the course. But in work, just like in cross-country, the purpose of being in the front is to win, not just to lead.

Unless, of course, you are the rabbit.

THE HOME STRAIGHT

CHAPTER TWENTY-TWO

THE BIG REVEAL

R eady? Here it comes…
  I hate running.

No, this is not a typo.

Now, I don't want to hate running, I really don't. I envy all those runners who trot along with their happy faces and glistening glow, wearing headphones and colorful outfits, while carrying a water bottle filled with some magic potion, probably water from the Fountain of Youth. The girls are joyfully bouncing along like Olivia Newton-John in her "Let's Get Physical" phase, while the boys try to look their macho best in their sleek sleeveless T-shirts, perfectly pomaded hair, and expensive, trendy running shoes. While they seem to be enjoying themselves, I will fully admit that I find these runners as annoying as sand in a wet bathing suit.

Okay…I guess I'm just very jealous.

It seems that somewhere along the way, I've had a falling out with running. Not a breakup, if you will; we're just at loggerheads. On one hand, maybe running is mad at me for not training and competing for a few more years. Okay, fine. Well, I'm mad at running for how much everything hurts right now. The stiffness, sore feet, tight calves, back pain…all lingering remnants from too many long-distance workouts and hard sprints, all while proba-bly wearing the wrong running shoes. Heck, the closest I've ever been to a runner's high was being lightheaded from throwing up after pounding out a workout on the track.

Another big reason I hate running is because I'm deeply conflicted. For my entire life I have adhered only to my emotional age while always fervently defying my chronological age. Because of this, I've come to realize that I have a four-minute mile brain and a fourteen-minute mile body, and I can't seem to reconcile the two. While I still work out to stay fit and healthy, I've come to also learn that I'm addicted to exertion, not exercise.

While Marty Liquori was my boyhood hero, Matt Centrowitz was someone that I looked up to in high school. A native New Yorker and a year older than me, Matt would eventually go on to make two Olympic teams and become the American record holder for 5,000 meters. Believe it or not, there was a time in his life when Matt was only the third-best runner in his family! His daughter, Lauren, was an American record holder while at Stanford, and her brother, Matthew, won Olympic gold in the 1,500-meters in Rio in 2016, the first American to do so in 108 years.

I first saw Matt at Van Cortlandt Park when I was a freshman in high school, when he was warming up before a race. Brawnier than most track guys, Matt wore a fierce look on his face as he prepared to compete. He almost looked like he was heading into a battle rather than running a race. His singlet was purple and gold, emblazoned with the word "Power," which described Matt's physique, maybe more so than the name of his high school, Power Memorial Academy, an all-boys Irish Christian Brothers school, famous at the time for an alumnus by the name of Lew Alcindor. Like me, Matt wanted to break four minutes. Unlike me, Matt's hero was Jim Ryun, the other runner who was shoulder to shoulder with Marty on the cover of *Sports Illustrated*. Matt did run 4:02.7 in 1973, at the end of his senior year at Power. He then attended Manhattan College for one year before transferring to the University of Oregon, where, under the tutelage of Bill

Dellinger, he broke Steve Prefontaine's school record in the 1,500. When his career was finally over, Matt's best mile time was 3:54.8.

Not bad for a kid from the Bronx.

Like it was for me, track was something that fell into Matt's lap by accident. When he realized that he may have a future in the sport, he came home from school one day and enthusiastically announced to his mother, "Hey, Ma! I finally found something I'm good at! I can run!" Yet for both of us, track was never a means in and of itself, but rather a means to an end. While we are both proud of our Bronx roots, it was no garden spot in the '70s, so running fast was a way to a better life and a way out.

In late winter of 1980, Matt came to stay with me in Florida to get some warm-weather training. We finished a long workout one afternoon, both spent and drenched with sweat, when Matt put his hand on my shoulder and said, "Just think of it this way: every mile we run is another mile in the bank. We're like squirrels collecting acorns for the winter. We are going to live to be a hundred years old, and we will be doing jumping jacks like Jack LaLanne and have beach bodies to the grave!"

Needless to say, Matt was hardly prophetic.

To this day, we are still track guys. We never, ever went for a run. We did a workout. We raced to win and hoped for our best time, whereas in a road race, most people seem happy just finishing. We are competitors, not participants. Because of a life in track, to this day we are competitive in everything we do. Whenever I fly somewhere, I not only have to be the first one on the plane, but I will also be the first one at baggage claim, even if I was seated in row eighteen. We are track guys even when we power walk through airports or ride the bike in the gym.

Yet should the day arrive when I can figure out how to actually enjoy this running thing, don't ever call me a jogger. That distinction was made clear to me by a T-shirt I spotted on a guy who was wrestling with a treadmill in a hotel gym. His soaked shirt said, "Those who run love running. Those who jog love cake."

———

In June 1964, Jim Ryun became the first high schooler to break the four-minute mile. Within a year he would go on to break four minutes another four times. In June 1966, Tim Danielson would become the second high schooler to go under four. And a year later, in June 1967, Marty Liquori would join the club as the third. The next high schooler to break this mystical barrier was Alan Webb. But not until 2001.

There are millions of people who should be grateful for the "running boom." It has sparked several industries, given birth to a wellness craze, and even created a new level of socialization. Just like the many colleagues I've worked with over the years, I have been blessed with a great life thanks to the "running boom." But along with this phenomenon came a simultaneous withering of the sport of track and field. Waiting thirty-four years for a fourth high schooler to break four minutes might be a glaring example. Or maybe it was the popularization of the famed New Zealand coach Arthur Lydiard and his long, slow distance-training method. Nonetheless, it's not fair to speculate, but it does cause me to wonder.

Two of my favorite sporting events are the FIFA World Cup in soccer and college basketball's March Madness. Part of both sports' popularity comes from the notion that anything can happen. A small nation or small college could come out of nowhere and take down a giant. Heart can sometimes win over talent. For me, these two events glorify the thrill of victory as well as humanizing the agony of defeat. While track and field has its showcase every two years with the IAAF World Championships, the sport has always been more associated with the Olympics, so its broad popularity expands every four years and then contracts two years later to a smaller yet passionate audience. Someone once told me that we should have the Olympics every year and Christmas every four years. That might give a boost to the popularity of track and field, but it would be a catastrophe for the economy.

The great British Olympic champion Sebastian Coe is the president of the IAAF, the governing body for track and field federations worldwide. He summed up his concern for the sport when he said, "My vision is to have a sport that attracts more young people. The average age of those watching track and field is fifty-five years old. This is not sustainable."

My affinity for the sport is endless. I never would have received a great (and free) education, seen the world, or had a four-decade business career if not for track and field. But Seb's goal to attract young people comes with a greater challenge, fitness for kids. In America, only 4 percent of elementary schools, 8 percent of middle schools, and 2 percent of high schools offer physical education. We trick ourselves into believing that our kids are healthy because we sign them up for soccer and other sports, but being active doesn't necessarily mean the same thing as being fit. On the other end of the spectrum, kids are being burned out in organized sports by an early age, and potentially they grow up to loathe physical fitness. When the U.S. men's soccer team didn't qualify for the World Cup in 2018, I wondered, What was the state of youth soccer ten years earlier? Another startling statistic is that one in every four U.S. men doesn't meet the mental or physical requirements of all arms of the military. Perhaps we are less safe as a nation because we are less fit?

I was introduced to track at my high school freshman field day. It changed my life. It's a simple sport that takes only a little heart and very little equipment. It's reminiscent of our innocent days on a playground, and it can inspire a set of life values that transcend sport while guiding a kid to a full and prosperous life, not to mention a healthy one.

Roy Benson is a legendary track coach who, among his many résumé brags, was the guy who shouted to Frank Shorter overhead from a bridge in Munich to tell him the size of his lead in the '72 Olympic marathon. Roy, very eloquently, had this to say about track and field:

"Isn't it great that our sport doesn't need human judges? No need for us to worry about 'artistic' merit, no one around taking off points for our form. All we've got to do is just put low numbers on the objective, nonpartisan, incorruptible clock. Best is least."

It's very easy. It starts with one simple step. You go out there, stay to your left, and get back as fast as you can.

CHAPTER TWENTY-THREE

MILE HIGH

"I really don't know why it is that all of us are so committed to the sea, except I think it is because in addition to the fact that the sea changes and the light changes, and ships change, it is because we all came from the sea. And it is an interesting biological fact that all of us have in our veins the exact same percentage of salt in our blood that exists in the ocean, and therefore, we have salt in our blood, in our sweat, in our tears. We are tied to the ocean. And when we go back to the sea, whether it is to sail or to watch it, we are going back from whence we came."

—John F. Kennedy, September 14, 1962, in Newport, Rhode Island

Long Beach, New York, is a barrier island on the south shore of Nassau County. Settled in 1623 and incorporated as a city in 1922, Long Beach is home to some thirty-five thousand people, smushed together on an island that is three and a half miles long and barely a mile wide at its broadest point. It is only eight miles from JFK Airport, and a fifty-minute ride on the Long Island Rail Road will have you in midtown Manhattan's Penn Station, which sits right underneath Madison Square Garden.

Once a summer community, Long Beach is now famous for its clusters of bungalows that have become year-round havens for its many proud citizens. The West End of Long Beach is known for its plethora of bars, which are a magnet for many young people who were absent that day in school when it was taught how to drink responsibly. One particular corner of Beech Street is called the Bermuda Triangle, since there are three popular bars within ten yards of each other where four kids can begin their evening together, but only two or three make it home. And oh yeah, Long Beach has one Starbucks.

While not known as a sports town, Long Beach does have a Polar Bear Plunge on Super Bowl Sunday to support the Make-A-Wish Foundation. More importantly, it also has a prestigious annual New York to California bicycle race. Now, it's critical to note here that the streets in Long Beach are named after U.S. states, and the bike race commences on New York Avenue and ends at California Street, which is one block away. The race is sponsored by Shine's Bar, a one-hundred-plus-year-old historic landmark, which is also historic for its early-morning opening and its loyal rise-and-shine patrons.

This book was written in Long Beach over a four-year stretch. A daily view of the ocean, which could be sleeping, dancing, or showing her anger on any given day, often served as inspiration as well as a calming influence, since 90 percent of writing is procrastination.

I do not feel that I am worthy of a memoir, as my life and its moments are just a long, hard grind, just like everyone else's. But the term *memoir* has both Latin and French roots, with loose translations to "personal memories" or "memory wars." Hence, I call this book a personal history.

For over forty years, I was in an industry that has been very good to me. And for twenty or so years prior, I had a hard scrabble and scramble that prepared me well. I have collected millions of snippets and sound bites that I tried to connect over the four years of this labor of love. Sometimes this collage of snippets looked like an impossible life-size jigsaw puzzle rather than the intended mosaic. Because of that, there were many starts and stops, charges and retreats, or hands furiously typing, and more frequently, arms thrown into the air in frustration.

This book may read like a career pursued with relentless ambition. The truth is, it was all just a hard effort to survive and hopefully thrive, all in the name of feeding a family. My regrets of constant travel, relocations, and missing important family milestones are permanently and painfully carved into my heart. However, just like you can't pass a driving test by putting the car in reverse rather than drive, you also can't learn how to drive in a parked car. As the sage philosopher Bono once said, "If you're not at the table, you're on the menu."

I've also learned along the way that the grass isn't greener on the other side. It's just a different type of grass, or maybe artificial turf, and sometimes it could be cement painted green. But in the good grass, there is always a four-leaf clover hidden in plain sight, which the Irish believe can ward off evil spirits. The Irish also believe that the four leaves represent luck, faith, hope, and love. I will spend my autumn years encouraging my kids and grandkids to roam the fields with zest while always looking for their four-leaf clover.

For those of you that I haven't had the pleasure of meeting, I hope that this book has given you a glimpse into a life well lived. For those of you who do know me, or think you do, you may know a little bit more about me right now, but you still don't know me. That mystery we all hold inside of ourselves ultimately allows us some form of self-preservation. If we were to be totally revealed, then our spirit would die.

However, for each of you, I leave you with this…

In 1979, Marty Liquori wrote a great book called *On the Run: In Search of the Perfect Race*. He signed my copy, "To Gene. I hope this book makes it all a little easier for you. Marty."

I don't propose for one second that this book will make it all a little easier for you, but I do hope that the tales I tell along my trail and the lessons embedded within will make you think, and hopefully inspire you, while you burn your own path as you chase your own dream.

EPILOGUE

I n the spring of 1980, all the air was sucked out of the ambition of every aspiring Olympian when President Jimmy Carter announced that the U.S. would boycott the Games in Moscow. This included Marty Liquori. To distract himself, Marty went skiing with friends in Colorado and came home with a slight injury. Prior to the ski trip, he had been asked to race in Kingston, Jamaica, at a meet called the Norman Manley Games, named after the first premier of Jamaica. Marty now had to withdraw from the race, but he asked the race director if he would take me in his place. While not exactly a fair swap, the race director reluctantly agreed, and a plane ticket was on its way.

I arrived in Kingston the day before the race, very anxious and excited. Since it was an Olympic year, the race was switched from the mile to 1,500-meters, often referred to as the metric mile. The field of eight runners was truly international. I was one of two Americans, the other being Paul Cummings, a great middle-distance runner from Brigham Young. The lineup included Filbert Bayi from Tanzania, who broke the world record for 1,500-meters five years earlier, as well as Steve Ovett, the brash Brit who would break the world record at 1,500-meters just two months after this race. National Stadium was sold out, and the thirty-five thousand fans loved the sprint races, as that's where the Jamaicans excelled, but they also knew that the 1,500 was the marquee event.

When the gun sounded, everyone went out cautiously until Ovett grabbed another English runner by his singlet and literally put him into the front of the pack to set a good pace. Malcolm Prince took us through the first quarter in fifty-eight seconds. We slowed a bit, passing eight hundred meters in two minutes flat. I felt surprisingly comfortable, with my eyes trained on Ovett and Bayi, who were settled in behind Prince. At the bell lap, Prince faded, and I found myself right behind two of the best milers in the world. Then, suddenly, Ovett shot to the front, and the race was on, or maybe it was over. Ovett hit the tape in 3:39, and Bayi just a second behind. I managed to finish third, with a time of 3:42.

Steve Ovett would go on later that summer and win a gold and a bronze in Moscow. Filbert Bayi would win a silver medal himself. After a great party at the hotel with these amazing athletes, I would fly back to Gainesville with the metric equivalent of a four-minute mile. Nearly two years of chasing four, and almost nine years to the day of being inspired by the cover of *Sports Illustrated*, my dream came true on May 9, 1980.

About twenty-five years later, I was looking at some clippings and mementos from my modest athletic career when I stumbled across the meet program from Kingston. It brought back a flurry of memories to that balmy Friday night. I remember how great I felt to be on the medal stand with two of the best runners in the world. That evening, we didn't get medals, but rather, we were given clay sculptures, mine being of a woman churning butter. She's been on prominent display in every home we've ever lived in. And I love that no family, friends, or guests realize that this simple sculpture was the most important trophy I had ever received in my life.

Then something hit me, something I never realized until that walk down memory lane in my quaint home library in Cohasset. While my dream came true on May 9, 1980, I suddenly realized that ten years later, to the day, on May 9, 1990, Patrick Jack McCarthy took his first breath. And with the grace of God, he didn't look at all like a skinned rabbit.

So I guess that while you're busy chasing your dream, make sure that all your senses are completely aroused, because you never know if you just might stumble upon a little magic along the way.

ACKNOWLEDGEMENTS

Thank you, Marty. For reading my letter and for writing me back. God bless the coaches: Morkan, Mulligan, Byrne, and Mitchell. Thanks for the confidence, the faith, and the trust as well as your patience while coaching the un-coachable.

To all the good ones in the athletic and outdoor industries that I've had the distinct pleasure to know and share the trenches with (you may not know who you are, but I do). As you all know, working in our industries is like going to a casino in Vegas…the lights are bright, the energy is high, and the oxygen is plentiful. But at the same time, there are no windows, no clocks, and… no exits! I hope that as you read this, you will nod, wink, cringe, smirk, and smile while always remembering to never take yourselves too seriously. After all, we sell sneakers and boots while the real problems in the world rage on.

To my great friend Chris Komisarjevsky, your illustrious business career is dwarfed only by your service to our country, with the many fearless missions you flew in Vietnam. I remain in awe. Thank you for allowing me to watch you author your fourth book, for keeping me grounded, and for going Dutch at the many lunches we shared at The Saloon in Long Beach. I couldn't have done this without you.

Deep thanks to Doris Huang for your energy and encouragement, and for relentlessly nudging me to pick up the pen and grace the paper. You and your Cornell MBA students continue to inspire me.

My dear Lydia Rumpf, thank you for helping me rescue this project from Apple Pages to Microsoft Word. Sure, simple for you, but a life-or-death ordeal for me. And you did this all while you were working toward your PhD. I can't wait to see what's next for you. I hope that someday that you will write a book.

Thank you, Ally Cuevas and Diane Martin, for your help and patience with my elementary laptop questions. And thanks for not rolling your eyes.

And deep gratitude to Jenny, Megan, Brian, and the team at Elite Authors.

Patrick, thank you for being my art director for this project. It means the world to me. I love you.

I had the privilege of a team of eight who read various drafts of this book. Two teachers, two professors, and two authors along with a real estate mogul and a fitness entrepreneur. Still, I admit to being a total wreck while Doris and Chris, as well as Susan McCarthy, Bernadette Mannion, Roy Hirshland, Mary Scott, Mike Haywood, and Assumpta Tucker, read different iterations of the manuscript. Thank you all for taking the time and for your critiques, your blunt suggestions, and your wide spectrum of encouraging words.

Then, of course, there is my own personal solar system, in which I find perpetual comfort while in my orbit.

To the eight brilliant stars in my Big Dipper, or as the Irish call it, the Plough. Messrs. Walsh, Centrowitz, Liquori, McHale, Lebeaux, Hirshland and Mses. Scott and Gentile. Throughout every phase of my life, each of you has inspired me at different junctures along the way. Most important, you each believed, and often when I didn't. I love you all. I promise to return the favor.

Absolutely most precious is the McCarthy family and all the families whose planets circle our sun. You are many, far and wide, but nonetheless a most beautiful constellation. You know who you are. I love each and every one of you. *So* much.

Love and kisses to the great eight who are my Medium Dipper (it's my solar system, so I get to create my own star networks). Alix, Dylan, Clancy, Jake, Maggie, Luke, Rory, and Rowan. Find and cherish your four-leaf clover and then heed no compass but your own.

And most especially to my eight little stars that twinkle so bright. My Little Dipper…Zoe, Hudson, Sloane, Mia, Hattie, Sullivan, Auggie, and Daisy. I never was and never will be good at baby talk or changing diapers, but I will always have an ear and a chair for you right next to me when you begin to chase your dreams. I love you…Grand.

To my shooting star, Olga. I see you glide every night. So do Jess, Pat, and Auggie. Your spirit shimmers.

Finally, to Pop. You are my North Star, the compass that leads me when my compass stalls. Thank you for always illuminating me, even when the darkness prevails.

Those last, hard five seconds were for you.

And of course, to the greatest star of all, my dear, sweet, beautiful Cassie. You continue to amaze. I look forward to you being canonized as a living saint, or at least having your own star on Beach Catholic's Walk of Fame. More importantly, I can't wait for the party that we will have after.

Good times never seemed so good!

ABOUT THE AUTHOR

Gene McCarthy is a well-known and respected leader whose varied career in the athletic and outdoor industries spans more than four decades. He has held executive and C-suite positions for legendary global brands including Nike, Jordan, Under Armour, Reebok, Timberland, and Merrell. His last role was as the president and CEO of ASICS America.

Mr. McCarthy has held seats on various boards in the footwear industry as well as for the Van Cortlandt Park Conservancy, where he founded the Van Cortlandt Park Cross-Country Hall of Fame. He currently sits on the board for The City Tutors, a nonprofit that serves the underprivileged in the five boroughs of New York City. As well, he is the chairman of the board for Foot-Balance System, a foot-health technology company based in Helsinki, Finland.

He is a frequent guest speaker at major colleges and universities that have included the University of Southern California, Cornell's Johnson Graduate School of Management, and Marquette University.

Mr. McCarthy currently lives in Long Beach, New York, where every day he can be seen on the boardwalk as he continues to try to reconcile his four-minute-mile brain with his fourteen-minute-mile body.

You can reach Gene McCarthy at https://linkedin.com/in/Gmccarthy56, or you can follow him on Instagram @alwayschasingfour.

Made in the USA
Middletown, DE
11 August 2024